MW01098409

THE
RAZOR
ANTHOLOGY

Copyright© 1995
Knife World Publications
P.O. Box 3395
Knoxville, Tennessee 37927

Copyright© 1995 by Knife World Publications

Published by Knife World Publications, P.O. Box 3395, Knoxville, TN 37927

All Rights Reserved

No part of this book may be reproduced in any form without written permission from the publisher, except for brief quotations embodied in critical articles or reviews.

Cover photograph by John Stewart

Layout and design by Kim T. Knott

ISBN- 0-940362-17-1

Printed in the United States of America

About the Cover

Cover photography by John Stewart

A variety of seven antique straight razors are pictured on the cover, representing manufacturers and brands from several countries. They feature handles that are relatively plain, though quite attractive, to those that are ornately carved or made of more exotic materials. Some blades are plain while others are decorated with elaborate etching or fancy file work. All are quite collectible and each has its own story to tell to collectors like Jim Matthews of Florida. Mr. Matthews' cooperation in permitting us to use this small but significant portion of his collection is sincerely appreciated.

1) W. R. CASE & SONS/BRADFORD PA razor handled in green pearl celluloid. From the c1905 - 1920 era, the razor's blade back is marked "Registered No 023/Warranted for Life."

2) Pearl handled razor with fancy file work on blade back. Blade is etched with the words "Our Best" and a crown separating the words. Tang is stamped "Ground and Made in Germany."

3) W. R. CASE & SONS/BRADFORD PA. The razor is handled in a beaded mottled brown celluloid that resembles mastodon bark ivory and has a bead-work edging. The blade tang is covered with a genuine pearl scale. Blade is etched with a star and the words, "Lone Star."

4) Fancy carved pearl handled razor from the1877 - 1928 era. Blade is etched "Challenge Cutlery Company" and "CCC." Tang is stamped CHALLENGE RAZOR/SHEFFIELD one side and B. J. EYRE/SHEFFIELD on the other.

5) CASE BROTHERS/LITTLE VALLEY NY razor with varigated green, black and red celluloid handle. From the 1867 - 1900 era and likely made by Napanoch.

6) CASE BROTHERS/SPRINGVILLE NY razor with ornately carved imitation ivory handle. c1912 - 1915.

7) MONDESIR/SOLINGEN handled in mottled brown and cream celluloid, with engraved sterling silver bolster wrapping on butt end. A scale of the same material as the handle covers the tang of this razor dating from the 1890 - 1938 era.

Introduction

Among the tens of thousands of cutlery collectors are a large number who either specialize in antique razors or who collect them along with their favorite knives. Collectors of knives have been very fortunate, especially during the past two decades, due to a continually growing list of reference works about their hobby. Collectors who specialize in antique razors have not been so fortunate.

Knife World's monthly publication is and does basically what its name implies; it publishes informative articles about knives. But razors and knives are closely related. They often shared a common brand name and manufacturer and most certainly their history follows a close parallel. For this reason and because we know that many of our readers have interests in razors, historical pieces about them are frequently included for razor and knife enthusiasts alike.

When we recently selected articles to reprint in the third volume of The Best of Knife World, the fact that razors had not been neglected during the past near two decades really came into focus. A large number of articles about them had been published; so many that they deserved a book of their own.

This is that book. The information it contains is the result of tedious and demanding research efforts by razor aficionados dedicated enough to do it and then write about their findings. The compilation of articles contained herein have been selected from those published during the past dozen years to offer razor collectors and enthusiasts a much needed source of information about antique razors and the companies that produced them.

Along with the authors whose works fill this book, we hope that you'll enjoy The Razor Anthology and that it will contribute to the pleasure you find as you pursue your hobby.

Table of Contents

Honing In On A Collecting Specialty

by Richard D. White

The art of collecting seems to have built into it an evolutionary process. As collectors gain more and more knowledge through reading, investigating, and talking to other collectors, they tend to gravitate toward other similar, but distinctive collectibles.

So it is with the collecting of knives. In fact, if one looks into the history of "organized knife collecting," you would find that knife collecting and trading started out as an offshoot of the collecting of firearms. As stricter laws were passed regarding the buying and selling of firearms, many gun collectors gravitated into the knife business. Certainly, the acquisition of sheath knives and pocket knives were an important byproduct of firearms trading. Even today, one of the best sources of pocketknives are the many gun shows which abound all across the United States.

For the knife collector, this evolutionary process starts with the branching out into other "cutlery related" objects. These related items are purchased so that the knife collector can put together a "complete collection." In many cases, the first knife-related item to be purchased tends to be old, original cutlery showcases (if they can be found). These cutlery cases once again serve their original purpose– that being to display knives. Now, however, these displays appear in knife shows instead of in hardware store windows.

Down the line, additional purchases often include original literature, advertisements or posters put out by the cutlery company, old knife rolls, knifepicks, or perhaps the biggest offshoot: straight razors made by your favorite knife company. As a serious collectible, razors are

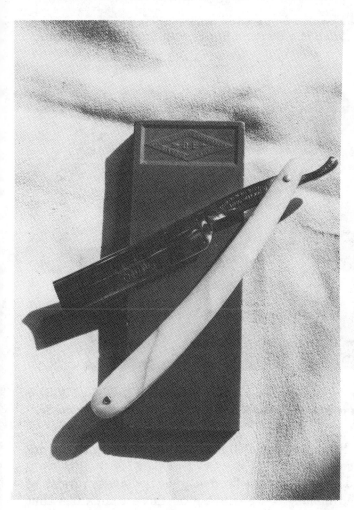

A Shapleigh "Diamond Edge" razor hone sitting below a Shatt and Morgan razor. Notice the distinctive "Diamond Edge" shield with the letter "DE" surrounded by the diamond.

A closeup of the Blish-Mize hone showing the intricate carving of the Mohawk Indian; a Blish-Mize trademark.

1

certainly a topic by themselves, with the razor market presently in a downturn stage.

My own individual introduction into the arena of razor hones came as a sidelight to the carving of duck decoys. Needing a "razor sharp" carving knife, I searched for a variety of sharpening stones in differing grades of coarseness. For a finishing stone, I discovered a razor hone as being the logical choice to polish the carving knife. After purchasing a couple of hones, I noticed that each stone was etched with a brand name– mainly Austrian by name.

Suddenly, I began to find these stones appearing at the local flea market, antique shows, and gun shows. In many cases, the sellers of these stones did not know just what their original purpose was– only that they were used to sharpen things. In fact, on several occasions, when I asked specifically about the price of the "razor hone," I then had to point out the stone to the owner.

With what appears to be a rather limited general knowledge of these hones, it would seem that the field of razor hone collecting is in its infancy. Will there ever be an interest in this specific field of collecting? Will razor hones ever match the price of razors produced by the same company? These are a couple of questions that need to be researched.

With several razor hones "under my belt," I began to find razor hones etched with names more familiar to the knife collector. I soon added hones etched "Keen Kutter," "W.R. Case," "Western States," and "Hibbard, Spencer, and Bartlett" to my growing collection. My readings led me to the conclusion that many companies which were thought to have produced only knives, in fact,

A mint Western States Cutlery and Manufacturing Co. razor hone in original box. Included is a Western States celluloid handled razor.

Two Keen Kutter razor hones showing the distinctive Keen Kutter emblem. Also included is a French ivory celluloid Keen Kutter razor.

produced a full line of cutlery-related items; among them were both razors and razor hones.

My quest led me to try to find a greater assortment of specifically etched hones– concentrating on those companies that produced pocketknives. One recently acquired purchase included a very intricately carved name plate etched "Blish-Mize-Silliman Hardware, Atchison, Kansas." In the center of this etching was a carved Mohawk Indian, the trademark for this particular hardware store. Having purchased several hardware store knives, I was particularly interested in this stone.

The second stone was, by comparison, quite simply etched with "CCC." Although it could be several different companies (like Cattaraugus Cutlery Company, or even Challenge Cutlery Company), my best guess is that this razor hone was produced by Curtain and Clark Cutlery, the most common company to use the "CCC" emblem. If this is the case, this particular hone is quite old since Curtain and Clark were in production around 1910.

A very special hone was sold to me by a dealer who is a member of my knife club in Denver, Colorado. It is mint condition, in the box, with original papers. More importantly, it is etched "C. Harvey Platts, Western States Cutlery and Manufacturing Company, Boulder, Colo." With the recent final demise of the Western factory, and with the increasing interest in Western States knives, I am sure that this purchase will be of special significance.

You noticed that I made a special point of mentioning that the C. Harvey Platts stone was "mint, in the box, with original paper." This statement illustrates a growing trend in collecting, found most evident in the collecting of toys. The value of any antique, whether it be toys, games, or even knives is enhanced significantly if the product is included with its original box. In many cases, the boxes which once contained the object are worth more than the items included therein. Old knife boxes are certainly becoming very valuable and are often included in published knife lists.

With razors, having the original box is especially important. In

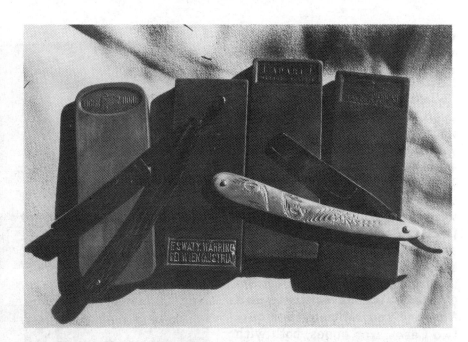

A selection of both American and foreign made hones. Included are common "Swaty" hones from Austria, "Tiger Hone" with oval shield, and a hone from the American Hone Company in Olean, N.Y.

Three hones produced by W.R. Case and Co. Although they show some slight chipping, they are still valuable because of the famous name and their ages.

most cases, the box and the instructions were discarded as soon as they got wet, which was frequently the case with razor hone boxes. Because of this, original boxes are highly prized.

Pricing

Because the collecting of hones is truly in its infancy, and since no "official" pricing books have been published, determining potential prices for these items is difficult indeed. One of the best

3

potential sources seemed to be the large sale book put out several years ago by Smoky Mountain Knife Works entitled *"Classic Collectibles."* This publication was used to illustrate a massive auction of straight razors along with the J.P. Huddleston Case knife collection. Although over 1700 razors were listed for sale in this book, only two razor hones were included. These two were a O.V.B. in original box for $35.00 and a Keen Kutter in original box for $40.00.

Sargent's *"American Premium Guide to Pocketknives and Razors,"* 2nd Edition, lists only two Case razor hones, both with original boxes, and both valued at $125.00 each. Krumholz's book entitled *"Value Guide for Barberiana and Shaving Collectibles"* proved to be little value also in establishing the potential selling prices of razor hones.

It would seem safe to say that "famous Maker" hones command potential prices which are much higher than ordinary hones, with Case, Keen Kutter, Western States, and other famous knife companies leading the way. Certainly, as mentioned above, those hones which also include original boxes increase the value of the hone itself; probably adding at least 30% to the value of the one. Finally, although of excellent quality, German and Austrian hones, because of their relative prevalence are priced less than American made hones.

Should collectors begin to include razor hones on their "shopping list"? I certainly did, adding hones to knife picks, showcases and other knife and razor related items. Although I have never found a knife pick in any show (I have certainly looked

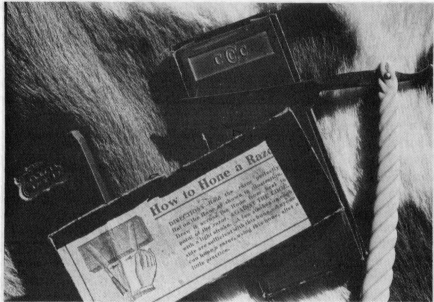

Top: A famous hardware store razor hone. Blish-Mize-Silliman Hardware was located in Atchinson, Kansa.. The lid of this hone box included honing instructions.

Bottom: Included in this photo are hones from Hibbard, Spencer Bartlett Company with their famous OVB Trademark, and the CCC Trademark representing probably the Curtain and Clark Cutlery Company. Notice that the middle "C" is surrounded by a larger "C."

in a lot of showcases), I have stumbled upon a number of unchipped hones in original boxes, and a greater number without boxes. What other field of antiques can you get in on the ground floor, especially when the item you are looking for is over 100 years old? Remember also that every man in the United States needed at least one razor hone to keep razors shaving sharp.

At least, by expanding your collecting vision, you will not go away from a gun show, antique shop, or flea market empty-handed. Good luck.

This article appeared in Knife World July, 1992.

Egyptian Designs

by Kurt Moe

Archaeologists are still digging in ancient Egyptian tombs hoping to find out more about that mysterious time over 3000 years ago. In fact the site of Princess Tia's tomb was only recently located and is one of those still being worked.

In recent years a group of artifacts from the King Tutakhamum tomb toured the country. Long lines of people waited to see the exhibition in the various cities it visited. What many people don't realize, is that the opening of the Egyptian King's tomb in 1922 also triggered a wave of interest across the USA. The priceless relics of precious metal and jewels from such a distant 1350 B.C. period sparked imaginations. These were knives buried with the king that live on in the dreams of collectors as well.

Egyptian designs were certainly used before King Tut's tomb was discovered and even today are still used. I believe, however, that during the decade or so following 1922 that many designs on razors, lather mugs, and knives attempted to take advantage of the King Tut popularity.

A razor which seems to have picked up on the Egyptian theme is one by Fox Cutlery.

The razor handle is an earth brown colored plastic with a nickel silver inlay. The inlay is fashioned to look like a beetle or scarab with wings.

Two mugs leaving little doubt as to Egyptian nature of their designs are marked with "Benedict Mfg. Co." trademarks. Both mugs are also marked "Karnak Brass" which I believe is the model line or series of the mugs referring to the Egyptian design and the brass material used in the mug or design. "Karnak" is the name of a South Egyptian village located on the river Nile.

The body of one mug is made of thin brass and is marked on the bottom with the Benedict trademark and the number 633. A green color was used to antique the design then a clear lacquer like covering was put over the whole mug. My U.S. Army training helps me distinguish that the metal where the coating has been rubbed off during use is tarnished brass. The fingers wore the mug in nearly the same place over the many times lather was mixed in the mug.

Remington knife showing Egyptian symbols. Winged figure and lotus blossoms decorate this side of the metal handle.

Second side of the Remington knife. Cobras and more lotus blossoms decorate this side. The knife is 3-1/8 inches long when closed.

Two more details reinforce the theory that this mug was used for making lather instead of some other use such as to hold hot cocoa. There is a milk glass insert for the soap and there is a curved projection on the handle that makes a good spot to hold a lather brush.

The central design of the mug appears to be a replica of the youthful King Tut's burial mask itself.

A second mug has a brass Egyptian figure and what appears to be a small amount of brass plating remaining on a pewter like mug. The number "881" is stamped on the mug's bottom along with Benedict's trademark. This mug has two projections on the handle that would keep a brush from rolling off. There is a rim on the mug top which was likely to hold a metal or glass cup insert.

Of more interest to the knife collector is the Remington knife using an Egyptian design. This knife's metal handles are full of Egyptian symbols. There are six lotus blossoms, and two cobras in the designs which are very Egyptian in origin. The female figure and out stretched wings can be considered Egyptian as well.

The larger blade has "Remington UMC" inside a circle and "Made in USA" around the circle stamped on its tang. On the tang back is stamped the number "R 730". The smaller blade has just the "Remington UMC" stamped inside the circle.

This "R 730" number created a mystery in itself. The circumstances of the knife's purchase led me to believe the knife was authentic, yet the R730 number couldn't be found on any of the Remington pattern lists that I located. Did I have a rare knife here?

The last digit of a Remington pattern number usually indicates the knife's handle material. An "O" represents Buffalo Horn. Even a razor collector can tell this knife has metal handles that are probably nickel silver and such pattern number should end in "9".

Close examination of the tang shows that there would be enough room to have an additional 9 on the number and still the number would be centered. The tang does seem to have a bevel dropping away slightly where the fourth number would be. Perhaps a 9 did not leave an imprint when stamped.

While thumbing through a Remington Catalog No. C-5 reprint one day, I saw it. There was a picture of the metal handled Egyptian design knife. It was listed with two numbers depending on the blades in the nickel silver handle. The "R 7309" has two blades and the "R 7319" has one blade and a file.

It may have been more rewarding financially to have a rare Remington knife not listed in the books, but I really don't mind that at least this Egyptian mystery was solved.

This article appeared in Knife World April, 1983.

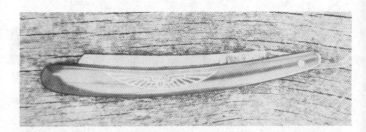

Fox Cutlery razor with earth brown plastic handles. Inlay is beetle of Egyptian design.

Karnak brass shaving lather mugs. Both Egyptian design mugs have brush rests.

6

Straight Razors and Accessories

by Ben Myers

The collecting of straight razors is a specialized branch of knife collecting, and it is becoming increasingly popular. Within that field there are many sub-specialties. Some collectors specialize in German razors or Swedish products. Other collectors are interested in the razors that were made by particular companies.

Razors sometimes have engraved blades, and many collectors are mainly interested in the engraving and search for attractive pictures or unusual subjects. On some blades the engraving is deeply cut and then filled with gold metal to make the picture stand out more clearly.

Other collectors are more interested in the handle. Older razors usually had handles made of natural materials such as wood, bone, horn or turtle shell. Modern razors usually have handles made of celluloid, other plastics or aluminum. Celluloid handles were produced and a collection of them can make a very attractive display. Celluloid handles were also molded to show hunting scenes, pictures of animals, women (including nudes), patriotic scenes and all kinds of decorative designs.

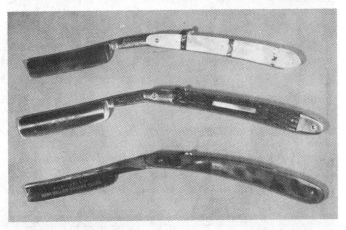

Top: A mother of pearl and abalone hanled razor from John Primble India Steel Works. Middle: A picked bone handled razor from the Torrey Razor Company. Bottom: A turtleshell handled razor from Wolff, Lane and Company.

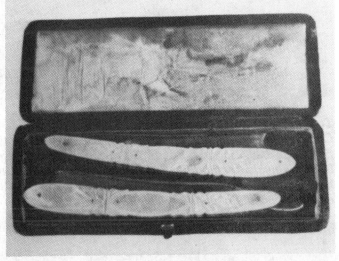

A matched pair of carved mother of pearl handled razors made by Joseph Rodgers & Sons of Sheffield, England. These razors recently sold at auction for $200.

Since celluloid could be made in any shape or color, it was sometimes used to imitate other materials. Handles that appear to be made of bamboo, turtleshell, or horn are often imitations that are really made of celluloid.

A few razors were made with handles of valuable materials, such as mother of pearl, ivory, gold, or silver. However, these are relatively rare. The mother of pearl often turns out to be plastic,

An assortment of 5 different "name" shaving mugs. Name mugs generally only have the user's name and gold rims on the mugs. Name mugs sell for considerably less than occupational or fraternal mugs. The mugs shown above sold for about $5 each at a recent auction.

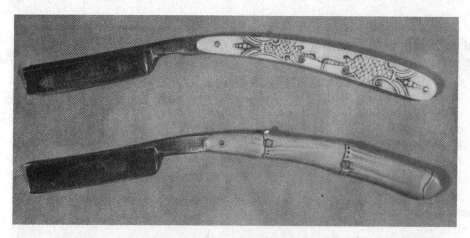

Top: A fine example of a celluloid razor handle with a pattern. Razor by Levering Razor Co. Bottom: A celluloid razor handle that has been designed to look like real bamboo by the Oxford Razor Company.

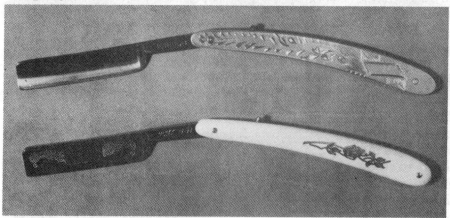

Top: A carved aluminum handled razor made by the Ranidae Razor Company of West Germany. Bottom: A modern plastic handled razor from the Bohlerstahl Razor Company of Solingen, Germany. The blade contains a modern etching filled with gold leaf coloring. The handle contains a flower pattern made of thin silver. Such razors can be bought for about $15 to $20.

A fine example of a celluloid razor handle. The pattern shows a woman's face and long hair. The razor was made by the Challenge Razor Company specifically for the Isaac Walker Hardware Company of Peoria, Illinois.

the ivory is celluloid, and the gold or silver turns out to be plated and not solid.

Elephant ivory and celluloid can usually be distinguished by the fact that ivory is stiffer and harder to bend. When the two sides of a razor handle are squeezed together, if they bend easily and touch each other - then the material is likely to be celluloid. If the two sides of the handle are stiff and resist touching each other, they are more likely to be elephant ivory.

Another characteristic is that ivory was a valuable material and the handles were usually cut rather thin to reduce the amount of material used. When the handles are thick they are more likely to be celluloid, which was cheap.

When ivory is inspected under a 10 power magnifying glass the cellular structure may be apparent. The material may look like a pile of soap chips that have been pressed together. Celluloid and plastics are more likely to have a smooth and milky appearance, with no sign of any cellular structure. However, the test is sometimes deceptive because if ivory is polished repeatedly, the cellular structure may be hard to see.

The market value of better quality razors has increased tremendously during the past few years as they have become more popular. The value of a razor is increased by the artistic quality of the piece, by the historical connections, by the materials used, and the general condition.

Defects in a razor reduce the value drastically. A razor's edge is extremely thin and is usually made from a very hard and brittle steel. Dropping the razor often chipped small pieces off the edge. Since a razor was often covered with a slippery, soapy lather, and it was often used early in the morning by someone who was only half awake, they were often dropped and damaged. Any damage reduces the value. In addition, razors often became rusted when they were put away while still wet. Rust marks reduce the value.

When a razor has a real ivory handle, the ivory often develops small cracks around the metal pins that hold the handle together. This, naturally, reduces the value.

Before buying an expensive razor, make sure that the blade and the handle fit each other properly. It is quite common for collectors to buy a razor with a broken handle, and then buy another razor with a broken blade, then fit the sound handle of one razor to the sound blade of the other razor. When this is done, the two units may not fit each other. The handle may be too long for the blade, or the blade may not close properly.

When blades and handles are substituted, a historical conflict may exist between the handle and the blade. If the blade is engraved in 1880 with a patriotic theme, and the handle is a 1920 art deco style, then something must have been substituted.

Collectors of straight razors often branch out into the collecting of related shaving items. One popular item is the wooden cases that were used to hold matched sets of razors. The cases were usually made of solid oak. They were sometimes inlaid with a brass plate that had the original owner's name or initials engraved upon it.

Matched sets of razors (often 7 razors to a set) were sold in an effort to solve the sharpening problem. Some men could not master the delicate art of sharpening a razor properly. So, the man would buy a matched set of 7 razors and from time to time he would take the entire set to his neighborhood barber, who would sharpen the entire set at one time - for a fee. The man could then take the set home and use it for a long time. This eliminated the necessity of making frequent trips to a barber shop in order to keep one razor sharp.

Another popular collector's item is the shaving mug, which first came into general use around 1830. At that time, an ordinary working man would shave himself at home. A prosperous businessman, doctor, lawyer, or professional person might visit the barbershop each day to be shaved by the barber. The town barbershop often became an important meeting place and social center for the prosperous people in the town. A man would buy a shaving mug and have his name and occupation put on the mug and then it would be displayed in the barbershop, along with the

Left: Rare occupational shaving mug used by New York Policeman Daniel Haviland. This mug sold at auction for $1,500. Right: Occupational shaving mug used by F.B. Davis who was an automobile dealer. This mug recently sold for $550 at auction.

Left: A fraternal shaving mug used by G.D. Renninger who was presumably a member of the T.O.T.E. fraternity. This mug recently sold at auction for $350. Right: A fraternal mug used by Mr. Ewen who was a junior member of the O.W.A.M. fraternity. This mug sold at auction for $125. Many fraternity mugs can be purchased for about this price.

mugs belonging to other important people. The display of mugs was often an important status symbol and a form of advertising. If a man could afford to visit the barbershop each day, this was proof of his prosperity and importance in the world.

So, the shaving mug was often carefully selected. The lawyer's mug would have his name, and a legal symbol. The doctor's mug would have his name and a medical symbol. Some men used the symbol of their fraternal society: the Elks, the Masons, etc. Shaving mugs became popular gift

The barber used "barber bottles" to hold liquids such as hair tonic and perfume. These bottles sell for about $50 to $60 dollars each.

items for Father's Day, or for an anniversary.

One type of shaving mug was called a "scuttle mug." It had two separate compartments; one was used for the soap and the brush, and the other was used to hold very hot water which would keep everything warm.

Straight razors and their accessories were in common use throughout the 1800's. In 1905 the safety razor started being widely distributed and within about 20 years it had taken over more than 90 percent of the market. Today, the straight razor is used only in barbershops as a kind of tradition. The millions of straight razors and accessories that once existed have disappeared except for those that are still left in the hands of collectors.

At a recent auction, straight razors of better quality sold for about $20 to $200 each. Shaving mugs sold for much higher prices, generally selling between $100 and $400. However some exceptionally fine items sold for $750 each.

For information concerning straight razors, contact Robert Doyle of Fishkill, N.Y. For information on shaving mugs contact Deryl Clark of the Shaving Mug Collector's Association, Road 6, Box 176, Bedford, PA 15522.

This article appeared in Knife World May, 1986

Original oak mug rack which was actually used by a barber in his barbershop. The rack holds 108 mugs. The lower drawers were used to hold supplies.

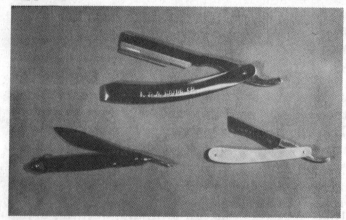

Top: L. & A. Razor Company stainless steel handled razor. Left: J.A. Henckels Co. corn razor with celluloid handle. Right: Henckels Co. corn razor with mother of pearl handle.

Razors of the Bowie Men

by Mark Zalesky

Bowie knife. The mere mention of the words brings to mind adventuresome men on their way to the gold fields of California in the late 1840's, of young soldiers in the Civil War, of the shifty-eyed gambler on board a Mississippi steamboat. In the period from about 1830 to 1870, bowie knives (and their close relatives, the folding dirks) were the close companion, the "trusty friend" if you will, of the men who helped forge a nation. From the statesmen to the cowboys down to the common man, many knew the warm comfort that the hefty lump on their belt, in their pocket, or up their sleeve provided. Today, these knives represent the top end of the knife collecting market, the high-dollar items that the majority of us can only dream of owning.

Now, these great (and not-so-great) men of long ago most certainly used their prized knives for a great number of purposes, but it's highly unlikely that many owners ever used these bulky instruments to remove their facial hair. Though perhaps a less glamourous job, the straight razor nevertheless performed an important task in the daily lives of the men who carried the bowies, the men who helped shape this country of ours. What's more, a small number of collectors are beginning to realize that the face-shaving companion of the bowie knife is well within the price range of the average collector today.

Straight razors from the same period (1830-1870) were as varied as the Bowie in outward appearance. They were sometimes extremely large and heavy, or they

Two 1860 period bowies by Corsan, Denton, Burdekin & Co. surrounding some razors of the bowie period of 1830-1870.

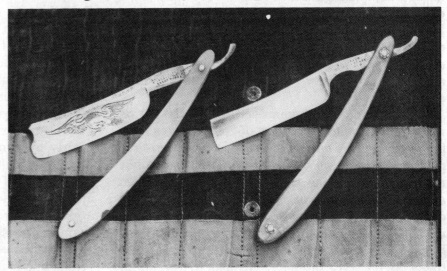

Straight razors by Wm. Greaves and Sons and Tillotson, Columbia Peace, respectively.

could be rather small and lightweight. They were often well-finished but were sometimes quite crude. Best of all, they could be handled of the same materials and decorated as elaborately as the finest of bowies. Handles could be pressed, carved, embossed, or inlaid with shields, pearl, or silver pins. Blades could be stamped or etched with fancy scenes, slogans, or wording, in many cases

11

Three I*XL razors. Top is marked "Rockingham Works," middle has pearl inlay, and the bottom is pressed "The American I*XL Razor."

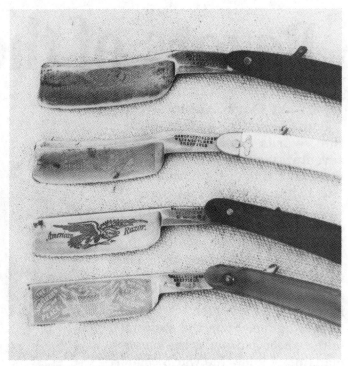

A group of Wade & Butcher razor sma during the bowie period.

the same ones that adorned bowies. It would seem, in fact, that straight razor blades were more often decorated than the blades of bowie knives and folding dirks of the period. This was undoubtably due to the fact that the large wedge-ground blades of the period presented a relatively large, flat surface, free of fancy bevels, which cutlers found quite easy to etch.

Cutlers and cutlery manufacturers of the period were generally not producers of bowie knives only, but, rather, they tended to produce other forms of cutlery as well, which usually included straight razors. Yet, while the marks of a certain maker on a given knife may make that knife a much more desirable (and thus valuable) piece, that same maker's mark on a straight razor often makes little or no difference to the value of the razor today. As collector interest continues to develop in this area of straight razor collecting, time may prove that "the razors of the bowie men" are the true bargains of today's antique cutlery market.

One of the most, if not the most famous of the bowie knifemakers was the firm of George Wostenholm and Sons, bearers of the famed I*XL trademark. They produced many thousands of both knives and razors for the American market from the early 1800's up to about 1970, both

elaborate and plain and of nearly every size and shape. Items marked as produced at the Rockingham Works predate 1848, at which time Wostenholm moved to the larger quarters available at the Washington Works. Knives and razors produced at the Rockingham Works are quite rare and the knives command a premium price. Production from the Washington Works is much more common, though still desirable. I*XL knives and razors are generally prized more highly by American collectors than most other English brands.

The firm of W. & S. Butcher produced not only many fine knives, particularly early ones, but also a great number of straight razors, perhaps more than any other English manufacturer. Most of the straight razors produced by this firm were marked "Wade and Butcher," referring to their partnership with Robert Wade. These razors, though common, are relatively popular in the collector market due not only to the famous name, but also to the great number of high quality razors produced by this firm, which include some of the finest etched blades in all of razor collecting.

Another famous English cutlery company is that of Joseph Rodgers and Sons, bearers of the "star and cross" trademark, located at No.6 Norfolk

12

Straight razor and folding dirk/dagger by R. Bunting and Son, Sheffield 1840-1850 period.

Street in Sheffield. Rodgers produced very high quality cutlery, perhaps the best in the world, using great amounts of ivory, stag, and pearl shell in the process. Though they produced large numbers of knives of all kinds, it seems that they produced many fewer razors than either Wostenholm or Wade and Butcher did.

While the great cutlery factories of George Wostenholm and Wade and Butcher produced thousands upon thousands of both knives and razors, the smaller shops of famed makers such as R. Bunting, T. Tillotson, Wm. Greaves, and Edward Barnes turned out many fewer pieces of cutlery, and are therefore much rarer than comparative I*XL and Wade and Butcher razors, though the difference in collector value is small for razors at this point in time.

I have not yet seen razors by the greatest majority of the famous Sheffield bowie makers, and yet we can safely assume that they are out there somewhere. But where are the straight razors produced by the likes of A. Davy, C. Congreve, G. Woodhead, and the dozens of other makers whose knives grace famous museums and collections across the country? Were they not exported to the same extent? Were they never produced? Or are they just hidden away in attics somewhere, waiting to be found by some lucky collector?

While the majority of bowie knives and straight razors produced up to 1870 were imported from England, a number of American makers began

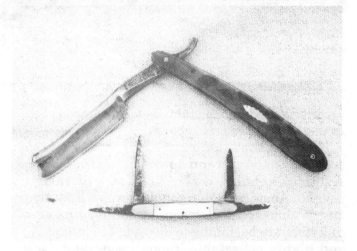

Straight razor and "Senate Knife" by Joseph Rodgers and Sons, No.6 Norfolk Street, Sheffield.

filling the market with their own production. These American knives and razors are much rarer than their British counterparts and command a higher price from collectors, though the difference is more pronounced in bowies. While some were produced by the early cutlery factories of firms such as Waterville (1843) and Holley (1844), many were also produced in the smaller shops of makers such as the Hassam Bros. of Boston or Michael Price and Will & Finck of San Francisco. And yet, to my knowledge, razors produced by makers such as Rose of New York or Schively of Philadelphia have not yet been uncovered. To a collector interested in this area, an American made straight

Edward Barnes and Sons made this beautiful pair– a straight razor and folding dirk. 1860 period.

razor produced in one of these small, famous shops would be a highly prized piece.

It seems that the majority of straight razor collectors today tend to collect either fancy celluloid handled razors or razors of various popular American knife companies (such as Case and Winchester). However, a small number of collectors are beginning to discover the interesting and highly collectable, though sometimes less elaborate, straight razors of the bowie era. I perceive the collecting of mid-nineteenth century razors to be in it's infancy, as Bowie knife collecting was in the 1960's. The time may be soon coming that, as the desirability of bowie knives has far surpassed that of the mass-produced Remingtons and Winchesters, so may the "razors of the bowie men" surpass the desirability of the mass-produced celluloid razors of the early 20th century.

This article appeared in Knife World July, 1990.

Copper Pins with Nickel Collars

By Kurt Moe

A razor has a copper colored pivot pin with a nickel silver collar. Usually this means that the pin is a replacement. When the pin is a replacement the blade is usually not original to the handle as well. There are exceptions, however. Some razors were apparently manufactured with this unusual combination of copper and nickel materials.

One such razor is marked on its shank, "Newton." "Made in German" and the number "230" is on the back. The blade is a "Copper King" etching. The flat metal handles are etched with leaves and flowers.

Sir Isacc Newton (1642-1727) was an English mathematician and astronomer. His principle contribution to science was the Law of Universal Gravitation. The connection between Newton and the Copper King etching isn't readily apparent. Perhaps it refers to Newton being master of the mint at London in 1699. The razor certainly doesn't date that early. Though the age of the razor isn't obvious surely 1910 would be a better guess than 1700.

The primary reason I believe this blade is original to the handle is that I've seen two examples of this razor that were exactly the same. They were like twins, both with copper pins and nickel collars. Several years and several hundred miles separated the two razors. With these circumstances in mind it would seem that the Copper King etch and the copper pivot pin could be more than coincidence.

A second razor is marked on its

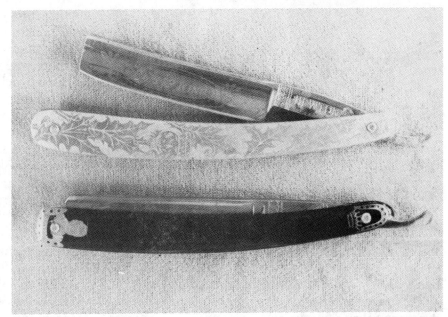

Two razors thought to be originally manufactured with copper pins but with nickel silver collars.

Top: Razor with leaf etching on metal handles. "Copper King" etching is on blade. "Newton" is stamped on the shank. Bottom: Star Barber Supply, Baltimore, Md. razor. "Benito" is stamped on the shank.

shank, "Star Barber Supply Co., Baltimore, Md," and "Made in Germany." The shank front is marked, "Benito."

The rounded handle in black has a very unusual copper colored inlay. The large end has on each side an inlay of a man's head and shoulders and is marked "Mussolini." The small end of the razor

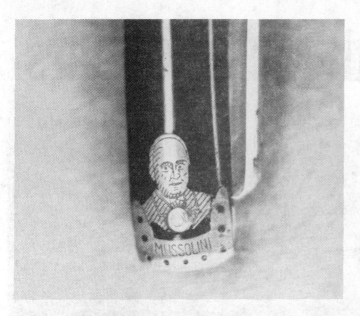

Mussolini inlay is on both sides of the black handle of the Star Barber Supply razor.

has a design on each side incorporating a crown.

This razor looked like it had been repined. The different colored materials of the pins and collars were one reason it looked that way. The pivot pin was also flattened compared to the other pin and there were nearby marks on the handle. I was disappointed because if the blade wasn't original to the handle the razor had less historical significance as well as less value to me than if it were original.

The space often reserved for the model name of a razor was marked on this razor "Benito." A trip to the encyclopedia confirmed that this was Mussolini's first name. It has been said that the odds of filling an inside straight poker hand are not good. The odds of Benito Mussolini having his first name on a razor shank and last name on the razor's handle without the razor being originally manufactured that way must be even smaller.

Knowing this information, lets look at the pins again. Pins on both ends of the razor are copper with nickel collars. Replacement pivot pins often do not match the pin and collar on the other end as there was no reason to replace both pins.

Barber school manuals often indicate that a blade should not be loose enough in the handle to fall closed by itself. The manual goes on to describe how to peen the pivot pin with a hammer to tighten a loose blade. Perhaps this explains the flattened look of the pivot pin and the marks on the handle around it.

My next thought was why would anyone produce a razor honoring this Italian, a dictator from 1922-1943? Perhaps the barber supply company served an area with a large Italian community. Perhaps it was because the Lateral agreement was reached in 1929. This treaty established certain rights for the Roman Catholic Church and the State of Vatican City. The razor is marked "Made in Germany." Perhaps a German manufacturer felt Mussolini's alliance with Hitler and Nazi Germany in about 1936 was reason to honor him.

In any case Mussolini's popularity began to slip in the years following. Germany began to treat Mussolini's government with contempt. Mussolini met death in 1945 as he and his mistress were shot and their bodies hung in public. Sources indicate that Hitler planned his last days so that he would avoid such a death and public ridicule.

This article appeared in Knife World May, 1990.

Damascus Razors

by Kurt Moe

Fine Damascus barrels were the standard of firearm excellence for many years. A French pinfire shotgun with figured barrels proved irresistible at a gun show several years ago. It is easy for me to admire the strength and beauty of Damascus knives as well.

The reputation of Damascus forged steel was envied and imitated by firearms manufacturers and as you will see, razor manufacturers. The cutlers probably wanted to identify with the Damascus reputation and wanted to make use of the pleasing pattern or design as well.

Some razors made use of blade etchings, with the words, "Damascus Blade." A "Thistle Cutlery New York USA" razor has such an etching coupled with an illustration of a camel.

One razor having a Damascus patterned blade is marked on the shank "Our Bullet." The shank back reads "East St.Louis B.S. Co." "East St. Louis, Ill." "German made." This barber supply firm has an unusual Illinois address also.

The Damascus pattern is not evident in the places where metal was honed off. The dull and shiny pattern was probably etched on the steel surface. The Damascus pattern is on the blade, shank, and tang surfaces, but did not prevent a large piece from being broken from the blade.

The razor handle is of an unusual pattern and appears to be made of black rubber.

Most razors found in the USA are either U.S. marked or from England or Germany. When it comes to Damascus razor blades,

Razor blades with damascus patterns. Top: Note shank stamping "Fradies A Paris." Tang is short, blade is wider at point. Pressed horn handle honoring LaFayette. Bottom: German made blade in black hard rubber handle.

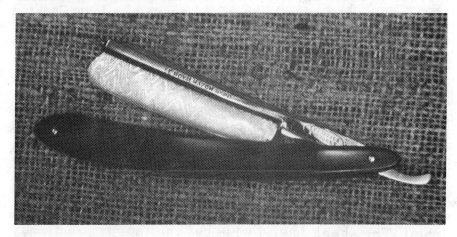

Removable razor blade with damascus pattern. French razor has dark horn handles.

however, most that I have seen are French marked.

A French frameback style razor has a removable blade that also appears to have its Damascus pattern etched. There is a small screw on the end of the frame which allows the thin blade to be removed and replaced. The frame is marked. "LeRoyal Razor No.20." The shank is marked "Lecollier" "A Nogent" in an oval and "France." The shank back is marked "Curley N.Y." and the frame is marked, "Depose." The blade has written in ink "450W/ 2 blds." Probably the razor was a sales sample and the razor was normally

Pile side of handle pressed the same as the front side, "D B 22," Gal, LaFayette bust, wreath, drum, and flags. This razor has characteristics of one from about 1800-1830.

sold with an extra blade.

The handle of this razor is a fine grained, glossy dark horn with a white bone spacer.

A very similar "Rasoir" but without a Damascus blade has markings, "Jaques Lecoultre Au Sentier Switzerland, M&M Co." This razor comes in a box with room for extra blades and has a small screwdriver to assist with blade changing.

Another frameback razor is marked on the shank "F. Georget" "France." The tang is marked "GRD." The thin blade has a Damascus pattern and is held by means of a lever locking mechanism in the frame.

The blade is stamped "Levier" (which translates to lever) and "Le Tourist." The blade back and shank back appear to be similarly marked "BteSGDG" and the razor handle is black celluloid.

This razor also came in a double box with room in one section for the razor and another section for extra interchangeable blades.

Another blade which appears to be etched or printed in a Damascus pattern is the most rare and oldest of the razors mentioned here. It probably dates from the first third of the 19th century.

The patterned blade is of an unusual shape, wider near the point. The shank is also wide but the tang is practically nonexistent. The shank is marked in a difficult to read script which might be "Fradies" and "A Paris."

The handles are flat semi transparent horn with dark spots. Design are pressed into the horn. The designs include a drum, flags, a wreath, cannon barrel and sword. The central design is a man's bust labeled "Gal Lafayette." There are other letters D,B and the number 22 near the hinge pin. The "Gal" may be an abbreviation of the title General. If anyone has an explanation of these letters and number, I would appreciate their help.

Both sides of the razor are pressed with the same illustrations. The handles are separated with a metal spacer and have brass pins with large iron caps.

The Marquis de LaFayette was born in 1757. As a young man he was a French volunteer and General active in our American Revolution against the British. Please do not confuse him with the French pirate, Jean Lafitte, who was involved in the New Orleans battle against the British.

There doesn't seem to be any particular great event during LaFayette's lifetime. Over the years he held various appointments and elected office. In 1830 he was forced to resign as Commandant in General of the French National Guard. He died in 1834.

What is remarkable is the length of time that LaFayette was involved in the politics of France. What is most remarkable is that he managed to survive the French Revolution while many around him literally lost their heads to the guillotine.

This article appeared in Knife World December, 1983.

George W. Korn Patents

by Kurt Moe

George W. Korn of Little Valley, New York applied for a patent in 1901 for a double hollow ground blade for razors. He was granted patent number 693,524 for this improvement on Feb.18, 1902. An "English hollow ground" blade is described as having a concave face from the cutting edge to the back of the blade. The specifications go on to say that such an edge is too thin and flexible and can have an unwanted vibratory characteristic.

A "Hamburg concave" is described as having a concave face on the top portion of the blade but is substantially convex near the cutting edge. This edge is described as satisfactory when new but that it could not be easily honed as required. The convex portion of the blade held the cutting edge from touching the honing surface.

Korn's patented double concave face allowed the blade to be honed when required, yet thickened the blade in a ridge. The ridge or rib is a short distance from the cutting edge and stiffens and strengthens the entire blade.

A razor blade using this patent is etched "American Double Hollow." The reverse side of the blade is marked "Geo. W. Korn Razor Mfg. Co.," "Little Valley N.Y." Very few razors are marked on the blade in this manner. A flattened area on the blade top is marked "Pat. Feb. 18, 1902." The same pearlized green handle material also covers the tang and shank of the razor.

A second razor is nearly identical except for company marking. This double hollow ground blade is marked "Cattaraugus Cutlery Co." "Little Valley N.Y." It has the same

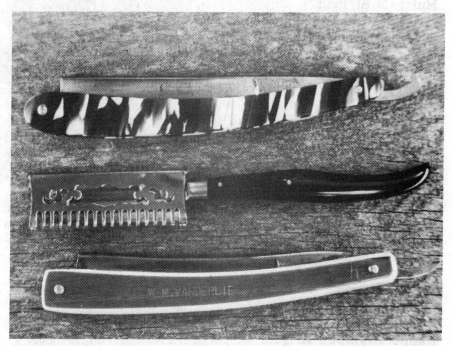

Three George Korn razors. Top: Green and cream mottled celluloid handle. Center: "The Real" safety razor with rigid handle. 1903 patent. Bottom: Red wood grain handle with red spacer between handles and a white border. Name imprinted in gold.

type of handle and material covering the tang and shank. The blade has the same markings on its top including "Pat. Feb. 18, 1902."

Steve Deer furnished information about his "Thomas Mfg. Co." razor using the Korn patent. The blade is etched "American Double Hollow." The back side of the shank reads, "US Patent No.693524." The gold pearlized celluloid handles are held together with pins that appear to be spun and have no collars on the front. The back sides of the pins have collars. These pins match the pins on the Korn razor previously described.

It is generally recognized in the industry that certain patterns of pocket knives were made by one firm and marked with the names of other firms in the cutlery business. It is my feeling that one company made the previously described Korn, Cattaraugus, and Thomas razors. They share many features and are all marked with Geo. Korn's double hollow patent date or number.

Other razors have double hollow ground blades but are not so nearly identical in their construction. One is marked, "Simmons Hardware Co. St. Louis," on the shank. It is marked, "Absolute Guarantee Pat. Feb., 18, 1902," on the shank reverse. Where the Korn razor has that information on a flat spot on the blade top, the Simmons razor reads, "No.8 Special."

Mr. Deer also has another razor with a double hollow blade. This one is marked "Hackett, Gates, Hurty Co. St. Paul."

A Robeson ShurEdge razor as well has a double hollow blade etched "New Science Concave."

Even more ordinary looking razors marked "Geo. W. Korn Razor Mfg." often had unusual features. Two such razors have white celluloid flat handles. One has a red wood grain face laminated to the handles, the other has a blue face. The beveled edge of the white celluloid forms a border around the edge of the handles. A detail of the construction is that the spacer between the handles matches the laminated color. One handle has a red spacer while the other handle has a blue spacer.

Both of these handles have names stamped in gold in the fronts of the handles. These names appear to personalize the razor for their owners.

George Korn received a number of U.S. patents. The book "An Introduction to Switchblade Knives," by Ben Myers and Lowell Myers, JD, has information on the patents Geo. Korn secured covering automatic opening knives.

Patent No.805,561 granted to G.W. Korn was for a razor handle improvement. The same handle would be used for a number of interchangeable blades without the need for tools.

Another patent application by G.W. Korn led to patent number 720,360. This safety razor has a guard next to the cutting edge of a hollow ground blade. The guard could be easily reversed to the other side of the blade.

A razor substantially the same as described in these patent specifications is etched "The Real," "Pat. Feb. 10, 1903." The blade is rigidly attached to the black

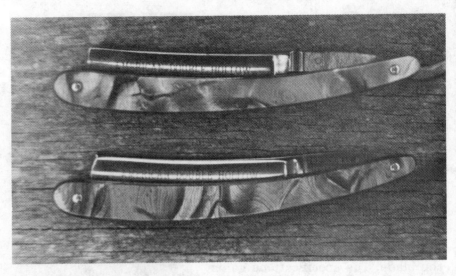

Two razors using the "Korn" patent. Top: George Korn razor with blade etched "American Double Hollow." Bottom: Thomas Mfg. Co. razor with the same blade etching and similarities of construction.

celluloid handle. It has the "Korn Razor Mfg. Co." marking on the back side of the blade. The box this razor came in is the size of an ordinary razor box, however, the part holding the razor slides into a sleeve like a matchbox.

Cattaraugus Cutlery has a small folding razor with a safety guard pictured in its catalog from about 1922. The guard appears identical to that on the Korn Safety razor and the blade is also etched, "The Real." The black handles appear to be "pinched" near the hinge pin. Another Cattaraugus razor has pearlized green handles and is also etched "The Real" on its blade. The reverse side of the shank is stamped "US Patent No.720360."

The last two razors described have indentations on both sides of the handle near the hinge pin. Patent number 815,355 was granted to G.W. Korn for handles with this design to allow the fingers to grip the handle better.

A small Robeson Cutlery Co. razor has a number on its tang that appears to be 730,360. Perhaps it and the similar "The Real" razors could have different patent numbers exactly 10,000 apart. This patent, however, pertains to a horse taming or training device. My guess is that the Korn patent number had a "2" mistaken for a "3" somewhere along the line. If so, this makes razors marked Cattaraugus, Robeson, and Thomas Mfg. with numbers or dates stamped on them linking them to Geo. Korn Razor Mfg.

This article appeared in Knife World May, 1984.

Jenny Lind

by Kurt Moe

Johanna Maria (Jenny) Lind was engaged by P.T. Barnum to sing for an American tour lasting from 1850 to 1852. Phineas Barnum had been greatly successful in the exhibition business. His name, however, was linked with freaks and hoaxes. He had been looking for an undertaking to lend some dignity to his reputation. The tour by Jenny Lind was just such a venture.

Without ever having heard Miss Lind sing, Barnum sent a representative to Europe to propose a contract for the tour of the United States. As soon as she accepted, a whirlwind media campaign was launched to make Jenny Lind a well known figure in the U.S. Barnum also conceived the idea of selling tickets to Miss Lind's performance by auction. What was to be normally a $3 ticket sold the first time for $225. Later in Boston a ticket sold for $625. In each city, Barnum would secretly approach several businessmen and suggest that if they bid the highest price for a ticket that they would receive a great deal of free publicity.

Jenny Lind was immensely popular with both men and women. She was a soprano with a bright and thrilling quality and could use her voice with skill and imagination. Sometimes called "The Swedish Nightingale," she was said to be a favorite of Queen Victoria. She was also said to be romantically linked with children's story writer, Hans Christian Andersen. During the U.S. tour, however, she married her accompanist, Otto Goldschmidt.

Medals and tokens were struck in Jenny Lind's honor. A connecticut bank even printed $3 & $5 bills with her face on the currency. It was no coincidence that P.T. Barnum was president of the bank!

Many items were sold carrying the singer's face or name. Cigars, poker chips, pipes, chewing gum, dolls, tea kettles, buggies, snuffboxes, hairpins, dinner service patterns, and matchboxes are just a few of the items. Even recent auction bills identify a type of bedroom furniture as being "Jenny Lind."

Wade & Butcher manufactured at least two differently etched razors honoring Jenny Lind. Jenny Lind was born in 1820 and both etchings

Etching of Jenny Lind by Wade & Butcher. Reference is made to a hospital gift.

seem to me to be of an adult woman. Both razors probably date from after 1840.

My guess is that that older of the two razors is the razor blade lightly etched "The Swedish Nightingale" above and "Jenny Lind" below her figure. The heavy blade looks typical of the old wedge style blades. There is a very slight concave to the surface, however, as a sharpening stone has removed metal from the blade's edge and back but destroyed only a part of the etching. The shank is deeply stamped "Manufactured by Wade &

Butcher Sheffield."

The handle is dark horn with a grain that makes it look much like wood. There is no spacer at all, the horn handles simply come together. The pins appear to be brass and the large collars have rusted like steel.

The second razor has flags and what appears to be an eagle above Lind's portrait and reads "Jenny Lind," "Hospital Gift" below. What appears to be monetary amounts of 500 and 1000 pounds are mentioned twice in the etching. The etching may have been lacking in detail even when new. Now some 140 years later a few spots of rust mask even more of the detail. One of the flags appears to have the side view of the figure of a lion.

In 1848, Jenny Lind took charge of a special benefit for Old Brompton Hospital for Consumptives. A part of the hospital was designated as the Jenny Lind wing.

In 1864 Jenny Lind founded a hospital for children in Stockholm.

Perhaps the razor etching refers to fund raising activities for one of these hospitals. Jenny Lind was frequently generous to charities, however, and there is nothing specific in the etching that ties the razor to either hospital.

The second razor has smaller brass pins and collars and a lead like spacer between glossy black horn handles. The mark on the shank reads the same as the stamping on the first razor. The mark is not nearly as deep, however, and appears to be etched. This practice is said to have begun in about 1850. Also included in the etching is the Wade & Butcher trademark using the letter B and the figures of an arrow and cross.

Some of P.T. Barnum's exhibitions before the Jenny Lind tour displayed a large sign inside the hall reading, "This way to the EGRESS." Some of the unsuspecting public would go through the door way expecting to see something called an Egress. They found instead that they were outside of the exhibition. P.T. Barnum seemed to enjoy fooling people because the word egress simply means a way out or exit!

This article appeared in Knife World August, 1990.

Wade & Butcher razor etching showing a figure of Jenny Lind and reading "The Swedish Nightingale, Jenny Lind."

Interchangeable Blades

by Kurt Moe

Stropping and honing were operations very necessary in preparation for the shaving ritual. The cutting edge simply wouldn't give a satisfactory shave without frequent stropping. This could be a time consuming operation to accomplish during early morning grooming hours. It is also doubtful that very many families had the multiple bathroom facilities common today. A leisurely shave was not often possible.

One solution to this problem was to have several blades that fit the same razor handle. The blades could all be properly prepared at one time and then each used in turn during the rest of the week. A type of set that dates from the early 1800's had a handle shorter than that of an ordinary straight razor and a number of interchangeable blades. Robert Doyle's article, "A Study of Sets Part III" in the December, 1981, *American Blade* magazine illustrates such sets with seven blades each by "C & J Morton," "Webster," and "Wade & Butcher."

Such a razor set with seven interchangeable blades has been seen in a case which reminds one of a pencil box. There is a leather strop bonded to the swinging lid. The whole box slides into a tight fitting sleeve which holds the lid securely shut. A small ivory handle is used to pull the box back out of the sleeve.

The short handle is ivory with a metal spacer. The blade holding mechanism is clad in a alloy that tarnishes green. There is a spring loaded button catch to hold the blades to the handle.

There are seven blades with shanks that are file cut top and bottom to prevent fingers from slipping. There is no makers name. The only marking is the number 5 on the tang end of each blade. The shanks do not become narrow but are nearly the same width as the blades.

Another set is in a deep maroon leather box with a hook fastener. The ivory handle is stored on its side. There is a metal spacer between the handles. The pins are brass with no collars. The blade holding mechanism is clad in brass. A spring loaded mechanism holds the blade until a button is pushed down to release it.

The seven interchangeable blades are etched on

Razor set from about 1820 with seven interchangeable blades fitting one ivory handle. Note that the shank is nearly the same width as the blade. No maker is shown on the razor.

Razor set with three blades marked "Clark & Hall." Lummus dates this maker 1797-1823. Ivory handle has design made up of about 200 small pins.

the back or top with the days the week "Sunday" through "Saturday." The bottoms of the shanks are file cut. The tops of the shanks are fluted. Each shank is stamped "Josh Roberts" with an anchor trademark. Six of the shanks are marked near the end with the number 5. The Saturday shank is marked 3. There is no obvious explanation for this difference. Perhaps it was simply a mistake due to poor eyesight.

The magazine *Antiques* in December, 1922, has an article by Henry T. Lummus on "Old Sheffield Razors." A razor set is pictured with a razor handle boxed with seven interchangeable blades. This razor handle is very unusual in that the head end has two knife blades in it. This could truly be a razor that even knife collectors would want.

Still another razor set has a handle of ivory with many small pins in a design around an inlaid shield. The inside of the handle shows the pin holding the shield in place.

The making of this ornate design must have been time consuming as there are about 200 pins in total with about four pins per 1/8 inch of design. The pins do not go all the way through the handle which is about 1/16 of an inch thick. The pins show only on the outside surface of the handle. There is a pewter like metal spacer separating the handle. The iron pins which hold the handle together all appear to have had iron collars worked into the shape of flower petals with the pin being the center of the flower. Some of the collars have been lost.

There is a tang of metal clad with brass and marked 3. The hollow tang has a spring mechanism with a button release.

This set has three interchangeable blades with each blade marked "Clark & Hall," "3." The blades are wedge shaped. The shanks are file cut top and bottom. Henry Lummus dated this firm from about 1797 to 1823.

A very large razor has pointed handles which are mottled light and dark brown. The possible tortoise shell handles are separated with a metal spacer.

There are three interchangeable blades. The blades are unusual in that they are double edged and have a slot in the end to hold a safety guard. The other end of the guard fits a pin on the blade. The guard protects both edges of the blade and can be placed on either side of the blade.

A small key fits a slot in the razors shank. When turned, the key releases the blade. The tang is unmarked except for the number 2. The three blade shanks are also marked 2.

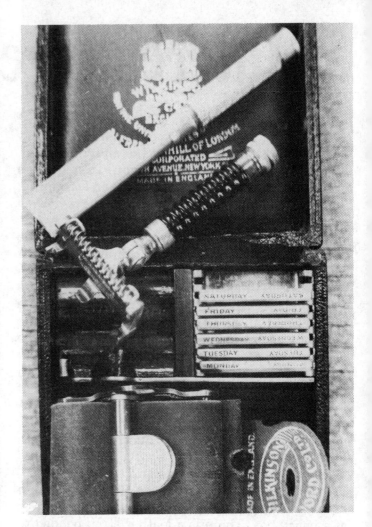

Wilkinson Sword Co. Ltd. made several types of seven day safety razor sets. This model has a silver plated razor, seven day etched blades, strop and blade holder fitted to a case.

An ordinary sized razor has dark glossy horn handles with a spacer that appears to be ivory or bone. This razor probably dates from about 1900.

The tang, shank, and back of the razor is a metal alloy with a shade of brass color. The pins holding the handle together resemble brass rivets. There is no marking of any kind on the razor itself.

There are seven blades marked JAQUES LE COULTRE, AU SENTIER. Each blade is marked with a N followed by a number from 1 through 7. The blades have a slight wedge shape and have a brushed finish. The blades are stored in wax paper folds. A screwdriver is included as part of the set. A screw at the end of the razor's frame tightens or loosens to hold or release one of the blades.

In about 1890 a whole new type of razor was

introduced. This type of razor had a round tube handle and a frame which held a short section of hollow ground blade.

One of these razors was the STAR brand razor made by the Kampfe Bros. New York, USA. These razors could be purchased with more than one blade. Some sets were fitted in elegant morocco leather cases lined with satin and could be purchased with one safety frame and seven blades. One blade for each day of the week. Some packaging had simple nickel-silver holders to use for stropping the blades. Other cases had stropping machines that automatically flipped the blades over after each stroke on a strop. Some of the machines had elaborate decorations and were silver plated.

A black leather covered case is lined in dark blue satin and velvet. The lid has a crest and reads, "Wilkinson Sword Co.," "Made in England," "Exclusive agents for the United States of America," "Alfred Dunhill of London." The case holds a safety razor frame with a guard that rolls across the face. Loosening the handle permits the angle of the head to be adjusted. The metal parts of the razor appear to be plated with silver.

There are sections of the case that hold a strop and a holder clamp used to strop the blades. Another section of the case holds seven hollow ground blades. Each blade is etched twice on the top with a day of the week from "Sunday" through "Saturday." The blades are also etched "Hand forged/ Made in England/ Wilkinson Sword Co. Ltd." There is an illustration of a hand holding a ball peen hammer. Some sets even have scroll etched on each side of the day etching.

Another set of Wilkinson blades

Three double edged blades with a guard fit a large razor handle. Small key is used to release blades from razor.

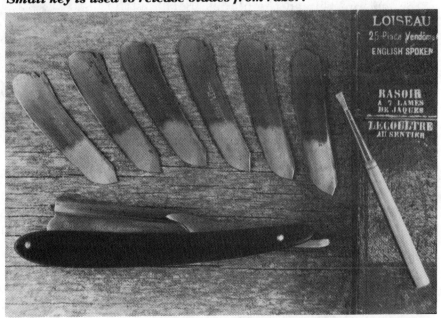

Blades numbered 1 through 7 are marked "Jaques Le Coultre, Au Sentier." Handle is dark horn. Screwdriver is used to release blade from frame.

and razor frame is in a chrome case and is probably much newer. The blades in this set are still hollow ground but are about half the size of the previous set. Each blade fits in a clamp marked twice with an abbreviation for a day of the week.

The case holds a strop which threads through the razor so that the blade need not be removed from the frame to be stropped.

The paper sleeve for this chrome case calls the razor an Empire Model. The printing goes on to say that the seven day set was manufactured by the Wilkinson Sword Co. Ltd. at their factory,

"Acton, London, England," "Established 1772."

The English "Rolls" razors are known to have companion cases with slot marked with the days of the week for extra hollow ground blades. Similar types of razor frames were also marked "J.A. Henckels Twin Works, Germany." These razors were also cased with slots for extra blades and compartments for strop and blade holder.

There are known to be "C.V. Heljestrand, Eskilstuna, Sweden," razor frames cased with slots for 31 blades. The hollow ground blades for these razors are known to have been marked with the days of the week in English or other languages or even with numbers from 1 through 31.

A leather box marked in gold, "Sextoblade Razor Style B, E. Weck N.Y." holds a Weck folding razor with a guard. The fitted green box has a brass plate marked with the days of the week opposite blade slots. While the Sextoblades were often disposed of when dull, some users may have stropped and reused the blades. Perhaps the blades were rotated in their use to "rest" them between shaves.

The country auction that yielded this box had two auctioneers calling at opposite ends of a yard of hayracks. There were hundreds of boxes of small items and some were sold by the box. It is remarkable that we discovered this Weck Razor box at all. More remarkable is that we could keep track of the Weck box location for the several

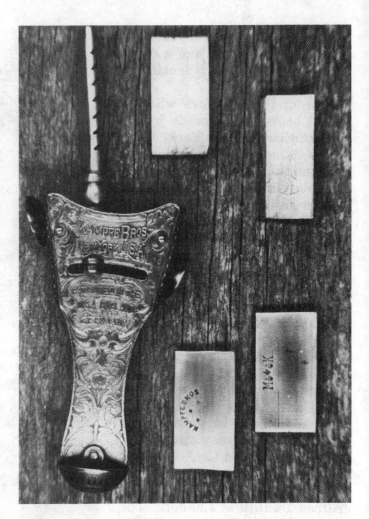

Silver plate Kampfe Bros. stropping machine with hollow ground razor blades of various manufacturers.

hours that we waited before my wife Cindy could get it for a single bid.

Gradually after 1900, disposable blades became more and more popular. Each of the World Wars was probably responsible for converting hundreds of thousands of young men to use of safety razors and disposable blades. Though some owners continued to hone and strop their safety razor blades, most didn't take the time and simply threw away blades that no longer gave a good shave. A new blade was then unwrapped and used.

Now in the 1980's advertisements tell us not to even bother to change blades but to throw the whole razor away. For those people decades ago that found it difficult to throw away a used blade, I'm sure the idea of a disposable razor would have been impossible to accept.

This article appeared in Knife World May, 1985.

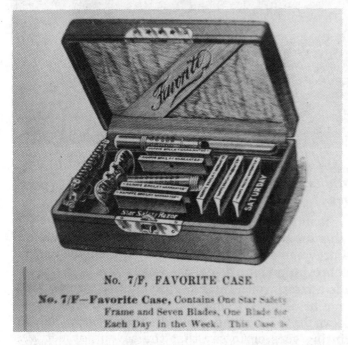

No. 7/F, FAVORITE CASE

No. 7/F—Favorite Case, Contains One Star Safety Frame and Seven Blades, One Blade for Each Day in the Week. This Case is

Illustration of Star razor set containing seven blades as shown in 1902 Witte Hardware catalog.

Shaped Razor Handles

by Kurt Moe

Razor handles in this unusual shape are sometimes described as a gunstock pattern or looking like a lady's leg. Razors of this shape are not particularly common even though they may have been sold over several decades.

A 1902 hardware catalog has a full sized picture of a black "shaped handle" razor. The razor is marked on the shank "Witte Hardware Co," "Made in Germany." It is etched on the blade, "Witte Hdwe Co." The handle is described only as being the color black.

Hibbard, Spencer, Bartlett & Co. has a pictured listing of this style of razor handle in what I believe is a 1933 catalog. The razor was etched "Our Daisy" in gold on the blade and had a double file tang or shank. The handle was described only as an oval rubber shaped handle.

I have no reason to doubt that similar razors were sold for a time before 1902 and for even a few years after 1933.

Some similar black handled razors with white spacers have several different markings. One is marked on the shank, "JBF Champlin & Son," and "Round Point," "Galvanic" on the reverse side. The shank is filed for grip and is curved to fit the finger.

Another razor is stamped on the shank, "Schatt & Morgan," "Titusville, PA." The tang bears the number 926.

Still another razor is marked "CW Hackett Hardware Co." This razor has a very unusual type of hollow point on it blade and also has a curved and filed shank. The

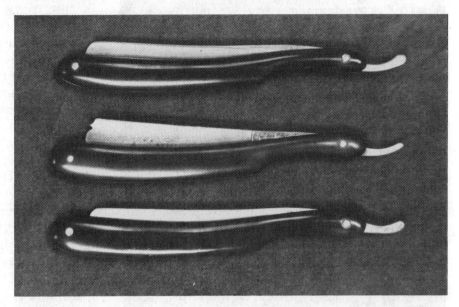

Three black handled razors all with gunstock or shaped handles. Top: J.B.F. Champlin & Son. Middle: C.W. Hackett Hardware Co. Note the unusual point on this blade. Bottom: Schatt & Morgan razor.

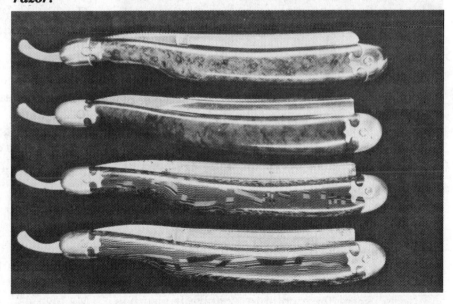

Four Clauss wood grain celluloid handled razors with German silver end caps.

blade is stamped "Our Best Diamond Steel" amidst some small designs.

Some traditional razor handles are found to be crudely scraped or cut down by their owner. Perhaps he was satisfied with his blade but wanted the feel of a shaped handle.

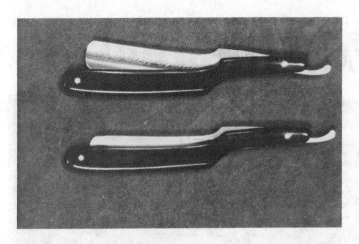

Matched pair of razors etched on the blades "The New Shape." Both blades and black handles are shaped.

Imitation tortoise shell handle and case. Marked W.H. Morley & Sons. Perhaps a mortician's razor?

A very pretty and unusual razor is marked on the shank, "Clauss" in script and "Fremont O." There is also a number "12802 E." The handles are an imitation wood grain using black lines on dark brown background. German silver end caps complete the design. Another razor is nearly identical showing the same shank stamping and handle but no E shows.

A third "Clauss" razor has a shank stamped similarly except for a definite 12902E. It also has German silver end caps but has a different wood grain celluloid handle. This razor has a handle design of a black and brown swirl that looks like walnut burl grain. A fourth "Clauss" razor has an imitation burl handle and is marked similarly but has no number. The top corners of the shank are file cut. The blade is stamped, "Steinman Hdw Co."

These Clauss razors were found individually. While they are similar, they are not matched pairs.

The next two razors were purchased as a pair in a thin, dark maroon box. The box appear to be leather covered and is blue satin and velvet lined. The lid is hinged and releases with a button to show the two black handled razors on their sides. Not only do the handles have the unusual shape, so do the blades. I suspect that these razors would feel and shave much differently than conventional razors because of the placement of their cutting edges. A traditional razor would need a blade at least one inch wide for its cutting edge to be in similar position relative to the holding thumb and fingers.

The blades are appropriately etched "The New Shape" in script. The shank has an illustration of a foot kicking a round ball. The shoe is quite detailed showing shoelaces and spikes. It is also stamped "Trademark Foot Ball." Since these razors have a European origin, a round ball would be as expected instead of the odd shaped American football.

The shank's reverse side reads, "Finest Sheffield Steel," "Forged and Real Hollow," "Ground in Germany." While it was apparently common for Sheffield steel to be used to manufacture razors and knives in other countries, it is unusual to find a razor so marked.

There are several other variations of the gunstock handle. Some of the handles slip into what looks like a toothbrush case of similar material. Sometimes the handle also forms one end of a case or sleeve.

A pretty imitation tortoise shell razor handle has the shaped handle also. The shank is stamped "WH Morley & Sons," "Cloverbrand" with a four leaf clover pictured and "Germany." This razor has a matching case of the same imitation tortoise shell celluloid.

A knowledgeable friend indicates that he's heard this style of razor called a mortician's razor. My own experience cannot confirm this particular use. The possibility of the piece being a mortician's razor, however, jumps into my mind every time I handle it and also prompted a more thorough than usual cleaning of this razor.

This article appeared in Knife World May, 1982.

Rollerback Razor Co. Part I

by Phillip Krumholz

When Raymond Albert Wittl first filed his patent for a "combined razor and stropper" on May 27, 1912, he must have thought that he had the world by the tail. THIS inventor was going to be rich!

By the time his patent #1,090,823 was granted on March 17, 1914, Wittl had probably had a strong dose of reality. It was one thing to invent an item, another thing to manufacture it in quantities efficient for profitability, and yet another to market the item successfully.

Thus marks the efforts of people involved in the short era of the Rollerback Razor Company, a time of tinkering, modification, assembly and marketing attempts. But what WAS the Rollerback Razor, really?

Only one other "self stropping" razor was known at the time that boasted a gear drive, and that was the AutoStrop razor patented some ten years before by Henry Jacques Gaisman. (It would become the Valet AutoStrop razor in 1920.) This hoe-type safety razor featured a flip-up blade cap that retained the blade, and was gear-driven to allow the blade to bear on a strop which was inserted into a slot in the razor's innards. The back and forth flip-flop action resulted in a honed blade on both sides.

Now, Raymond Wittl's invention did much the same thing, but in a different manner. His razor resembled a straight razor (a safety guard was added later) that actually had a metal roller running along the back of the blade; it had a gear on one end of the roller that

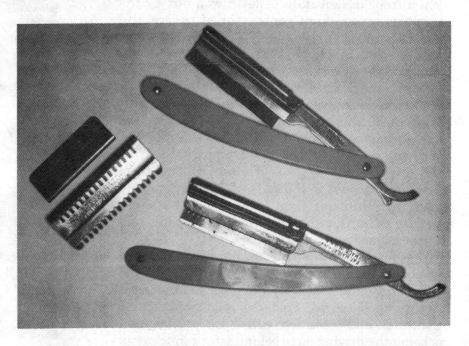

Small gear Rollerback, top, and large gear Rollerback, bottom. On the left is a safety guard and a stropper blade insert.

meshed with a gear on a stationary spindle collar. The gear on the spindle collar meshed, in turn, with a gear on the "slitted substantially C-shaped pivotal mounted blade holder." With ordinary stropping action, the razor blade would bear down with the correct pressure to strop the edge. At the end of the motion, the blade holder would automatically flip over for the return stroke. This was an excellent idea for barbers with carpal tunnel syndrome!

That leads us to the first problem- barbers. They would be the ones most likely to have used or needed the Wittl invention, having a large amount of shaving and needing a quick, easy method of stropping. Clearly, this was a barber's invention. Barbers, however, were taking it on the chin (I couldn't resist) in 1914 from legions of former customers who had learned the quick, convenient method of SELF SHAVING. The customers were actually using one of the hundreds of different types of safety razors available to shave in their own bathroom, rather than making the onerous and stubbly trip to their nearest barbershop.

Then there was the second problem. Wittl's invention depended upon extremely close tolerances and careful manufacture and assembly. The tiny gears could get worn or teeth could break off, and the stropping function would then be no better than with the conventional straight razor. The gear train was quite delicate, and this problem would prompt design changes later on.

Of course, the major hurdles were capitalization and marketing

29

strategy. It is known that a few Rollerback razors were made up and submitted to the U.S. Navy during the early days of the razor "standardization committee." Eventually Gillette won out as the primary government contractor of razors and blades. Apparently, the U.S. Navy was not interested in the Rollerback, nor was any other branch of the armed services.

Wittl WAS able to interest his brother, Frederick, in the venture. Frederick J. Wittl was living in Milwaukee with his wife Jessie, and he was a foreman at the Gem Hammock & Fly Net Company at 326 Florida Street. Apparently Wittl had some large degree of clout at the Gem Company, because in the early 1920s the company split into another firm located on the same premises, the Gem Leather Goods Company, and Wittl became its manager.

This movement towards leather goods (and, in particular, barber strops) gave Frederick Wittl the opportunity and contacts to market his brother's invention. Of course, Frederick was no slouch at innovation and invention, either. He is attributed as being the driving force behind later refinements to the design and improvements to the product line.

So, the Rollerback Razor Company was established during World War I. It never had an official location or factory, but was run during its brief life span from Frederick Wittl's home at 567 Stowell Avenue.

One of the advanced features of the Rollerback razor was the replaceable blade, a la Durham, Curley Brothers, Weck and others. Advertising stated that one could obtain a hundred shaves from one of the long single edge blades, using the honing action of the roller back, of course. Osroe Clark's Clark Blade & Razor Company of 119 Sussex Avenue in Newark, New Jersey, produced the blades for Wittl. You may recall that Osroe Clark invented his own safety razors and was involved in a nasty patent infringement suit with King Gillette's razor company from 1909 to 1911, and Clark lost. There is evidence to suggest that Clark made two sizes of blades for Wittl, based on a 1923 pricing letter. This, it is assumed, was the result of design changes from the small to large gear style of razor.

Meanwhile, Wittl was developing his razor blade stropper. It is not known who manufactured the parts for Wittl, but it is assumed that most were subcontracted in small quantities. Perhaps

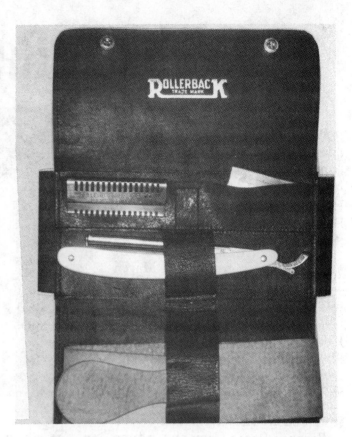

Complete Rollerback set in Morocco leather pouch.

some were produced for Wittl at the Gem Leather Goods Co. (Certainly the leather pouches of the razor sets, and the strops, were produced there.) Since Wittl operated Rollerback from his home, it is conceivable that most razors or stroppers were assembled by him.

But, back to the stropper. Wittl realized that a broader market existed for folks who wanted to quickly strop their razor blades, than folks who wanted a Rollerback razor. Based on the same patent, then, a stropper was marketed "for all makes of safety razor blades." Literature and even the company letterhead stated that the "roller automatically turns the blade at every stroke on (the) strop." The C-shaped blade holder mentioned earlier would accept metal-backed single edge blades such as the Rollerback, Gem, ASR, Ever-Ready, etc. For unbacked or wafer-thin blades, a nickel silver insert of folded metal was provided that would allow a blade to be slid into the insert, then the insert slid into the blade holder. This device promised to be much more salable than the Rollerback razor.

But was it?

This article appeared in Knife World May, 1991.

Rollerback Razor Co. Part II

by Phillip Krumholz

In last month's Knife World, we traced the roots of Chicagoan Raymond Albert Wittl's invention of a gear-driven straight/safety transitional type razor, and the subsequent manufacture and marketing of the device by his brother, Frederick J. Wittl. A razor blade stropper based on the same design was developed by Frederick Wittl.

You may recall that Frederick was operating the Rollerback Razor Company from his home at 567 Stowell Avenue in Milwaukee. It is interesting to note the optimism that Wittl exhibited when he had a run of business letterheads and store display signs printed up. He failed to place an address, other than Milwaukee, Wisconsin, on the printed matter, undoubtedly hoping the business would take off to the extent that he could move the operation to larger quarters and manufacture the products in large quantities. Unfortunately for Wittl, his dream never materialized.

As mentioned in Part I, the original Rollerback razor was of a delicate nature, and would have been a product that appealed mainly to barbers of the day. The original razor strops featured the same tiny gears and the need for close tolerances and careful assembly.

Several prototypes exist which trace the evolution of the Rollerback products, all from the 1920 era. There is the original razor and stropper, with a tiny gear drive. There is a stropper with early small gears and a solid metal knurled handle tapering to the gear assembly. There is another featuring larger gears with a hollow handle. There is another with large gears and a hollow handle with a soldered spindle collar. There are two models with non-movable gears that feature soldered collars and hollow handles. There is another stropper prototype with a brass roller on a hollow handle with a pinned and soldered spindle collar. Finally, there is the late model production stropper with a solid metal handle, large gears, and pinned and soldered collar.

Some evolution is seen, too, with the small nickel-silver blade inserts. An early hinged example exists that was a forerunner of the folded metal insert.

Similar evolution occurred with the razor itself,

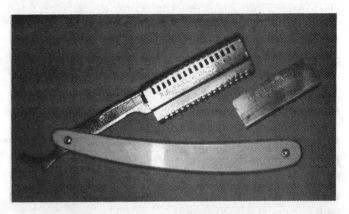

A small gear Rollerback transitional razor with guard installed.

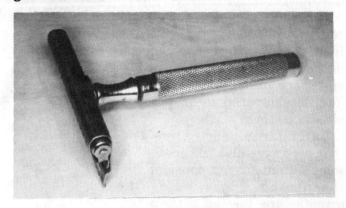

An unfinished prototype hoe style safety razor.

and there exists a partly-finished prototype of a hoe-type Rollerback safety razor. Speaking of the razor, it was mandatory to develop a safety guard that would clamp over the roller and the "C-shaped holder." These guards were large nickel silver affairs prominently stamped with the Rollerback name. They were made in such a manner that they may have fit some traditional straight razors, but the author has no knowledge that the company sold only the safety guards.

What is known, however, is that Frederick Wittl contracted for a large quantity of razor blades in 1923, which perhaps was the heyday of his razor operation. Meanwhile, his bread and butter came from his position as Manager over the fledgling Gem Leather Goods Company at 326 Florida Street in Milwaukee.

Gem Leather Goods began in the early 1920s

and lasted until the late 1940s. In 1942, Gem had relocated to 2430 North 3rd Street in Milwaukee, and it was still managed by Wittl that year. Rollerback by that time was just a memory. Gem Leather Goods, as an aside, produced its own brand of razor strops as well as Wittl's Razor Strop and Wittl's 2 In 1 Razor Strop. Gem manufactured Brandt Strops and, under license, strops patented by Sunusack of Chicago. (Is there a link between Raymond Wittl, the brother who started it all, and whose activities by this time are unknown, with Sunusack?) Also manufactured under license was the Meehan Razor Blade Stropper.

It is assumed that Wittl contracted for his razor strops from the Gem firm. Early strops packed with the razor sets were elaborate items, and later ones had deteriorated to basically a piece of leather.

Later large gear razors and stroppers were also "cheapened" to some extent, if you consider the cheapening an ease to manufacture. Instead of threading and assembling the gear drives with tiny screws, for example, pins were pounded in and solder applied. The products themselves were still of sturdy construction, perhaps better than the earlier ones.

These "cheapened" production methods probably helped Wittl's profitability, however. The $5 Rollerback razor sets came in attractive Morocco leather pouches with a strop, three blades, the razor and guard. The stroppers and blade inserts were intended to sell for $1.

The life of the Rollerback Razor Company is thought to have lasted until the mid-1920s. After that, a few remaining stroppers and razors were offered by Wittl to

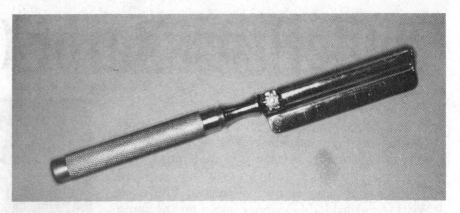

The final large gear production stropper had a solid metal handle with fine knurling.

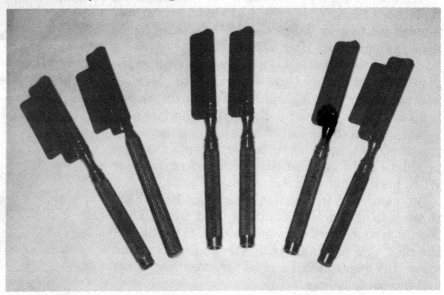

An evolution is seen in stropper prototypes and production pieces. From left, large gear hollow handle; small gear, solid tapering handle; large gear, soldered collar hollow handle; two non movable soldered collar hollow handle stroppers; and brass roller, pinned and soldered collar hollow handled stropper.

customers of the Gem Company. He is believed to have died in 1945.

Another dream of wealth had ended, and with it the dream of producing a quality cutlery product. Collectors can relive this dream as they seek to uncover rare artifacts of the Rollerback Razor Company. There IS an interest in this and other pioneer razor operations that only stayed in business a few years, especially ones with unique designs.

As Wittl himself put it, "The Roller does the trick!"
This article appeared in Knife World June, 1991.

Demonstrator Razors

Kurt Moe

Many brands of razors were offered by the manufacturer at no cost or reduced cost directly to the shaving public. The business concept behind these wonderfully generous offers was that more razors being used meant more blades being purchased. More blades sold meant more profit. A key part of the program was that the blades should have a unique quality or shape to encourage razor users to purchase their blades from the original manufacturer.

The 4 S Razor Company sold a folding razor with replaceable single edge blade and guard. The razor's name is obtained from the first letter of the words, Simple, Sanitary, Sharp, & Safety. The instructions found with the company's razors emphasize its similarity with the old fashioned straight razor. The blade could be stropped and honed. The firm even recommended that the guard of its razor be removed before shaving if whiskers have become long.

THE JUNIOR ADVERTISER. The metal parts of this specially made starter razor were of high grade nickeled steel. The handle was a tough black fiber. The razor with reasonable care was said to last a lifetime. It was offered, however, for the purpose of showing the user the superior shaving qualities of the razor design and blade. It was expected that the user would want to purchase one of the firm's better models at a later date. Perhaps after a few months of exposure to water and soap the sight of a cheap looking fiber handle would encourage the user to do just that. Price 50¢.

One such advertiser razor is found in a blue and white paper box. The box is marked "The 4 S Razor, Patented Sept. 22, 1914, Patents pending, Ness City Kansas." Further printing advises, "This razor is only a working model of our better grade razors. After you become thoroughly familiar with it you should buy one of our regular Sets if you want the keen, velvety 'De lux' shave. Notice: This razor is sold with the license restriction that it may be used only with the blades manufactured by us. These blades may be purchased from your local dealer."

It is also thought that some razors with black fiber handles may have been given, compliments

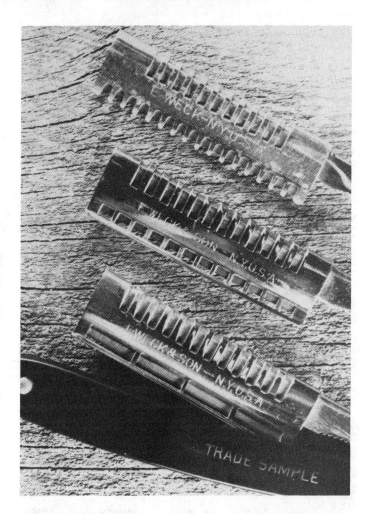

Trade Sample Weck razors with three variations of blade guards.

of retail advertisers.

A September 22, 1914 patent was granted to Volney T. Miller of Ness City. The application for the Combination Razor was filed June 27, 1913. The specifications of this patent #1,111,164 describe a movable blade arm and movable right and left guard arms with a locking device in the handle. The blade shown in patent specifications has a notch on each end. The actual razors described here have a frame consisting of two arms which hold the blade and a removable and reversible blade guard. The actual blades have two holes in them. The actual razor has no locking device in the handle.

Since the razor and blades look very similar to the patent drawings and since the inventor and

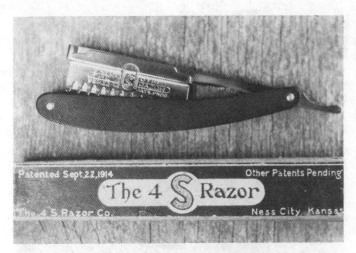

The Junior Advertiser razor sold by the 4 S Razor Co. with its paper box. Black fiber handle.

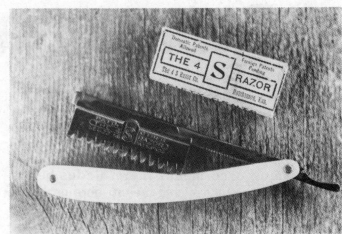

The better white clluloid handled version of 4 S Razor with a package of six blades.

The Junior Advertiser with its guard and blade separated.

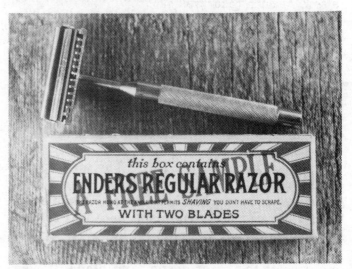

Enders regular razor with its Free Sample Box.

the 4 S Razor both list the same Ness City, Kansas, address, it is likely that this is the correct patent in spite of small design differences.

Other models that the 4 S Razor Co. hoped customers would want to buy after trying their demonstrator razors and their blades are as follows.

THE ARMY MODEL. This boxed outfit consisted of a Junior Advertiser razor, a package of blades and a strop. Price $1.00.

LITTLE BEN MODEL. A boxed razor with transparent pyraline handle and package of blades. Price $1.50.

OUR SPECIAL. Seven blades and razor with white celluloid handle in a leather case. Price $2.50.

A 4 S Razor with white celluloid handle and

nicely finished nickel plated blade holder arms can be found in a black slide case. The case while a little larger is similar to the case in which many straight razors can be found. The case is marked in silver, "The 4 S Razor" and has room for a package of blades.

DE LUXE MODEL. Silver plated razor with white celluloid handle and seven blades in a limp leather case. This set also includes a nickel plated collapsible camel hair brush, shaving stick container, and shell horsehide strop. Price $5.00.

Blades were sold six to a pack for 50¢. The single edge was rather inflexible and had a cutting edge 2 1/8 inch long. The 4 S Razor Co. stated that they were building their business on blade sales. They therefore were putting their best efforts and material into that area of manufacturing.

34

A complete line of strops was sold priced from 75¢ to $2.00. The strops were especially made for safety razor blades.

The set of instructions much of this information comes from shows a Hutchinson, Kansas, instead of Ness City address. It is likely that over the years the packaging of the different models of 4 S Razors may have changed as well.

The more common Durham Demonstrator folding safety razor can be found with handles of a cheap looking black fiber material also. One such razor was packaged in a red & white paper box. The box is printed "This Safe Razor Demonstrates the Superior Shaving Qualities of Durham Duplex Blades." The guard of this razor is marked Durham Demonstrator rather than the usual "Durham Duplex." The Demonstrator metal parts may not have as nice a finish as Durham's other razors.

There are several variations of the black fiber handle designs ranging from plain to the more ornate pattern shown here. Durham Demonstrator razors may also have been marketed in special holly leaf and berry trimmed Christmas packages. What better gift for a customer than one which keeps him coming back to buy blades? The Demonstrator program may have worked so well that higher quality white celluloid handled razors were offered in Demonstrator packages with Demonstrator marked guards as well.

A Durham Duplex razor given "Compliments of American Machine & Foundry Co. New York" advertises the A-M-F Sickle Bar— The Safety Razor of the Fields." The gold printing on a black handle also reads "Don't

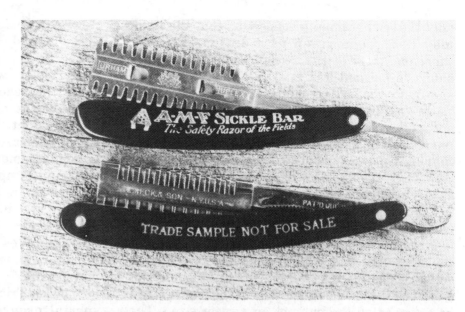

Top: A-M-F Sickle Bar Complimentary razor. Bottom: Weck handle marked "Trade Sample- Not For Sale."

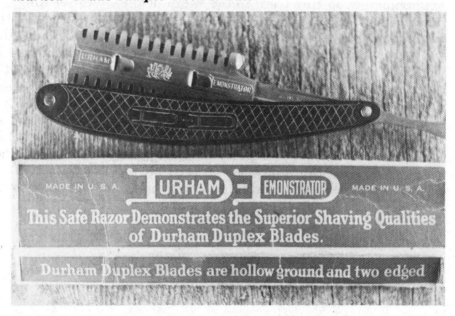

Durham Demonstrator with design on black fiber.

Change the Mowing Machine Knife, Slip a New Blade in the A-M-F Sickle Bar."

The Durham Duplex blade was larger than many blades used by other razors of the time. The blades were stiff and had a distinctive shape. Durham Duplex hoped that after using one of their demonstrator razors a customer would like its ease, quickness, and comfort. The customer would then want to purchase one of their nicer regular sets and continue to use and purchase the Durham Duplex blades.

"E. Weck & Son Sextoblade" folding razors can be found with black handles marked with variations of "TRADE SAMPLE NOT FOR SALE" wording. The razors appear to be of good quality with only the gold stamping suggesting that the razor may have been given as a demonstrator to increase sales of the replaceable blades. The shank is marked PAT'D JUL 27, 09." The blade slides into the holder and has a reversible guard.

An "Enders Regular Razor" is found in a specially printed box. The box is marked on the narrow sides, "This Package Not for Sale." It is marked in red on the widest sides, "A FREE SAMPLE." The box itself seems evidence enough that the razor was not sold. The razor with instructions does not appear different in any way from those sold in the usual way.

The Enders box also reads "The razor hung at the angle that permits Shaving. You don't have to scrape." The blade is behind the comb guard-not on top as with some other razors. The blades could be stropped on the palm or on a razor strop. The benefit of stropping being that the edges approximately 30 tiny teeth to the width of the human hair can be straightened and aligned for better cutting.

Both the razor guard and blade are marked with the "Wm Enders" signature and "Trade Mark Made in U.S.A."

Enders also offered the E-7 set for $2.00. A flat strop is built into the razor storage case.

One of Gillette's programs from the 1930's sold ten blades at the regular price of $1.00 and included the Goodwill razor free. It is probably no surprise that the blades used in this razor had a new slot design instead of the old three hole design already being sold by competitors.

There are a great number of give away programs known as combination offers. In these cases the razor manufacturer contracted with third parties who gave the razor to users of their own product. The desired result was still the same. The razor manufacturer hoped to realize a greater volume of blade sales.

Some examples of combination offers include Gillette razors given to purchasers of Palmolive & Colgate shaving products, Wrigley gum, even to purchasers of clothing or soap. Every flea market has examples of the Autostop Valet razors in familiar domed boxes marked with names of newspapers.

"Clark's Trial King Razor" was also offered in special programs to improve dealer sales of blades. One such razor was marked "Clark's Silver King."

It seems that some firms may have profited more than others from the programs to sell razors at a reduced price or give them away in order to obtain repeat blade sales. Clark Blade and Razor Company seems to have been one such firm. They sold their #2 blade to fit their own Silver King razor. They also sold their #4 blade to fit the Autostrop, the #5 blade to fit the Enders, the #11 blade to fit the Weck, and the #13 blade to fit the Gillette!

This article appeared in Knife World September, 1993.

The Phenomenal Spike

by Jon Reinschreiber

"It's the steel behind the temper, behind the grind, behind the edge, that makes the Spike the blade you like...The Phenomenal Razor." Thus proclaimed the advertisement in the November 1927 issue of the "Barber's Journal." Phenomenal it was, by 1927 the Union Cutlery Company's Spike Razor had become the largest selling wedge ground straight razor in the United States. The Spike was the most popular of over one thousand brand name razors made by the Union Cutlery Co. The reasons that this unassuming, plain handled razor enjoyed such overwhelming popularity at a time when silver tips and colorful, fancy handled razors were plentiful is a mystery.

The marketing of the Spike Razor was originally aimed at the professional barber, and was heavily supported by full page advertising in the "Barber's Journal, Master Barber Magazine and Beauty Culturist," and other trade publications of the times. Later Spike Razors were sold to the general public through barber shops, hardware stores, and drug stores.

The exact date that the Spike Razor went into production is unknown, as production records for the early years of the Union Cutlery Co. are no longer in existence. It has been determined, however, that production was started soon after Union Cutlery Co. relocated from Tidioute, Penn. to Olean, N.Y. in 1911. Mr. Dick Sturm of the Kabar Cutlery Co. estimates the start of production between the years 1912 and 1915. The Spike Razor remained in constant production in Olean until early in 1952. That year the Board of Directors of the Union Cutlery Co. sold the American Hone Co. and all of the Union Cutlery Company's razor tooling to a gentleman in Moravia, Iowa. The Board of Directors then voted to change the company name from the Union Cutlery Co. to KaBar, Incorporated, and ceased production on all razors. Included in the sale were 4000 pairs of Spike Razor handles. The buyer in Iowa, who had previously been purchasing privately branded razors from the Union Cutlery Co., contracted W.R. Case and Sons Cutlery Co. to grind blades for these handles. The blades produced by W.R. Case and Sons were stamped

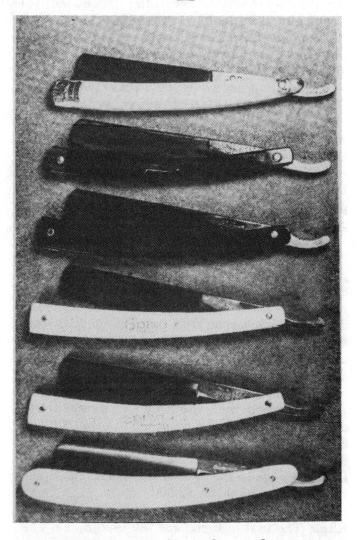

Some Spike Razors from the authors razor collection.

with the SPIKE trademark on the mark side and UNION CUTLERY CO., OLEAN, NY on the pile side. As of this writing, the blades produced by W.R. Case and Sons cannot be distinguished from those manufactured by the Union Cutlery Co. in Olean. The reason for this is that no W.R. Case & Sons produced blade has yet to be positively identified.

On May 8, 1952, 4000 razors bearing the SPIKE trademark were ordered from the Fritz Bracht Cutlery Co. in Solingen, Germany. An additional order for 4000 razors was placed on September 16, 1952. At this time the production of the Spike

Razor in the United States and the usage of the Union Cutlery Co. name on straight razors and other cutlery products came to an end. The Union Cutlery Co. name was revived in 1967 when KaBar issued a limited edition BiCentennial Commemorative folding knife with a Union Cut. Co. tang stamp. KaBar continues to use the Union Cut. Co. stamping on occasional limited edition knives.

The razors produced by the Fritz Bracht Cutlery Co. were of typical German design utilizing three pins in the handles instead of two. The handles were white plastic with the SPIKE trademark hot stamped in gold. The blades were stamped with the SPIKE trademark on the mark side and UNION CUTLERY CO., MORAVIA, IOWA on the pile side. Both of these stampings were also in gold.

The Spike Razor manufactured by the Union Cutlery Co. in Olean was a square point, wedge ground straight razor. It was forged from a 3/8" x 3/16" high carbon steel bar. The blades produced by W.R. Case & Sons were forged from 5/16" diameter high carbon steel rod. The handles were either translucent green celluloid or cream colored celluloid with a fine horizontal stripe in a slightly darker shade. Some examples are known to exist with the stripes running vertically. All handles were stamped with the Spike trademark and occasionally with the name of the distributor. Spike razors came in four blade sizes: 3/8", 4/8", 9/16", and 5/8". These dimensions were measured from the edge to the back of the blade. The Spike razor originally sold for $2.00.

There were several variations on the Spike Razor. The first of these was the Gold Spike. The Gold Spike was nothing more than a Spike Razor

with a bronze shield in the shape of a railway spike pinned to a translucent green celluloid handle, instead of the stamped in SPIKE trademark. The tang and back of the blade were covered with a thin gold plate. A second variation was the Special Spike. This razor was uniquely designed to eliminate the biggest drawback to shaving with a wedge ground razor, the weight. Wedge ground razors have a thicker blade profile than a hollow ground razor. This thicker profile allows a stiffer edge and better edge control and feel. This results in an easier shave but a much heavier blade. The blade of the Special Spike was hollow ground starting 1/16 of an inch up from the edge and continuing to the back. By doing this the wedge ground edge was retained while excess weight was eliminated. The handles of the Special Spike were of straw–colored celluloid with nickel silver tips. The blade was marked SPECIAL SPIKE on the mark side and Union Cutlery Co., Olean N.Y. on the pile side. The Special Spike was available in three different blade sizes: 4/8", 9/16", and 5/8". It sold for $2.50.

Other Spike Razor variations were the Number 100 Spike, Hand Forged Spike, and the Red Spike or Red Fox Spike. There was also a transitional or safety Spike. The Spike Safety Razor was a basic Spike razor with a safety guide that attached to the back of the blade with two knurled thumb screws.

Next time that you are at a knife show take a close look at the straight razors, and the popularity of the Spike razor will immediately become evident. You will see a good many well used Spikes, but the collector who finds a mint Spike razor will have a hard to find treasure indeed.

Union Cutlery Company Factory Olean, New York c 1940

This article appeared in Knife World November, 1982.

Tally Ho Razors

by Kurt Moe

The running fox with its bushy tail flowing behind him has long been used in combination with the phrase "Tally Ho" as a trademark. We identify "Tally Ho" as what a hunter cries out when sighting a fox. What can come to mind is a morning scene of English countryside. Riders on spirited horses fly over obstacles to head toward the cry of "Tally Ho." No one wants to be left behind.

The easy to remember fox symbol on a razor distinguishes the maker's name from those of his competitors. The trademark and reputation may have been as valuable to the makers as the building or equipment used to actually manufacture the razors. The Tally Ho with the figure of a running fox was used by several firms over the span of decades.

F. FENNEY

Frederick Fenney is usually shown to have been a Sheffield, England maker of razors during the period 1824 to 1852. His mark can be found on some razors of high quality. The following Fenney razors were probably made late in that 28 year period.

The razors described here may even all date from the final ten years. All the handles are made of a grained dark natural horn material. There are, however, a great number of differences in blades, handle shape and pin construction that are difficult to explain if they were made within a few years of each other. Perhaps one explanation could be that all the razors with the F. Fenney were not completely made from start to finish by one cutler or even at one

Top: Dark horn deeply pressed handle with running fox and "Tally Ho." Probably a F. Fenny razor c 1845. Bottom: Geo. Wostenholm & Son razor box label printed in tones of gold and brown. 1919 Register shows Wostenholm's use of the Tally Ho mark.

place.

Had the razors been marked G R (before 1830), W R for (1830-1837), or V R (1837-1901) dating them would have been much easier. There are no such markings used here.

It is disappointing for collectors not to be able to date their razors precisely. Many features such as handle, etch, and blade styles do suggest time periods in which they are likely to have been manufactured. It is believed by many, however, that specific razor features did not exist to a certain year then cease to be used by all cutlers at the same moment. The world that they lived in and that we live in now is not that orderly!

A razor is shank stamped with the running fox trade mark and the words, "Tally Ho." The razor also reads in three lines, "F. Fenney, Sheffield, Warranted" in a rectangle. There is a stamping on the sway backed blade which appears to read, "A Real Tally Ho." There is no spacer between the handles. Brass pins and small collars are used.

A second razor has the same Fenney trademark. The mark is so large that on most razors it cannot leave a complete stamping. The razor shanks are not flat and one part or another of the stamping usually does not leave a good impression.

A large square ended blade has a faintly etched scene of a train engine, coal car, and passenger car. The boxy old fashioned train engine looks like those that used wood for fuel. The scene is so detailed, however, that the fireman is obviously holding a shovel.

The horn handles have no spacer. Brass pins with iron collars are used.

Another blade has a homemade handle. A common fault of the dark horn material used was that it would start to crack at one of the pins. The crack would continue along the grain until the handle no longer held together. The user could try to repair the damage, replace the handles or discard the razor entirely. Most probably decided to repair or replace the handles!

The large shank has the usual Fenney trademark. The blade has a very thick back.

A Fenney razor has a pressed design in its dark horn handle. The fully pressed front handle reads, "Tally Ho Razor" with the running fox trademark in the center. The back handle is plain. The handles are held together with brass pins and small collars. There is no spacer. The razor pictured has had its blade replaced.

Henry Lummus published a number of articles in the 1920's about straight razors. One Lummus article shows a similar razor with a running fox pressed into its horn handle. Its blade is etched "Adamatine Edge." Lummus dates the razor from about the year 1845.

Some of the razors have dark grained horn handles separated by metal spacers. A razor with the "Tally Ho" trademark has a beautifully deep etched blade showing the running fox and the words, "American Tally Ho Razor." The pins and small collars are brass.

More examples of the usual Fenney mark have nickel silver

Fenney marked razor with deeply etched blade reads "American Tally Ho Razor."

Top: Thick back on blade etched "C.T. Bingham's Patent Concave Tempered by Thermometer" in script. Shield on horn handle. Center: Green C.T. Bingham label. Bottom: Lighter, more modern hollow ground blade probably still made before 1890 by F. Fenney.

pins and collars. One has a lightly pressed scroll design with a running fox ad the words "Tally Ho" in the dark horn handle.

Lastly a plain horn handle holds a blade of a different shape etched with symbols. Some of the symbols include a balance scale, cornucopia, hand, feather, eye, bow & arrow and the letters FLT in circles.

C.T. BINGHAM

At some point the Tally Ho running fox trademark began

appearing in a different form. The variation of the trademark reads, "C.T. Bingham, Late F. Fenney, Sheffield" in three lines. There is no box around the words.

The word "late" has a great number of definitions. The meaning and use of the word late as it was used about 140 years ago in England may not be the same as it is used today in the U.S.A. It is assumed, however, that the word "late" used here doesn't mean a tardy arrival. In the context of the word "late" followed by a person's name it likely meant that the person had recently died. Another usage of the word was such as "the late employer." Its meaning that employer just previous to the present one. If we accept that the "F. Fenney" marked razors were made during the period 1824-1852 it is my guess that those marked "Late F. Fenney" were made after 1852.

An 1801 Act of Parliament made special provision for a life interest of a cutler's widow in the cutler's mark. She would be allowed to use the mark herself or sell the use of the mark for the remainder of her lifetime.

Robert Doyle's book *Straight Razor Collecting* shows a photograph of a razor which appears to have the "C.T. Bingham" version of a Tally Ho trademark. The etched blade reads, "A Real Tally Ho Razor Set With Care & Warranted To Shave" in a ribbon surrounded with scroll. He dates this type of razor from about 1850-1860.

A second razor has the "C.T. Bingham" trademark on its shank. While the "Late F. Fenney" line is quite deep and even in its stamping the "Y" is missing. Perhaps the stamping die was defective.

The blade grind is unusual in cross section. The blade back is thick but about 1/3 inch from the cutting edge the blade becomes abruptly thin. An etching on the thick part of the blade is very, very faint. So faint, in fact, that it was overlooked many times. The etching reads, "C.T. Bingham's Patent Concave Tempered By Thermometer" in script.

The dark horn handles have metal spacers. The pins have no collars. The bar shield is pinned to the handle. The metal used appears to be nickel silver.

A final blade also has the "C.T. Bingham" version of Tally Ho trademark. The blade is found in a celluloid molded bamboo pattern handle. An original celluloid handle in this pattern would have suggested a date of manufacture much later than the previous razors. There are marks though, near the pin which create doubts about the originality of this handle.

The blade of this razor also suggests that it is later than the previous razors. It is much lighter and has a hollow ground blade. Examples are sometimes seen of older wedge shaped blades having been professionally hollow ground. These examples still have a heaviness or bulkiness to them. The hollow grind of this blade is characteristic of one manufactured after 1875.

All of the razor shanks mentioned here are marked "Sheffield" without the word "England." The U.S. Tariff Act of 1890 is said to have required a permanent identification of the manufacturing country on imports from after the year 1891.

SAMUEL FOX & CO. LTD.

Samuel Fox & Co. Ltd. of Stocksbridge Works near Sheffield used the Tally Ho running fox trademarks for steel and wire. Marks may have been granted to different companies for use at the same time on different classes of products. The Fox company used similar running fox marks on tires, axles, umbrella frames and other non cutlery products.

U.S.A. USERS OF THE RUNNING FOX MARK

Safety razors with the name E.L. Schmitz can be found having a running fox mark. Straight razors with the Koeller & Schmitz or Fox Cutlery Co. names also can be found with a running fox mark. The marks used on these razors do not include the words "Tally Ho" and probably date slightly before to shortly after the year 1900.

GEO. WOSTENHOLM & SON

A colorful Geo. Wostenholm & Son Ltd. label is printed mostly in tones of gold and brown. The label was to be used on a box holding a dozen razors. The label is proof that the "Tally Ho" trademark didn't disappear with the fading of either the F. Fenney or C.T. Bingham names. *The Register of Trademarks of the Cutlerys' Company Sheffield* dated 1919 also shows that the running fox Tally Ho mark lived on with one of the great names in razors, Geo. W. Wostenholm & Son. This Tally Ho trademark lived not just for decades but for a century.

This article appeared in Knife World October, 1993.

Case Brothers Tested XX

by Kurt Moe

The trademark "Tested XX" is said to have been first used by the Case Brothers cutlery firm. The firm was founded by three brothers, John D., Jean, and Andrew J. Case. Various stampings used by the firm show its different factory locations over the years.

There are many excellent reference books available to those collectors wanting more detail about this place and time in cutlery history. Most of the books feature the Case family. *The First 100 Years, A Pictorial and Historical Review of W.R. Case & Sons Cutlery* by James S. Giles is a recent book containing about 200 pages of relevant information.

The list of Case family members involved in the cutlery industry is both long and confusing. Careful study is needed to sort those members with the same name but different middle initials and those with similar sounding names into their proper place in the industry. There were also situations in which the same individual may have worked for different firms at different times.

A razor stamped on the shank's side with "CASE BROTHERS" "LITTLE VALLEY, N.Y." in two straight lines was probably manufactured in about 1910. The Little Valley factory was destroyed by fire in about 1912. Available reference sources, however, sometimes disagree on the precise date of this event as well as some others.

The top edge of the shank has the "TESTED XX" mark. The XX is said to mean that the product so marked had been double tested for proper

Case Brothers razor from about 1910. Handle is honey colored celluloid in the twisted rope pattern. Blade has round point.

Frozen food knife with its blue box, patented in 1954. Genuine pearl folder with two blades above shows relative size.

hardness of the blade. This example of stamping is deep on the left and gradually becomes lighter as it reads to the right. Even with a magnifying glass only one X can be seen. The blade can be described as shoulderless and has a round point said to be for general use.

The celluloid handle in the twisted rope pattern is a very pretty honey color with streaks of rust color in it. The red box holding the razor is marked "CASE BROS. LITTLE VALLEY N.Y." "TESTED XX" in black lettering.

Another book has been especially informative to me because of its coverage of razors. That publication is Jim Sargent's *American Premium Guide to Pocketknives & Razors, Identification and Values,* either 2nd or 3rd Edition. There are pictures of razors (some in color) and razor values included.

In about 1914 the Tested XX mark was sold to W.R. Case & Sons. The good news is that their cutlery products with variations of the XX marks are still being manufactured and sold. The diversity of a century of products stamped with the XX mark certainly keeps them from becoming boring to cutlery collectors.

The observant reader may notice some early W.R. Case & Sons letterheads or advertising pieces that include the information "Case Tested XX since 1847." It is believed that this information should be disregarded. Most sources agree that the year 1847 was W.R. Case's date of birth and that the firm bearing his name was not even founded until about 1902.

A good many collectors concentrate their efforts on only folders. An old story is sometimes told of a very large fellow who had a lucky streak and won a great number of silver dollars. The fellow was just beginning to complain that he preferred the convenience of folding money when the sweet talking casino cashier interrupted him. She offered the observation that even the silver dollars could be folded, if he were man enough.

A similar tongue in cheek observation might be made concerning this frozen food knife, but why destroy something so unique?

This odd looking knife blade has several pieces of information etched on it. "CASE XX STAINLESS FREEZ-CUT" tells us the maker and the material of the blade as well as the knife's use. This special blade would not wedge tight like an ordinary knife would when cutting frozen food. The blade would not mix pieces of wrapping with the contents of a package like might be expected of a saw.

This knife was designed to be a frozen food cutter specifically adapted for severing frozen vegetables and other food packages. No longer would package contents need to be thawed before being divided into portions of the needed size. The user would be able to have variety without waste. Frozen packages could be cut without even removing their wrapping.

"NEVER NEEDS RESHARPENING" and "PAT NO. 2,685,131" were two more pieces of information etched on the knife's blade. The patent was granted on August 3, 1954 to Fred B. Seeberger of Yeadon, Pennsylvania who assigned one half to Harry H. Kennedy of Greenwich, Connecticut. The blade does not have a thin sharp edge which might require maintenance but has an edge more like many small chisels.

The knife is about 14-5/8 inches overall. Its look is

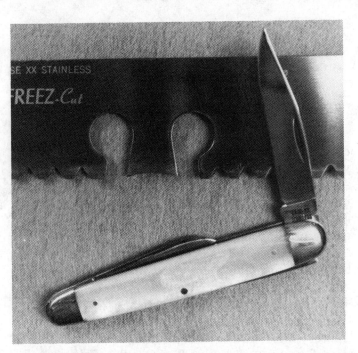

Close up of same Case XX Stainless marked knife.

similar to that of a long broad blade bread knife except for its teeth. The handle is a black plastic type of material applied with three rivets.

The knife blade is protected by a cardboard sheath and was found in a long box with its blue cover printed CASE TESTED XX FREEZ-CUT.

A pocket knife is stamped CASE XX STAINLESS which is a marking said to date from about 1950-1965. The FREEZ-CUT knife and the pocket knife share some features. Both knives are marked CASE XX and STAINLESS and may have been manufactured about the same time.

The remainder of the features are not similar. The folder with genuine pearl handles has its master blade marked 079. This is said to be the handle pattern number for a 3-1/4 inch sleeveboard pen knife. The master blade of this example is in the wider end of the handle. The smaller pen blade is in the smaller end of the handle as is usual. Both ends of the handle have bolsters.

The joints are not prominent on this knife. There is a notch cut out from the back handle so the nail nick of the pen blade can be used. Some strength was apparently given up so this knife could have the smoothness achieved by use of a sunken joint.

Don't stop with just cutlery if you like collecting the Case XX trademarks. Current catalogs include such interesting items as brass belt buckles and baseball style caps to help advertise your collecting interest.

This article appeared in Knife World March, 1992.

Cattaraugus Razors

by Kurt Moe

In a cover letter to a Cattaraugus Cutlery catalog, J.B.F. Champlin starts his story in the year 1880. The letter says that the bulk of the American trade at that time obtained its supply of high grade cutlery from England and its cheaper goods from Germany. American shops filled small gaps in the cutlery industry as well as they could.

The letter goes on to say that it was in 1880 that John B.F. Champlin, grandfather of the letter writer, started in the cutlery business on a small scale. Tint Champlin, the company's president at the time of this catalog, continued the tradition of

Illustration on the back cover of the Cattaraugus catalog. The boys are consulting the Cattaraugus scout knife with a compass in its handle.

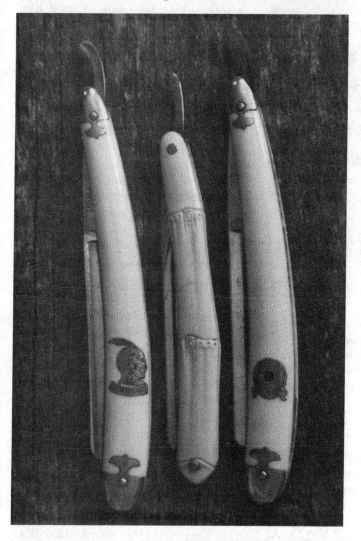

Three imitation ivory celluloid handled razors. The razors with nickel silver ends and inlays are included in the 1930 price list.

using the best of materials and the most skilled of workmen.

While this catalog is not dated, there is a price list in it that is dated July 15, 1922. The razor stock numbers shown in the catalog can be found in the price list.

A semi transparent emerald green handle with a figure of a lizard embossed in gold is pictured in the catalog and included in the 1922 price list. The blade points offered on the razor were the round point, the square point, and the needle point. The needle point is shown to have a very sharp point

Cattaraugus Cutlery Company, Little Valley, New York.

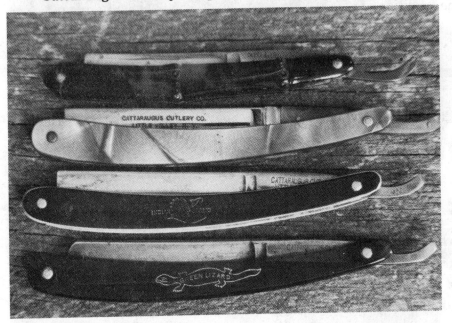

Top: Small imitation tortoise celluloid handle in bamboo pattern The following razors are in the 1922 price list: Mottled green handle with same material covering shank, Cattaraugus stamping on blade; Blue veneered on white celluloid handle embossed with Indian; Transparent green handle embossed with Green Lizard.

while the similar square point is slightly rounded.

Other semi-transparent green razor handles are plain with the "Green Lizard" illustration and lettering etched on the blade. There is also a slimmer variation of the lizard embossed on some handles.

The catalog also shows a semi-transparent red celluloid handle with a magnetized blade. An amber celluloid handle and an imitation oak celluloid handle are shown as well. There is a blue veneered on white handle with the illustration of an Indian and

the words "Indian Brand" embossed.

Slogans found on the razors in the catalog include: Every Day, Barbers Friend, Pleazal, Galvanic, Double Hollow, Cobalt, and a moustache razor slightly smaller than the usual razor was etched "American Junior."

Cattaraugus at some time also offered small blades in imitation tortoise and imitation ivory handles shaped to look like bamboo. These were probably moustache razors also. Cattaraugus blades can be found in rounded handles of mottled yellow, orange, or green celluloid. Another has a handle shaped like an ear of corn.

The "Galvanic" razor has the peculiarity of being marked "J.B.F. Champlin & Son" rather than "Cattaraugus Cutlery."

Another razor has a pearl tang so has the Cattaraugus stamping on the blade. The catalog has a drawing identifying razor parts. The word "shank" is not mentioned and the tang is shown to include that part of a razor usually marked with a company name.

Some confusing information appears on two green pearlized razors with the same material covering their tang. Their stock number 129 appears on the 1922 price list but the razors are not in the catalog. One razor blade is marked on its back, "Pat. Feb. 13, 1902." The other razor blade is marked "Pat. Feb. 18, 1902." A 16 power magnifying glass shows the "Feb 18" stamping to be even and clear while the "Feb 13" stamping is uneven as if done with a damaged tool. Perhaps a piece of the "8" had broken away leaving the imprints to read like 3's. Patent information at the library indicated that patents were issued on Feb. 11 and Feb 18, 1902. No patents were issued on Feb. 13, 1902. On Feb 18, 1902, patent No.693524 was issued to George W. Korn for the Double Hollow Ground blade that these Cattaraugus razors have.

A lifetime guarantee and insurance policy was issued to razor purchases according to the Cattaraugus catalog. The razors could be returned free for rehoning and were insured against accidental breakage from any cause whatsoever. This was not always the case with Cattaraugus razors, however, as I have seen some boxes with the following warning label: "This Razor is ground very thin and is highly tempered. It should be handled with great care as it is easily broken, and no broken razors will be exchanged." Which policy came first, I don't know. A fancy eight razor display case shown in the catalog featured a copy of the razor guarantee and had compartments inside for stock under lock and key. The case was mahogany and titled, "Cattaraugus Little Injun Razors." There were figures of stick men which appear to represent Indians with tomahawks. There were descriptions under the razors such as "Med. Beard, Tender Skin," or "Tough Wiry Beard, Skin exposed to weather." These descriptions read much like the "Robeson" display of about the same time period.

While the company offered to rehone razors without charge at least at the time the catalog was in effect, the same catalog offered at least a dozen different hones for sale. One had a green lizard embossed, others had cartoon like Indians or more realistic Indians. Some hones were colored blue, others were in the more usual

Carving knife and fork bearing Cattaraugus trademark similar to the brightly colored Indian inside the lid of a hone box. The handles of the knife and fork are mother of pearl and sterling.

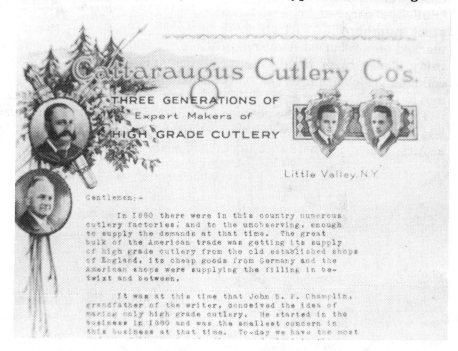

Photo of an original letterhead.

hone colors of brown or grey. One hone box has a colorful Indian illustration on the inside of its lid.

The same design on the hone box is also on the blade of a carving knife. Both the knife and fork handles are mother of pearl and sterling. The knife's blade is also marked "England."

Many of the pages of this catalog are similar to pages of knives reproduced in *"Romance of Collecting Cattaraugus, Robeson, Russell, Queen Knives"* by Mrs. Dewey P. Ferguson.

The catalog's line of knives included a number of silver and enamel handles and 10K gold or sterling handles. The knives were

47

featured on full color pages while the rest of the catalog is in black and white.

Two letters are reproduced in the catalog. They refer to Cattaraugus knives that gave service for 20 and 30 years. The first letter is from Taylor & Van Dien, a Ridgewood N.J. firm and is dated Nov. 17, 1921. The other letter is from a Newcastle, Pennsylvania hardware firm Kirk, Hutton & Co., dated Aug. 13, 1910.

A second price list is in a pocket of the catalog. This one has a different numbering system for the razor stock numbers and is dated Jan. 1, 1930. It mentions a "BullsEye" razor and one with the stock number "B 52T" which is marked on a razor with an Indian inlay. These razor handles were celluloid grained to look like ivory and have nickel silver ends.

The back cover of the catalog has an embossed picture of three scouts checking their compass.

Cattaraugus Cutlery Co. "Little Injun" razor display case featuring lifetime guarantee certificate. Note the stick man trademark.

One of them says, "That's North, Phil." The Cattaraugus American Scout Knife 42209B in the catalog includes a compass set into what is described as a stag bone handle. This knife had brass liners and nickel silver bolster. This knife sounds just like the gimmick some of us country boys could use to find our way around the city after knife show hours.

This article appeared in Knife World February, 1984.

Clauss Cutlery Razors

by Kurt Moe

"If you can remember Santa Claus, You can remember that Clauss Cutlery is the best." This motto circles a Santa Claus trademark shown in a Clauss Cutlery catalog from about 1920.

Mr. R.W. Van Hook, president of the Clauss Cutlery Company, kindly furnished that general catalog and another pamphlet that they prepared to celebrate the company's first 100 years. This catalog and pamphlet were the source of much of the information that follows about Clauss Cutlery.

According to the booklet commemorating the firm's century in the cutlery business, its history begins in 1877. John H. Clauss, his young brother Henrie Clauss, and five others started "The Elyria Shear Works" in Elyria, Ohio. Ten years later the business was prospering and chose to expand in Fremont, Ohio. Articles in the Fremont Daily News indicated that Fremont was excited about the addition of 40 to 50 families to their population. The construction of the factory and housing for the Shear Works employees would result in jobs and work for others in the area.

The new facility included a Corliss engine housed in its own building. It was customary at the time for power to be transmitted to areas of a factory by line shafts. Long belts then transferred the power from a rotating shaft to individual machines.

In January 1890, the Clauss Shear Works at Ohio Avenue and Pine Street in Fremont was completely destroyed by fire. The fire started in the forge room and rapidly spread through the wood structure. The fire temporarily put 125 men out of work. In less than a week, however, construction was started on a new building. Fremonters heavily subscribed to the stock offered after the fire. Some of those families are still shareholders today. The Fremont Journal wrote that electric light enabled construction to continue until 9 o'clock each evening. In less than four months, the Shear Works was back in production in their new four story brick building at State Street and Sandusky Avenue. Again a single engine powered the plant's equipment through line shafts and belts.

Clauss made use of national advertising to sell

Santa Claus trademark as shown in catalog from about 1920. The word 'Clauss' is in script as usually found stamped on the razors.

its razors, shears, and scissors. Magazines such as Woman's Home Companion, Delineator, Harper's Monthly, Godey's Ladies Magazine, Cosmopolitan, Munsey's and Scribner's were used at various times from 1895 to 1910. Two ads from 1895 show the word "Clauss" in block letters. The ads from 1896 and later have the word "Clauss" as if hand written in script with the "C" extended in a line under the rest of the letters.

We know that Clauss razors date back at least to 1896. An ad from that year described Clauss razors as water hardened, gas tempered, and hand forged. The ad offered a fine shell handled razor for two dollars.

In 1899, John Clauss moved to Toledo and commuted to Fremont. A short time later, John Clauss was involved in the "Never Fail" Company of Toledo. A product of this firm was the Clauss

Never Fail Razor sharpener for old style and safety razor blades.

Also at about 1900, cartoonist Palmer Cox did a number of advertisements for Clauss. One such item, a "Clauss Primer" used Mother Goose rhymes "up dated" with reference to Clauss products. One rhyme example was, "Deedle, deedle dumpling, my son John. Went to bed with his breeches on. Got up early in the morning feeling very brave. Stropped his good Clauss razor and proceeded for to shave." The example was accompanied by an illustration of John shaving. A rhyme example in the Alphabet Primer was "X is for Xmas. Santa Clauss has been here. Left Pa a Clauss razor, and Ma a Clauss shear."

The cover of the Clauss Centennial picture book shows a pair of scissors specially made and engraved for the 1907 Jamestown Exposition. The pair of scissors features an illustration of Pocahontas and Captain John Smith.

One page in catalogs from about 1910 and 1920 showed awards the firm received at International Trade Expositions. The World's Columbian Exposition of 1892 and Pan American Exposition of 1901 are just two of many award metals shown. The 1910 catalog included 379 different kinds and sizes of shears, scissors and tinner's snips and 42 different models of straight razors. The catalogs show many pictures of steps in manufacturing shears, scissors, and razors. Two pictures show workers straightening razor blades after hardening and assembling the blades with handles.

Henrie Clauss filed a patent application in 1905 for a safety razor blade that consisted of a thin blade with a strengthening back much like that on a frame back

The most unusual pattern in the Clauss catalog is the Indian handle. The fancy scroll handle along side shows some similarities. Both are celluloid stained to antique the design.

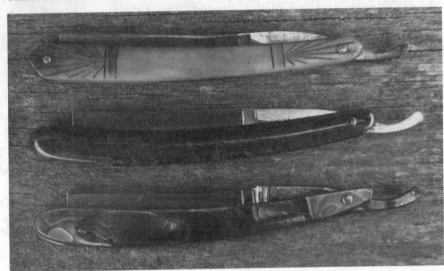

Three Clauss razors. Top shows Diamond End pattern cut into the bone handle. The middle razor has imitation wood grain handle in red and black celluloid. Bottom razor has tang mounted with celluloid material similar to handle material.

straight razor. The back which appears to be nearly 1/4 inch in diameter and running the length of the blade was to stiffen the blade to allow honing and stropping. One of the other benefits was that the back could be of relatively cheaper material than the cutting edge of the blade.

Patent No.851,066 was granted for this invention on April 23, 1907. I have not seen or heard of a blade of this type and do not know if it was ever produced.

In 1919, a Henkel-Clauss merger was announced. The Henkel Company, apparently named for August Henkel, had been incorporated in 1906. The new Henkel-Clauss firm was headed by

Clauss Razors

Catalog illustration showing how razor was held by a person shaving himself. Other grips were often used by barbers when shaving another person.

Paul Schaaf with John Clauss serving as Chairman of the Board. Later in 1919, John Clauss died after having been in failing health. Henrie Clauss started another scissors company in 1920. This Tipton, Indiana firm used the tradename "H. Clauss." There are probably razors with this marking as well. Henrie continued to live in his elegant Fremont residence until his death in 1927.

Another catalog has a very similar cover to the 1910 catalog. It identifies itself as Clauss catalog No.44. The date Feb. 7, 1919, is part of one of the printed pages and Henkel Clauss is identified as the owner and operator of the Clauss factories. This probably dates the catalog from about 1920. Factory and offices were identified as in Fremont, Ohio, with export offices at 258 Broadway, N.Y.C.

The catalog indicates that Clauss would supply helpful advertising and window displays. In addition to window trim and electrotypes, oak or mahogany cases were available to display razors and other items. They featured the Clauss name etched on the glass.

Items shown in catalog No.44 were mostly shears and scissors. Other products included ink erasers, cigar clippers, surgical instruments, razor blades, and razors.

The ink erasers used to scrape away mistakes were available in spear point or knife shapes. Handles were cocobolo, ebony or bone.

At least two variations of cigar clippers were sold. One was a 3-1/2 inch pair of scissors with a curved cutting edge where the handles met. The other clipper did not have scissor blades.

The many surgical instruments included several variations of "Mayo" scissors and an unusual shaped instrument called an "Umbilical Scissors."

Cards of 12 or 24 packages of razor blades are shown. The packages with 8 blades in each sold for 50 cents and fit Ever Ready, Gem Junior, Sharp Shaver, The King, ADS, Shavewell, The Hubbs, Very Sharp, Star, Columbia Junior, and US R Razors. These blades do not appear to have been individually wrapped with paper. The card suggested that safety razor blades be stropped lightly both before and after shaving.

A Clauss safety razor which looks very similar to a "Christy" razor was pictured in the catalog. The case with velvet linings holds two small blade boxes, one marked "sharp" and the other marked, "dull." The Christy Company was last located in Fremont, Ohio.

The No.44 catalog includes a large selection of straight razors. Six different point styles were offered. The Square point (S), the Round point (R), as well as the more unusual Grooved (G), Honed (H), Irish (I), and Wedge (W), points were offered. The letter S,R,G,H,I, or W marked on a razor shank along with the stock number indicated the point style. Usually 4/8, 5/8 and 6/8 inch wide blades were offered. Grinds were often available as half concave, medium concave, or full concave. Not all razor handles were offered in all combinations of grind or width. Examples in my collection do not always have numbers and some have numbers that are not shown in the catalog.

The "Royal Tiger" pattern is shown with a tiger etched in gold on the blade. The handle appears to be real carved ivory with a design like tree buds carved on each end. Another illustration in the catalog showing razors as part of a group, shows a similar razor with carving only on the tang end.

Some razors had handles with "mounted" tangs covered with material matching the handle. Other molded celluloid handles are described as Fancy Scroll (801-11), Bamboo (1501-11), Twist (2101-11), Wreathed (7401-10), Fancy Matted (7101-11 and 7301-3), and Fancy Beaded Antique Handles (9301-11) in assorted colors. Since three blade widths and three grinds produces only nine combinations, most number sequences were missing the 4 and 8 leaving three sets of three numbers. For example, the Fancy Scroll pattern had numbers of 801, 802, 803, 805, 806, 807, 809, 810, and 811.

Two more such handles deserving special attention are the "Vampire" and "Indian" patterns. The ladies head with long flowing hair in art nouveau style was called the "Queen" in a Thomas Mfg. Co. catalog. Clauss called its lady of the same pattern, the "Vampire Antique" (7701-11).

The most unusual handle in the catalog is called the Indian Handle (9301-11). The large end of the handle has a dancing Indian warrior in a head dress and holding a tomahawk. The smaller end of the razor has another tomahawk and pipe crossed. There is scroll around both ends as well. This is a very desirable pattern among razor collectors. The few razors that I've seen of this rare pattern were Clauss Cutlery razors. This particular example is ivory colored celluloid antiqued with a rich brown stain. The catalog indicates that there may be different colors of celluloid or

The razor on the bottom has a carved handle shaped like a tree bud. The middle razor has a celluloid handle in an unusual pattern with leaves and berriers. These razor handles are not listed in the 1920 catalog but are shown in a razor roll or case that is illustrated. The razor at the top has a metal star and ribbons of metal through the pins.

stain for this model. As is the case with the other patterns mentioned, this pattern is repeated on the back side of the razor also.

Another unusual design of lines etched in a flat handle is called the Diamond End handle. The catalog indicates these are celluloid in assorted colors, however, there are examples of the pattern which appear to be bone or ivory.

Stub End Oval or Stub End Flat handles are shown in the catalog as well as Silver Tipped Celluloid handles.

Other patterns included Gun Metal Tang and Back illustrated as marked 5102 but identified as GMT-1-7. "Barbers Extr Special" was BSX B for black handles and BSX W for white handles.

There were several semi transparent handles shown. Colors include Lavender, Ruby, Green, Blue, and Yellow. These were identified as T for transparent and L,R,G,B, or Y after the number for color. Another transparent yellow handle had a gold plate back and tang and a "Bullet Point" which looks like the Irish point mentioned earlier.

Clauss razors which are not mentioned in the catalog are many. There are two different wood grain celluloid handles in the gunstock handle pattern. One looks much like brown burl grain wood, and the other more of a straight oak grain.

Nearly all the razors have their "Clauss" marked in script. There are at least two exceptions, however. An aluminum handled razor has "Clauss" in block letters arranged in an arch over "Fremont, O. U.S.A." on the shank. It is stamped 2502 S on the tang. The S probably designates the square point.

Another razor has "Clauss" in block letters on a straight line

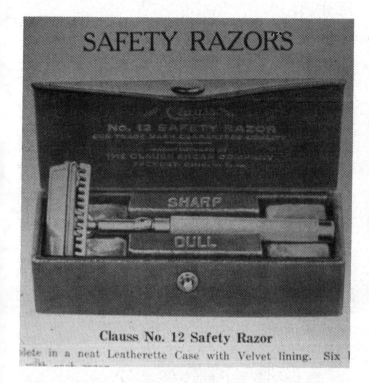

SAFETY RAZORS

Clauss No. 12 Safety Razor

Clauss safety razor which looks much like one made by another Fremont, Ohio, firm, Christy. Illustration is from 1920 catalog.

over "Fremont, O. U.S.A." These marking are etched into a tang and shank mounted with real mother of pearl. The green pearlized celluloid handle is of the Stub End and Flat type.

Still another nice example of a Clauss razor has an ivory colored celluloid handle molded in the "nude picking grapes" pattern.

An unusual pattern has leaves on each end of the handle and some berries on the large end. The blade is etched in gold, "The Razor of Quality" on the sides of a Maltese type cross. This pattern probably predates the catalog as it is in an illustration of a razor roll but is not separately listed.

The publications furnished by Clauss do not have any information on pocket knives but we know Clauss knives exist. John Goins in his book "Pocketknives," shows a two blade jack marked "Clauss." Another example is a 2 blade mother of pearl handled knife with shield. It is marked "Clauss" in script on the tang and etched on the larger blade.

In 1920, Henkel-Clauss acquired the Unsinger Razor Blade Co. at Bidwell and Ewing Streets. It was renamed the Cu Ply Company. Within a few years that name disappeared from company

Inside view of Clauss plant shows line shafts and belts that powered machinery. This illustration is also from the 1920 catalog.

records.

In 1921, Germany was permitted to ship shears and scissors duty free into the United States. The purpose was to allow Germany to pay its WWI debts and reparation costs. During the years that followed, the Henkel-Clauss company suffered.

After the Great Depression, the company pulled itself out of debt under the leadership of its president, Carl Wieber.

Production during WWII was almost 100 percent surgical scissors and instruments. The pent up demand for ordinary shears and scissors led to a post war boom for business.

In July 1946, operations at the plant stopped for the time it took to honor 54 employees with over 25 years of service with Clauss. Three men were honored for over 50 years each of service to the company.

In 1947, a new factory was built and employment was expanded to almost 300 people. A display card of "Clauss Gold Metal" razor blades probably dates from about this time. Each of the 20 boxes held 5 blades individually wrapped in paper matching the box.

Over the years, there had been some confusion of the firm's Henkel-Clauss name with the name of the German firm, J.A. Henckels. In 1954, the corporate name was changed to Clauss Cutlery to eliminate this confusion. Also about this time, plans were made to emphasize industrial instead of consumer products.

In 1966, Tom Weiker retired with a total of 62

years of service. He had spent 15 years with Clauss Shear, 35 years with Henkel Clauss and 12 years with Clauss Cutlery. He had lived the company's history from lunch hour boxing matches with John Clauss to the current company president, Robert Van Hook. In the next year the firm became a part of Alco Standard Corporation.

Current Clauss product lines include Florist shears, snips, and knives. Industrial wire strippers, poultry scissors, and aviation snips are some more products. The new literature mentions the use of molybdenum alloys in some products, however, the basic shears, scissors and snips business remains relatively unchanged.

The "roaching/fetlock," description of one pair of shears led to some speculation as to the exact nature of its use. Finally it was found that trimming a horse's mane could be called roaching and the fetlock was another part of the horse just above the hoof. The more imaginative speculation concerning insects and drug culture was at this point discarded.

I've enjoyed learning about this cutlery firm and want to wish Clauss Cutlery a successful second century. Thank you to Clauss and Robert Van Hook for the information they shared.

This article appeared in Knife World April, 1984.

Eagle Razors

by Kurt Moe

The eagle design has long been associated with military insignia. One military item featuring an eagle design is the "Gillette U.S. Service Set." By 1915 Gillette had their pocket edition safety razors. At least five types of metal cases in the 4" x 1-7/8" size were offered. They were the plain metal case, the basket pattern, the shell pattern, the flower pattern, and the empire (scroll) pattern. Also, about this time, a special nickel plated set was designed for use by servicemen.

An embossed design on the special set's hinged cover shows an eagle with outspread wings. Several military branch symbols were incorporated into two composite designs. A close look shows what seems to be one infantry rifle, one cavalry sword, an artillery cannon, the engineer's turreted castle, a Navy anchor, a signal corps flag and the medical corps staff. The cover also has a flat spot without any design that is an excellent spot to engrave the owner's name. I have seen examples of the serviceman's name and unit engraved in this spot.

The Gillette set contained a razor, 12 blades in a metal container, and a metal mirror. The razor needed blades with three holes. One hole was needed in the center to accommodate the screw-on handle and another hole on each side of the center was needed to accommodate holding posts. By 1918 this kit was also being offered to civilians through mail order catalogs.

Some of the small metal blade boxes I've seen with the kits have another unusual feature. There is a striking surface on some of the boxes similar to those seen on tobacco cans and match safes. The box that originally held blades could also hold matches long after the blades lost their usefulness. Now I'm no longer surprised to see the name Gillette appear in a match safe collection.

This next style of razor was described in a mail list as a razor made in Germany for Union soldiers and was part of a sale of Civil War items. A drawing showed the razor to be decorated with an eagle in the handle center and stars and stripes diagonally on both ends. I never did receive an answer to my letter to the mail order coin firm requesting the source of their information. I was

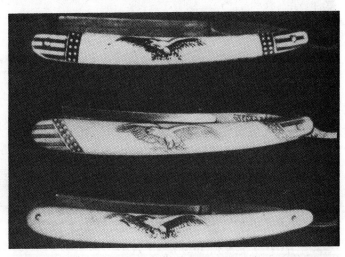

Eagle razors similar to the alleged Civil War razor. Top: McGill Cutlery Co. razor shaded in brown. Center: Oxford razor shaded in blue. Bottom: John Primble razor without star and stripes.

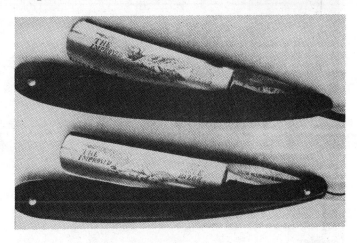

Two nearly identical razors except marked differently. Top: Salem Markos and Bros. Bottom: Salem Alloway and Bros. Belonged to my great, great uncle.

doubtful at that time and am now even more skeptical that this razor could date back to the 1865 end of the Civil War.

There are indications that an ivory colored plastic like material did not exist until several years after the Civil War. One such indication is that in 1868 a cash prize was offered by a New York firm to anyone developing a substitute for

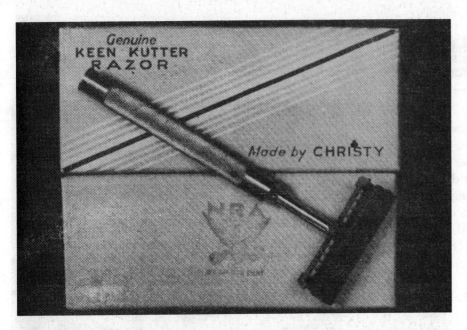

Keen Kutter razor box with NRA recovery eagle dates the razor near 1933-1935.

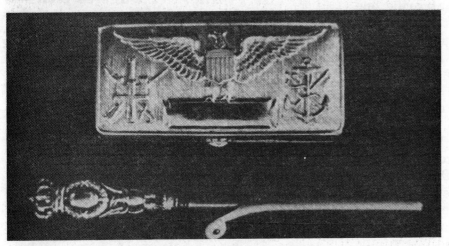

Top: WWI Gillette US Service Set. Note the composite military symbols. Bottom: Curling iron with sterling handle. The design seems masculine enough to suggest that it could be a mustache curler.

ivory. Another indication is that in 1869 a plastic like material called celluloid was patented. I feel it is unlikely that these events would have occurred when they did if the handle material already existed earlier during the Civil War.

It would certainly make the eagle razors more desirable and valuable to have a connection to the Civil War. The following three razors were purchased from razor dealers without any alleged Civil War connection at a total cost of less than the asking price of the single razor offered by the mail order house.

The first eagle razor handle has a wing spread eagle carrying arrows and the olive branch in his claws. The symbols of war and peace. Both ends of the razor have stars and stripes. The whole design of eagle, stars, and stripes have a blue color. The back side

of the handle is plain. The handles appear to be an ivory colored celluloid and have only a pin at the blade pivot end.

The razor shank is imprinted in three lines, "Oxford Razor," "Warranted," and "Germany." The reverse side reads in three lines "Germania," "Cutl. Works," and "Germany." This razor most closely resembles the alleged Civil War razor.

Another eagle handled razor is quite similar and could be mistaken as a duplicate. The biggest difference is that the stars on the handle ends are vertical instead of diagonal. This handle is narrow grained ivory colored celluloid and has a pin at each end. The stars, stripes, and eagle are a brown color. The blade is gold washed "American Beauty." The shank is stamped in two lines, "McGill" and "Cutlery Co."

The third eagle handled razor looks a little bare without stars and stripes on the ends. Its eagle is nearly identical to the other two eagles. The handle is made of a yellowish ivory colored celluloid with a wide, less defined grain showing. This razor handle has the customary two pins and has a black spacer between the handle pieces.

The shank is stamped "John Primble, India Steel Works, 1024-5/8." The 5/8 fraction probably refers to the blades width in inches. The reverse side is stamped "Extra Ground & Mfd in Germany."

Another razor is decorated with eagles both on its handle and its blade. As a Civil War period razor, this example is much more convincing. The handle is made of semitransparent horn. The pins and washers are of brass. There is no spacer between the handle halves, just a thickening of the natural horn material. Pressed into the horn on the front side only is an eagle carrying a ribbon and some arrows. The ribbon says "American Razor." The imprint has a gold color to it showing even the detail of many feathers.

The blade is heavier than that of a more modern razor and is of a wedge shape instead of being hollow ground. The surface that is etched is nearly flat instead of concave or curved. The blade has been etched to a dull finish except for another flying eagle holding arrows which is bright and shiny. The words, "American Razor," was not manufactured in the U.S. The shank is deeply printed "Warranted Razor, Sheffield, England." Even this razor might not date back to the Civil War, however, in spite of the horn handle and wedge blade.

An eagle that I've found on a Keen Kutter safety razor box dates the approximate manufacture or packaging of that razor. The eagle has its wings spread and appears to be holding a gear in one claw and lightning bolts in the other. The printing includes NRA and the words "Member" and "We do our part." I believe these initials refer to National Recovery Administration. Any firm that conformed to the administration's code was allowed to use a blue recovery eagle symbol in its advertising and apparently on packaging or on the product itself. This symbol was to indicate that the manufacturer was cooperating with the NRA in its efforts to recover from the great depression.

The National Recovery Administration had a short life, (1933-1935). The products or packaging which carry the recovery eagle were quite likely to have been made during 1933,

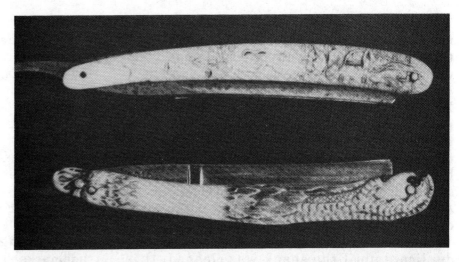

Top: Hibbard, Spencer, Bartlett eagle head and claw razor. Bottom: Simmons Hardware razor showing eagle carrying snake.

Brass door from large Post Office box. Except for the eagle, it would never have found its way into this razor collectors home.

1934, or 1935. Even allowing for unsold inventory would make manufacture of a marked product shortly before, during, or shortly after that time period.

I have also seen the blue eagle printed on a package of razor blades and in that case the eagle seems to have been part of the original printing. The recovery eagle on the Keen Kutter razor package made by Christy appears to have been applied after the manufacture and printing of the boxes. Some stampings are relatively clear while others are faint and all are a blue color different from that used on the rest of the box.

These next two razors have nearly identical handles with white spacers and eagle blade etching. The long necked eagles face left and carry arrows in their claws. The words "The Improved Eagle Razor" are stamped along the sides of the eagle. The bottom razor is one of those pieces which has special meaning for a collector. I knew the man that shaved with this razor and he was a relative, a great, great uncle.

One of the stories my grandparents tell about him kind of cools my wish for going back to "the good old days." That's the tale of a country doctor taking Uncle Dore's appendix out on a kitchen table. It makes me realize there are a lot of things better today than they were in the past. The shank of this special razor is etched "Salim Alloway & Bros." The cardboard box the razor came in was also marked.

The other razor appeared to be an exact duplicate until the shank was cleaned. It is imprinted "Salem Makos & Bros, Warranted."

Other razors have the eagle incorporated into their designs in different ways. One razor with an imitation tortoise shell handle has a nickel silver inlay of an eagle appropriately labeled "Eagle."

Another razor has a pair of eagles patterned after the US Great Seal etched on the blade. Also etched is the phrase "E Pluribus Unum," the national motto. The razor, however, was made in Germany.

Razors mentioned in previous articles that deserve mention again because of their eagles include two marked "Keen Kutter." The horn handled Royal Keen Kutter razor has a deeply imprinted eagle on its blade. While many Simmons Hardware razors are marked Germany, this one is imprinted England on its shank. The Simmons Hardware razor with an eagle carrying a snake on the fancy handle also deserves mention.

I never tire of looking at the Hibbard, Spencer, Bartlett & Co. razor with the eagle head at one end and the eagle claw at the other end.

The eagle symbol itself certainly can be considered part of the appeal of a number of collectables. For instance, stamps and coins often feature eagles. There are many other items carrying eagle designs as decorations or trademarks. This razor collector even fell for a curling iron (perhaps a mustache curling iron) with a sterling handle featuring a crown and an eagle. An etched glass door and a brass post office box also found their way into my home because of their eagles. It is just as likely that someone without the slightest interest in cutlery would take home a straight razor, service kit, or knife just because of its eagle design. That piece could remain out of circulation for years as a result. Personally I hope a knife or razor collector gets first chance at the nice eagle cutlery pieces!

This article appeared in Knife World January, 1982.

Electric Cutlery Razors

by Kurt Moe

The Electric Cutlery Co. was responsible for some very uncommon razor handles. Applications for design patents were submitted in July, 1891 for an unusual design by Louis Fuller and five more designs by Marshall Lefferts. These men are shown to have assigned the patents to the Electric Cutlery Co. The patents likely make those handle patterns exclusive to the Electric Cutlery Co. blades except in those circumstances where the original blade was replaced. While many razor inventions were patented and trademarks were registered, I am not aware of design patents for razor handles except for these five for Electric Cutlery.

Some razor shanks stamped "Electric Cutlery Co." on the front can be found that are also stamped "Friedmann & Lauterjung" on the shank back. The Electric Cutlery Co. marking is also found on pocketknives. The John Goins "Pocketknives" book furnishes more information about the firms, markings, and pocketknives along with illustrations as well.

A similarly named company "St. Louis Electric Grinding Co." 109 N. Broadway, St. Louis, M.O. also appears on razor shanks. This firm, however, doesn't appear to be related to the Electric Cutlery Co."

One Electric Cutlery Co. razor is pictured in "The Encyclopedia of Collectibles" as part of an owl collection. In fact, my razor also was a part of an owl collection for a time. The difficulty in locating this razor may be in part due to the additional demand for the piece because of the owl design.

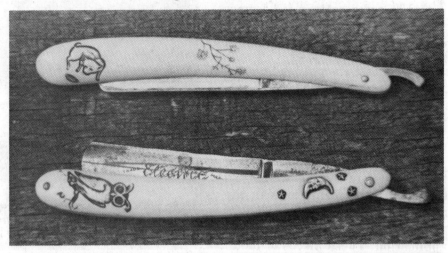

Two "Electric Cutlery" celluloid razor handle designs of the five patented in August 1891. Top: The back side of the monkey creature razor. Bottom: This razor was recovered from an owl collection.

A rare and delicate celluloid handle that looks as if it was braided. Blade shows one of Electric's etchings. Back of handle is marked, "Design Pat. Aug. 18, 91."

The blade of this owl razor is deeply marked "TradeMark Electric." The shank is similarly stamped. In both cases the word Electric has been designed to include various "Z" marks to represent lightning of electricity. The back of the shank reads, "The Electric Cutlery Co," "Newark N.J." The top edge of the shank has checkering and the bottom edge has file cuts. The top edge of the blade is also worked to some extent.

The handle material is celluloid which is grained and colored to look like ivory. The design differs from most others in that the owl sitting on a branch appears to be cut into the handle.

Design patent No.21014 refers to the ornamental owl figure as being intagliorilievo. This means the figure in relief appears to be cut or carved below the surface of the handle. After seeing several razors with the same pattern it becomes apparent that the handles were molded in this design instead of being individually carved.

Months of shaving and accumulation of dirty soap scum tend to darken parts of the design making the pattern look nicer than when it was new and clean.

The second unusual feature of this handle are three stars in gold color and a crescent "man in the moon" in silver which are described as "heavenly bodies" in the patent application. These pieces of metal have been applied onto the celluloid rather than inlaid.

The back side of the razor handle is plain except for the raised letters, "Design Pat. Aug. 25, 81." If this razor was manufactured within the seven year term of the patent, it would be about one hundred years old now.

Apparently the pin by the owl on this razor was a repair by the razor's owner. One of the characteristics of Electric Cutlery Co. razors that I've seen is that they have no pin at the large end of the razor.

A second razor pattern is also celluloid which is grained and colored to look like ivory. Designs are molded into the handle on both sides. The front side has an animal with an almost human body. It could be a monkey sitting on a branch and eating some kind of fruit. There are various flowers that look like thistle blossoms.

The animal on the back side of the razor has a similar head but has a body which is more dog like. This animal is looking at an object that could be a dish, a football, or perhaps half of a large piece of fruit. I had hoped that the specifications

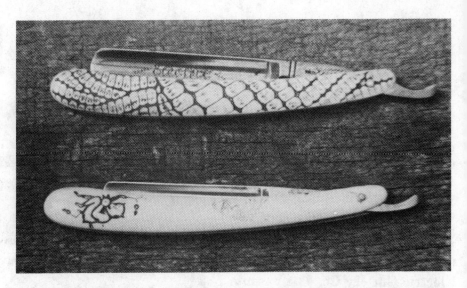

More 1891 Electric designs. Top: Simulated alligator leather. This pattern is also found in brown celluloid. Bottom: Monkey creature molded to look like it was cut into the ivory like celluloid.

of design patent No.21013 would identify the figures. The description, however, is simply "ornamental figure." The rest of the decoration is described as "conventional flower and branch forms" in the manner of "Chinese Decoration."

This design has been found with blades etched "20th Century Razor."

Some other razor handles look like a simulated alligator leather and are described as such in the specifications of design patent No.21012. This pattern was produced by Louis Fuller and can be found in both ivory color and in brown celluloid. The blade on the brown handled razor differs from the others described here in that its shank is etched with a sort of wreath trademark and the shank back shows the location to be "New York" instead of New Jersey.

The next Electric Cutlery Co. razor described here is a fragile design molded to look like celluloid was braided or woven to form the handle.

The specifications of design patent No.20997 describe the design as "vine like forms intertwined by a cord." There are several open spaces through the handle. The purpose of the spaces was to permit the exhibit of the blades ornamentation according to the patent. Uneven shrinkage of the celluloid might be the cause of some of the hairline cracks in this handle. The back side of this razor is marked in raised letters, "Design Pat. Aug. 18, 91."

Design patent No.21015 was issued for a pattern that I can't remember having ever seen. While the patent specifications refer to a drawing, the library that I visited could not furnish an illustration of the pattern. The description includes "a conventionalized flower form" and "pennant forms" also in relief. Rounded forms are "interspersed in the folds of the pennant forms." The designs are similar both on the front and back of the handle. I am looking forward to the day I might find this pattern to complete the grouping of Electric Cutlery Co. design patents of August 1891.

This article appeared in Knife World July, 1983.

Farwell, Ozmun, Kirk & Co.

by Kurt Moe

The St. Paul firm of Farwell, Ozmun, Kirk & Co. is known for its "Henry Sears & Son" and "Queen" marked cutlery. John Goins' book titled "Pocketknives" shows Farwell, Ozmun, Kirk & Co. to have started using that name in 1881. The book also shows that they acquired Henry Sears & Son of Chicago in 1897.

The Farwell, Ozmun, Kirk & Co. catalog from about 1932 shows that the firm also identified itself as "F.O.K. & Co." and as "Farwell Hardware." The catalog was expected to last about three years and had nearly 60,000 items represented in it.

One picture in the catalog shows some of F.O.K. & Co.'s delivery trucks of that time. The identification on the trucks featured the name "Farwell" and indicated that the firm was a manufacturer and distributor of wholesale hardware. Dealers could also call for their freight at the loading dock just off St. Paul's Third Street.

A title page of the catalog No.1432 indicates that F.O.K. & Co. was a manufacturer of sheet metal goods, paints and varnishes. There is a very large paint section in the catalog including some color samples.

The distribution of auto parts was also a part of the firm's business. The pages list parts for different cars including names like Auburn, Cleveland, Overland, Pierce-Arrow, and Stutz. Some names not so familiar as auto makers are included also. These names include Ajax, Case, Davis, Erskine, Jewett, Kissel, Marmon,

Henry Sears & Son 1865 razors. Top: Marked "Queen," Center: Blade marked "Made in Germany," Bottom: Blade etched "The Rob Roy Razor."

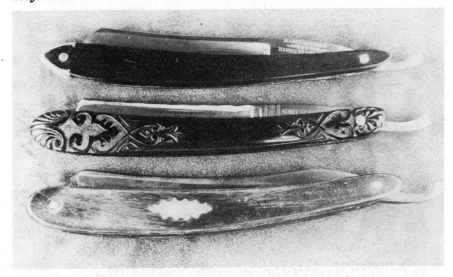

Top: "Manufactured by Henry Sears & Son" razor with dark horn handle with end grain on large end covered with a metal cap. Center: Worked back blade etched "Henry Sears & Son 1865" with black molded celluloid handles. "Mfd. in Germany." Bottom: Dark horn handles with metal and pearl shield. Shank is stamped "Henry Sears & Son, Rockford, Ill."

Moon, Rickenbacker, Roosevelt, Velie, and Wolverine. There are dozens more names that I've never heard before. The truck parts list has dozens of unusual names.

A page listing officers of F.O.K. & Co. shows C.H. Bigelow as the

Illustration from Farwell Hardware catalog dated about 1932. Their fleet of "modern" delivery trucks is shown at their loading dock.

Henry Sears & Son glass front display case. According to one long time retailer, the ten compartments were meant to hold packages of razor blades.

President. He was shown as being with the firms since 1888. There are no Farwell or Ozmun names listed as officers or directors but there is an E.B. Kirk, Director, shown on the page. His first year of service with the firm was shown as 1892.

An all too frequent occurrence is for a flea market dealer or antique dealer to say, "This razor dates to the Civil War. See, the 1865 date is stamped right here." The dealer then points to the shank of a Henry Sears & Son razor. The date of manufacture is rarely seen on a knife or razor. In the case of Henry Sears, the date 1865 is the date the company started doing business. This 1865 date has become a part of the firm's marking as one of its trademarks. Henry Sears & Sons knives in the 1932 catalog often have the trademark "1865" etched on their master blades. It is obvious that these knives are 67 years too new to be associated with the Civil War period. The premium prices that primitives of the Civil War period bring should not be applied to Henry Sears & Son knives or razors marked 1865.

A hunting knife assortment in the F.O.K. & Co. catalog includes eleven carbon steel blades with lengths 4-1/2 to 6 inches long. These are tang marked "OLCUT Union Cut. Co." One knife with a fish blade is marked "Union Cutlery Co." "Stainless Steel" on the blade.

A page of Henry Sears & Son hunting knives is not totally as one would expect. Some do have "Queen" trademarks. However, one illustration has an obvious "KaBar" mark inside a diamond on the handle. The description of this knife is that it has a Henry Sears & Son quality blade. A fancy cast aluminum handle with a guard has a removable cap with compass. The hollow handle serves as a match holder. Perhaps a mistake was made in assembling the catalog and the wrong illustration and description were matched.

A catalog illustration shows a

window or counter display for Henry Sears & Son knives. The display features a horseshoe and says, "You're in luck if you own a Henry Sears & Son pocketknife." The catalog has nine pages of Henry Sears & Son pocketknives. There are also several more pages of assortments and special price packages shown.

The stock numbers of the Henry Sears & Son knives shown in the catalog are chosen to give a description of the knife. The first digit from the left shows the number of blades, the second digit shows the composition of the handles and the last two numbers show whether the knife has a punch blade. If the last two numbers are 50 or higher, the knife has a punch blade. Handle composition numbers are identified as follows: 1 Rosewood, 2 Ebony, 3 Stag, 4 Pearl, 5 Celluloid, 6 Genuine Stag, 7 Bone, 8 Cocoa, 9 Nickel Silver.

From pictures in the catalog the handle identified as 3 Stag appears to be what is often called Pick Bone. There are very few knives shown that are identified 6 Genuine Stag. Examples of the numbering system given in the catalog are as follows: Knife No.2508 has two blades, a celluloid handle and does not have a punch. Knife No.3351 has three blades, a stag handle (pick bone?) and has a punch.

Today's pocketknife user might want to make new holes in his belt to lengthen it after a holiday season of good eating, or may want to shorten it after a successful diet. Many pocketknife users at the time that his catalog was printed still relied on horses for transportation or to do work. The catalog had a large harness and strap section. After looking at pages of this type of leather goods, I believe that a horse owner had many opportunities to use a punch blade.

A display shown in the catalog has a group of American made Sword Brand knives shaped like baseball bats. The assorted celluloid handles have Babe Ruth's signature, two blades and a shackle to use with a watch chain.

One Geo. Schrade knife is offered in the catalog, and a surprise to me was the six pages of Remington pocketknives included in the catalog. Most of these knives have "Remington" etched on the master blade. Three knives are shown with what the catalog calls the "cartridge" shield; they are the R1173, R1123, and R1306.

There is a page of Remington hunting knives and a large variety of Remington Sticking, Skinning, Boning, Packer's, Butcher's, Bread, and Paring knives. There are even Remington marked spatulas. There is a page of Remington carving sets. The packages for many of the Remington knives bear the "Klean Blade" trademark.

There are several pages of "Marbles" knives, axes, and specialties. There are also Remington glass front display cases shown as well. The knives were mounted with their blades partially open on an orange panel. The catalog said that this was the proper way to display pocketknives. The stock number and prices were shown on individual celluloid buttons. Thirty six compartments in the rear held reserve stock. Some displays included Remington kitchen knives and shears as well as pocketknives.

The catalog from about 1932 does not have any straight edge razors with "Henry Sears & Son," "Queen," or "Remington" markings. There are only four straight razors offered and they are "Genco" brand razors which are very plain.

There is a large variety of safety razors offered. There are several models of Gillette and Valet Autostrop razors. There are Gem, Ever-Ready, Enders, and Segal razors. There are models of the English "Rolls" razor including a silver plated variation that was more expensive than the usual nickel plated model. The Rolls razor case held a hone and strop to keep the old style hollow ground blade in shaving condition.

Some of the more unusual and collectible safety razors shown include the repeating Schick safety razor. This razor had a clip of twenty blades stored in the handle that could be shot into the shaving head one at a time. The chromium plated Ronson razor had a self contained sharpening device.

There were many brands of safety razor blades available. One package is marked "Henry Sears & Son 1865" "Farwell, Ozmun, Kirk & Co. Swedish Charcoal Steel." The blades appear to be wrapped in plain wax paper.

There are counter displays shown of Liberty, Speedway, Probak, Star, ShaVeZee, and AMMCO blades. The illustration of a counter display of Remington safety razor blades would rate a second glance from most collectors of knives and guns as well as razor collectors. The display is lithographed in three colors. The card contained twenty packages of five blades each. The double edged "Klean Shave" blades were among the most expensive at five blades for 45 cents. Speedway and Liberty blades were cheaper at two blades for 10 cents and ShaVeZee blades were twelve for 40 cents.

Besides blades for the safety razors stocked, other brands of blades offered included "Durham Duplex," "Christy," "Keen Kutter," and "Sexto."

Shaving creams and soaps were offered. "Burma Shave," "Williams," and "Colgate" are among those brands shown packaged in tubes as well as the more traditional cakes, sticks, or jars.

There are, of course, many Henry Sears & Son razors in circulation. One of the earliest that I have seen is one marked "Rockford Ill" on the shank. The horn handles are separated with a metal spacer. Brass pins and collars hold the razor together and there is a decorative metal and pearl shield. The blade is very large and heavy.

Another horn handled razor held together with brass pins and collars is marked "Manufactured by Henry Sears & Son" on the shank. The handle spacer is a pewter like metal. This spacer wraps around the large end of the razor so that none of the horn handle end grain is exposed.

There are razors marked "Farwell, Ozmun, Kirk & Co." on the shank. The blade of one is etched "Acorn Razor" with an illustration of an acorn.

One of the prettiest Henry Sears & Son razors has a flat celluloid handle which is a transparent red with yellow and green plaid. The pins are unlike those on other razors. The front side of the pin appears to be of one piece like the head of a rivet. The back sides of the pins are the more conventional pin and collar. The deep etching on the blade reads, "The Rob Roy Razor."

Another transparent red razor with flat handles has pins that look like rivets also. There is a "Queen" trademark and some scroll design in gold on the front of the razor handle.

Catalogs from the 1920's show Henry Sears & Son razors with "Queen" embossed in the handle. Often the blade is marked "Queen" along with the blade's width. A frequent blade width is marked "5/8" inch. There are examples in both black and ivory-like celluloid handles. Some razors had their shank and tang covered with real mother of pearl. Other razors had their shank and tang covered with celluloid material that matched the razor handle.

Other examples of Henry Sears & Son razors with black celluloid handles were embossed "Sears." At different times various colors of celluloid were used in the razor handles. The colors ranged from tomato soup color or transparent amber in flat handles to mottled yellow or green colors in rounded handles.

While most razors have blades of the usual hollow ground type, one blade has a thick back and very thin blade. After the first 1/8 inch of width, the blade is paper thin instead of having the usual taper. The shank is marked "Extra Ground" and "MFG in Germany" on the back. The blade when moved in the light is not uniform but shows dimples and ripples as it is turned. There are very few blades of this style seen so it must not have become a popular item. It may have been useful for only the fuzz-like whiskers in a very light beard.

Many communities still have O.K. Hardware stores. According to one store owner, the O.K. stands for Ozmun and Kirk. The home office of Farwell, Ozmun, Kirk and Co. remains on Farwell Avenue in So. St. Paul, Minnesota. The warehouse serving this area, however, was recently moved to South Dakota.

There is no longer a large catalog to use for ordering stock. The information for ordering is all contained on micro film. Stock numbers are put into a small computer which transmits the order by telephone. Wouldn't that have impressed a customer in 1932 looking for a fan belt for his eight year old Rickenbacker automobile?

This article appeared in Knife World March, 1985.

Fox Cutlery

by Kurt Moe

A water marked and worn catalog cover states that the Fox Cutlery Company was the manufacturer of the well known Fox Razors. The factory is shown as in Solingen, Germany. Two other locations for the firm are shown at 48 Center Street, New York and 928 Main Street, Dubuque, Iowa.

"We can hardly call to mind at the present time, any article so much used, and in which so much fraud and deception is found, than in a Razor," "Do Not Experiment, Get the Fox, and be Protected from Inferiority."

These quotes give examples of the style of language and advertising statements used in the catalog. Much detail is given about the old ways of tempering, hardening, and hand hammering the razors. Methods were still used as they had been used for generations. No new machinery had entered the making of Fox Razors to cheapen their production. The catalog shows only straight razors. There are no safety razors of any type shown.

Unfortunately this catalog is not dated. It does say that Fox Razors were known in the old country for nearly 80 years and that Fox Razors were then introduced to the United States in 1856.

Perhaps a clue to the age of the catalog is the lack of "Solingen, Germany" markings on the illustrated razors. *Levine's Guide to Knives and Their Values* tells me that manufactured goods imported to the United States in 1891 and after were supposed to be permanently marked with the

This catalog illustration shows the grinding and repair department at work. Razors could be concaved, honed, or repaired.

country of its origin.

A second clue to the age of the catalog is a statement about a great change that the grinding department has undergone in the last decade. The catalog discusses perfection of the art of hollow grinding or concaving.

The concaving was done with grinding wheels ranging from 4 inches to 1-1/2 inches in diameter. The types of grind used were flat ground, quarter hollow, half hollow, three quarter hollow, and full hollow ground. The thick or flat ground razor was said to shave as smoothly and easily as the thinnest hollow ground razor. The thin razor was less work to keep in good shaving condition.

Full sized illustrations of Fox razors cover the catalog pages. Razor shanks show a running fox trademark most times with the word "Fox." Other shanks read "Fox Cutlery Co." Even an end view of the blade is shown to indicate the type of grind.

Some etchings shown are "Damaskus," "Platina," "The Pride of America," "Fox Cutlery Co.," and "The Celebrated Fox No.44." This last razor had a full concaved blade and its stock number was 44. Another razor is shown etched "The Celebrated OK Fox" with "OK FOX" embossed in the handle.

One page describes Fox Razor No.444. The shank on the illustration reads "46 Koeller & Schmitz Cutlery Co." Certainly if one obtains a nice specimen of a Fox razor handle with a Koeller & Schmitz blade in it one shouldn't conclude the razor has been rebladed. The catalog doesn't describe the relationship between the Fox Cutlery Co. and the Koeller & Schmitz Cutlery firm but one does exist.

Some blade backs are elegantly worked. Some tangs and shanks are pearl or ivory.

Two Fox razors are without "Germany" marking just as those in the catalog. These razors have variations of the Fox trademark in the center front of their black handles. One of the razors has an ivory tang. The metal shank of the blade is pinned between layers of the ivory tang. The metal doesn't even extend to the hinge pin. These blades are marked "Fox Cutlery Co." on the shank front and have a stamping of a running fox and the words "Trade Fox Mark" under it on the backside of the shank.

The Grinding and Repair Department could sharpen shears, razors, knives and horse clippers as well as a list of other items. New handles could be put on razors for 25, 35 or 75 cents for the fancier handles. When ordering a new razor, a fancy handle could be fitted for only 25 cents more than the plain black handle. Razor handle patterns offered include a running fox in black, a running fox with scroll over entire handle, an imitation bamboo, rope, antique finish, and the wreath pattern. All handles appear to be celluloid with no ivory, pearl or horn handles offered. There is a statement that the handles were offered in different colors, however, I've seen only variations of the patterns in black and white.

Selection of a razor is covered in

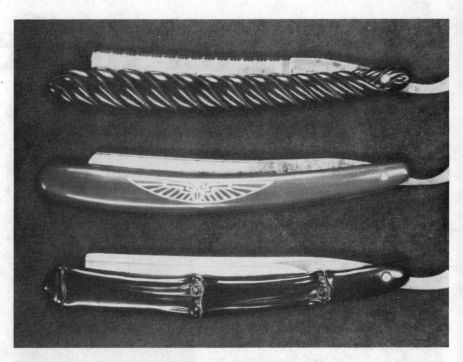

Fox razors. Top: Fancy worked blade in black rope pattern. Center: Earth brown handle with Egyptian design. Bottom: Bamboo pattern in black.

Two variations of Fox Cutlery Co. trademarks. The fox and surrounding design are different. White stain was used on design to better show detail.

the catalog. The person who shaves often and has indoor skin should select a full or extra concaved blade. Men with outdoor occupations and those that shave but once or twice a week should use a one half to three quarter concaved blade. "The full concaved razor always has the advantage of being easier to keep in shape on

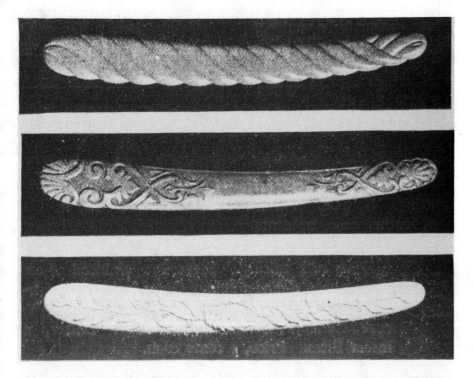

Catalog illustrations showing some handle patterns available for use as replacements. From top to bottom: rope pattern, antique finish and wreath pattern.

Fox razors with imitation ivory handles. Top: Unusual running fox design on handles with metal ends. Bottom: Running fox in 2nd variation of scroll handle design.

the strop."

Stropping suggestions include using canvas or linen first for only a few strokes then finish on leather. Always turn the blade on its back. Never turn on the cutting edge. A blade with its edge rounded will pull.

A keen sighted young man with steady hand and nerve can choose a light blade, perhaps as narrow as 3/8 or 4/8 inch wide. An older man would be better off with a heavier blade 5/8 or 6/8 inches wide. Fox Razors could even be ordered with blade of extreme widths of 7/8 or 8/8 inches for people with extreme

shaving needs.

The slightly rounded point is recommended for most shavers unless one were timid and used to a perfectly round point.

The catalog goes on to give detailed instructions on how to prepare the beard then actually begin to shave. Here I have a confession to make. I am too "timid" to put something so obviously sharp against my facial skin. I don't want to see my own face looking back from a mirror and bleeding! Furthermore, if someone else wants to take a chance shaving with what is commonly called a "cut throat" razor I would suggest that they not use a scene from a movie or television show as a model for their shaving style. Countless times my wife and I have groaned aloud as the star uses a blade perpendicular or at right angles to his face to scrape off the lather. I can almost guarantee that unless it is held flat against the skin, a sharp blade will cut the face.

This article appeared in
Knife World June, 1988.

68

Geneva's Genco Razors

by Kurt Moe

The Geneva Shear Co. had its shear manufacturing operation in Geneva, New York at the beginning of this century. Management of the firm was convinced by new employee, Walter Althoff, to take his father's equipment from a plant in Newark, N.J. and move it to Geneva. Geneva Cutlery's new razor department grew rapidly. The shear part of the business was dropped entirely by 1903.

Now known as the Geneva Cutlery Co., the firm directed its early efforts to winning the barber trade. The barbers were considered the most critical of razor buyers. If the Geneva razors satisfied barbers, it was thought that self shaving customers would be happy with the firm's product as well.

Three razors with plain black handles and etched blades probably date from these early years of Geneva Cutlery Co. One has an etching of a ship, AMERICAN LINE, S.S. ST. LOUIS on the blade and an antler trademark on the shank with the company identification. This ship etching is very similar to one that can also be found on H. Boker razors.

The second razor has an etching of several camels and the words, SILVER STEEL.

The third razor is etched GENERAL GEORGE WASHINGTON, REGISTERED and has a gold washed portrait of Washington. The shank reads, GENEVA CUTLERY CO., EXTRA HOLLOW GROUND, GERMAN GROUND. It is unusual to see a

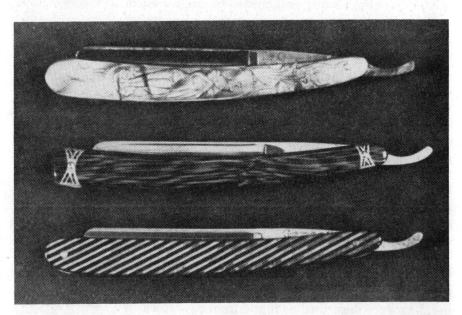

Top to Bottom: "Jessop" nude molded in a mottled green and silver celluloid. "Old Dutch" imitation wood grain handle. "Nubak" handle diagonally striped in gold and black.

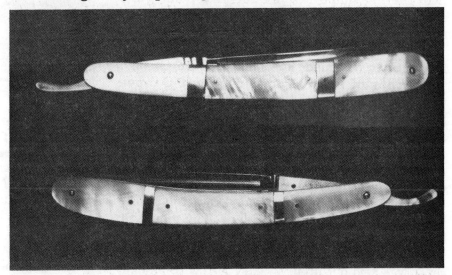

Top: Pearl razor with "Master Cutler" etching. Pearl tang and shank. Bottom: Genco "General" razor with three pieces of pearl on each handle pinned to an alloy silver liner and separated by alloy silver bands. Pearl tang and shank.

Geneva Cutlery razor marked with reference to its being German Ground.

Articles from *The American Cutler* give much of the credit for production of a quality Genco razor to the Walter Althoff mentioned earlier. In about 1918 Althoff was vice president and production manager. Wallace Page is credited for coining the Genco trademark in about 1916 when he became secretary and director of Geneva Cutlery Co. Page's duties included management of sales and advertising. The successes in areas of production and sales resulted in shipments each day of over 900 dozen razors.

A trip through the Genco factory would have resulted in seeing about 100 tons of steel stock waiting to be cut and sent to one of 16 drop hammers. Each worker specialized in a small part of the process of making a razor. The third floor grinding and polishing room contained some 68 workers. The blade polishing and buffing room held another 70 men. Inspection and testing was frequent. Every day some 5 to 6 dozen blades were consumed by testing to insure the Genco product was uniform and of good quality.

The Geneva Cutlery Corp. also boasted of its machine shop where manufacturing equipment, repair parts, and dies were produced. Razor handles were described as made from raw stock in the handle department. Gold lettered cases were produced in the casing department. These cases held the individual razors after final honing and stropping. Fifty seven sizes and designs were available.

The Genco News was a house newspaper offered free to those who made or sold Genco razors.

Another of several articles about Geneva Cutlery that appeared in *The American Cutler* tells of the quick response given to the U.S. government's war needs. A government order received at 9 a.m. for 10,000 razors was completed, packed, and delivered to the railway on the same day that the requisition was received.

A "Genco Safege" razor had a rotating safety guard on its hollow ground blade. The guard fit into a hole on one end of the blade and clamps to the shank on the other end of the blade. A similar razor was also put up in a khaki case with a hone, strop, and a mirror for use as a military kit.

The cutlery industry discovered that when products were scarce during the war that the public did not require such a large selection of sizes and patterns as before. By 1925, an advertisement in the Barbers' Journal listed only 14 kinds of Genco Barber Razors. The names listed in the ad included, Old Dutch, Head Barber, Nubak, Gold Seal, Gold Seal Jr., Forge Mark, Fluid Steel, Tonsor, Senior, De Roma, Master Barber, Wedge, Vanadium, and Expert. The ad

(L To R) Geneva Cutlery razor with an unusual variation of intertwined wreath, vines, and berries. Genco razor with metal red cross inlay. Geneva Cutlery razor with unusual variation of round faced lady with foot through flowing hair. Genco razor with unusual line design from about 1920.

proclaimed, "A Genco must make good or we will."

The "Old Dutch" was a razor with oval imitation wood grain handles and metal reinforcement at the pins. The "Head Barber" razor had flat imitation wood grain handles.

Genco razors did not always have a certain model of blade in the same type of handle. For example, the "Nubak" marked blade can be found in a celluloid wood grained handle molded to look rolled back to show flowers and vines. A second "Nubak" blade is in a diagonally striped gold and black handle.

Razors such as the "Gold Seal" had been

available for over five years at the time of the *Barbers' Journal* ad. The Gold Seal was a razor with gold semi-transparent handles and a gilt tang and back of blade. The "DeRoma" had an oval imitation ivory handle with fancy design metal reinforcement at the pins. The DeRoma and Vanadium razors had been available for several years as well. Other razors such as the "Seneca Chief" appear to already have been discontinued by 1925.

Molded celluloid handles with scenes were probably all discontinued by 1920. This would include razors like the "Jessop" with a handle of mottled green and silver celluloid molded in a nude pattern. Other examples would be the two variations of a lady's face with long hair flowing over the handles.

A very unusual pattern in molded celluloid shows a man standing in a boat and hauling in a net. The ocean and a lighthouse are in the background. The rare scene covers nearly the whole front of the handle. This razor is marked, GENEVA CUTLERY CO., WARRANTED, GENEVA, N.Y.U.S.A.

There is no doubt that the Genco "General" is very collectable. The tang and shank are inlaid with genuine pearl. Each handle has three pieces of pearl pinned to an alloy silver liner and separated by bands of the same alloy silver. The catalog specifications for this razor say, "Nothing that could be added to either quality or finish has been omitted." A variation of this razor is unmarked except for a MASTER CUTLER etching on the blade. This etching has been seen on other razors by the firm.

A Farwell, Ozmun, Kirk & Co. catalog from about 1931 still shows several Genco razors. The previously mentioned "Expert" is shown and described as having a very flexible blade. Another razor is identified as the "Grant." The razors appearing in the catalog seem to be rather plain and ordinary from a collector's view.

Some Genco razors marked BRADFORD, PA bear a striking resemblance to some W.R. Case & Sons razors. Several parties knowledgeable in the cutlery field have indicated that W.R. Case & Sons made those Genco razors marked BRADFORD, PA. Certainly the razors look like they could have been manufactured by the same firm.

Compare the Genco "Easy Aces" razor handle with a "Case's Ace" handle. First of all, there is a similarity of names. Secondly, there is a similarity of the imitation pearl material that makes up the handles. Thirdly, the shape of the flat handle is similar. Finally, the pins on both razors lack the collars found on most razor pins.

Another Genco razor sharing features of a W.R. Case & Sons razor has an inlay "Next." It also has similarities of size and shape of the handle and pins without collars.

A recent Doyle mail auction offered a razor with light blue semi transparent handles. The razor was marked GENCO MASTER BARBER and on the reverse side was marked, W.R. CASE & SONS, BRADFORD, PA. This dual marking certainly indicates a link between the two firms.

One obvious place to pursue a shared history including W.R.

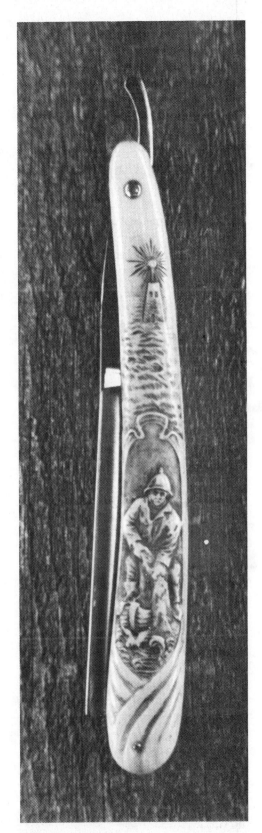

Geneva Cutlery Co. razor with rare celluloid handle pattern of man standing in boat and hauling in net. Ocean and lighthouse in background.

Case & Sons and Genco is with W.R. Case & Sons Cutlery Co. still in business. Unfortunately, my two inquiries about the possible link between the two firms did not yield any information.

The rich Geneva Cutlery Co. history and its razors span over three decades of this century. Its factory and its volume of U.S. made razors seem to have played a large part in capturing the razor market from foreign manufacturers. Certainly a large variety of razors were made. It is in finding those examples of yesterday's workmanship and in learning the history of their makers that makes today's collector truly happy.

This article appeared in Knife World September, 1986.

Top: Genco "Next" razor marked "Bradford, P.A." Center: W.R. Case & Sons "Case's Ace" razor with similarities in handle shape, material and pins to Genco Razors. Bottom: Genco razor with "Easy Aces" inlay marked "Bradford, P.A."

Gibford's Shaving Devices

by Kurt Moe

Edward B. Gibford of Adrian, Michigan invented several items related to shaving and received a number of patents for these designs during the first twenty years of this century. One such patent, #951,240 was issued for an improved stropping machine on March 8, 1910, and assigned to the Gibford Specialty Co. of Adrian, Michigan.

A device marked "ZIG ZAG Automatic Stropper" is nearly identical to the specifications of patent #951,240. The stropper is also marked, "GIBFORD SPECIALTY CO. MAKERS, DETROIT MICH. USA, PAT MAR. 8-10."

The device has a wooden handle painted black. It was said to be designed for stropping water type safety razor blades but could also be adapted for stropping of thick backed "STAR" type safety razor blades. The blade holding jaw could even be used to clamp on ordinary straight razor blades.

A strop was drawn through the device with the blade being held to the strop's surface. When the direction of the strop was reversed, a gear mechanism flips the blade over to strop the other side of the blade's cutting edge. This is a simplification of the workings of the device. The patent specifications consist of nearly two full pages describing how the stropper is made and how it works.

Gibford received several other patents over the years. Number 1,074,095 was issued in 1913 for a Razor Stropper Machine. In 1914 Number 1,089,832 was issued for another machine to strop razors. Number 1,257,078 was issued in 1918 for a combination razor hone and strop. There are other patents as well.

Most of the patents granted to E. Gibford seem to be related to strops and stropping machines. The Gibford Specialty Co. seemed to do most of their business in the stropper field as well.

E.B. Gibford did, however, receive patent Number 1,309,726 on July 15, 1919, for an improvement in razors. The patent drawings show a folding razor that held a thin replaceable blade. The object of the invention was to provide a means of ejecting or sliding the used blade out of the holder. The pivot pin of the razor could move in a slot in the razor shank. The pivot pin pushes

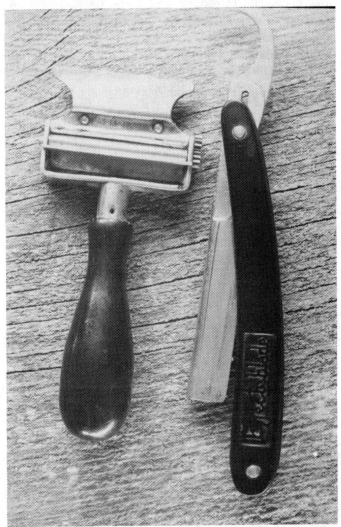

Left: Zig Zag Automatic Stropper. Gibford Specialty Co., Detroit, Michigan maker. Pat. March 8, 1910. Right: Ejectoblade razor by Pike Manufacturing Co. Gibford's Patent 7-15-1919. This example is missing both blade and safety guard.

against an ejector stem in the hollow shank. The ejector stem punches out the used blade enabling it to be removed with less danger of fingers being cut.

A black handled razor very much like the patent drawing is marked on the shank, "PIKE MFG CO., PIKE N.H. USA" & "GIBFORD'S, PAT. 7.15, 19." The handle is embossed "EJECTOBLADE."

The May 1988 *Knife World* contains an article

by Cindy Rabb, now Cindy Taylor, titled *Norton-Pike*. In this article Cindy describes Pike's Ejectoblade as a combination straight/safety razor. She indicates that the razor was supplied in two patterns, the standard two piece handle and the one piece Victory pattern. The razors were said to be supplied with safety guards but could be used with or without a guard.

Often when a patent date shown on a manufactured product is researched, the original concept or invention shows little resemblance to the actual item. The ZIG ZAG Automatic Stropper and Ejectoblade razor are unusual in that they are easily recognizable from the patent drawings. There is very little difference between the original concept of the product's design and the product as it was actually manufactured.

This article appeared in Knife World April, 1991.

Griffon XX Razors

by Kurt Moe

Chances are very good that if you see a sterling razor with a handle only 3-1/4 inches long, it is marked GRIFFON. One particular razor is marked in such a way on the shank front and is marked GERMANY on the back of the shank. The blade etching leaves no doubt as to the maker and purpose of this item either. The etching reads, GRIFFON CORN RAZOR. The blade is shaped much like a knife blade and was meant to be used to remove corns from feet.

The handle appears to be brass with a layer of sterling that covers each side of the razor. The pins do not show. The design is one of raised flowers and leaves along the outside of the handle. The handle is stamped in tiny letters on the front, STERLING and on the back side 925/1000. The second marking refers to the purity of the alloy being 92.5 percent silver.

A second small razor is also etched CORN RAZOR on the blade. The handle is real mother of pearl that shows pink and green colors when the handle is turned in the light. The razor's shank is marked GRIFFON XX and the back of the shank has the firm's trademark and GERMANY. The trademark is an odd sort of beast. It is very much like a mythical animal with the body and rear legs of a lion and the head, wings, and front feet of an eagle which is called a griffon. There is, however, a slight difference in spelling. Griffon is also a type of vulture and a breed of dog. The Griffon trade mark most closely resembles the mythical griffon.

The slide case that the pearl corn razor was packaged in looks like the

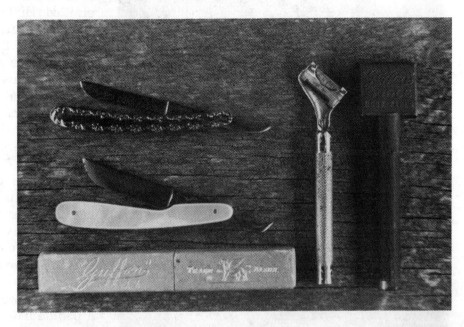

Griffon corn razors about 3-1/4" long. Top: Corn razor with sterling handle. Bottom: Pearl handled corn razor with box showing trademarks. Right: Griffon angle corn parer and its metal container.

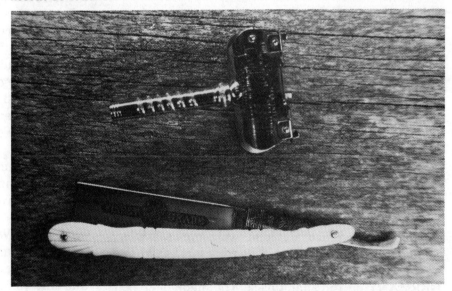

Top: Griffon safety razor and bottom: Griffon straight razor.

case for a straight razor except that it is only 4-1/2 inches long. This case has silver embossing of Griffon XX and the firm's trademark.

A small container with a tube the diameter of a pencil is embossed GRIFFON ANGLE CORN PARER. The container holds a small razor with a single edge blade. The blade, which is about 3/4 inch long, is marked GRIFFON ANGLE on the front side and CORN PARER on

Trade card with Wrigley's Safety Razor offer. Upper left shows Griffon razor. Lower right shows paddle-like stropping machine.

the back side of the blade. The razor is similarly marked and has the word GERMANY in addition. While one could easily slip and cause problems with the blades of the sterling and pearl corn razors, the Angle Corn Parer looks like it would be more manageable in removing thin slices of a corn. Aside from the function of the item, my view as a collector is that the pearl handled corn razor is a more desirable piece than the Angle Corn Razor. The sterling handled razor would be still more desirable.

There are some fine straight razors marked on the shank GRIFFON XX. One has the trademark and GERMANY on the shank back. The blade is etched THE FINEST GRADE GRIFFON XX. The hollow ground blade is in a thin ivory or bone handle carved on both ends like a tree bud.

Other razors are etched CARBO MAGNETIC REG U.S. Pat Of. An advertisement in the *Literary Digest* of March 9, 1907, tells that the blade is made of the most perfect steel produced in England. A secret process of electricity is used in the tempering.

The razor could be obtained with a DOUBLE CONCAVE grind for extra heavy beards. The ad suggests that a prospective customer write to the firm of A.L. Silberstein in New York for a booklet entitled "Hints on Shaving."

Another straight razor is etched on the blade GRIFFON XX. The same wording and the trademark is on the shank. The steel of the blade, however, stops just short of the pivot pin. The tang of the razor is all ivory. The shank of the razor has the single piece of ivory extending on each side of it.

The New Griffon safety razor is marked with several patent dates starting Sept. 22, 1896, and ending Jan. 7, 1902. The razor stamping also shows the firm A.L. SILBERSTEIN, MANUFACTURERS. There are small screws on the razor head. These are used to adjust the blade to give an ordinary shave or a close shave. This razor has also been seen packaged in a round tin container. With that package there was probably a small blade holder for stropping the blade on an ordinary strop. The razor pictured, however, was packaged in a large box with a paddle-like stropping machine. The strop shows English, French, and U.S. patent dates. A.L. Silberstein is again shown as the manufacturer. The instructions with the box illustrate other cases for Griffon razors with up to six slots for extra blades.

Some years ago I acquired a colorful trade card in browns, purple, green and blue. The card read, WRIGLEY'S SAFETY RAZOR OFFER. Time wasn't taken to study the card and my incorrect thought was that the card referred to the Gillette razor offer of about 1923. Dealers purchasing a box of Wrigley's gum received a free Gillette razor set. About a million razor sets were distributed as a result of this promotion.

Closer examination of the razor illustration shown on the card indicated the GRIFFON written across its hollow ground blade. The razor and automatic stropper was free with eight boxes or 160 five cent packages of Wrigley's Chewing Gum. This offer was for Juicy Fruit, Pepsin, and other assorted flavors. Both $8 retail worth of gum and the shaving outfit was only $5.50.

"Every man his own barber" is one phrase shown on the trade card. Another phrase "Shave yourself in the dark or on horseback if necessary" is probably meant to show the ease and safety of shaving with a Griffon Safety Razor. Personally I've enjoyed trying to picture a man lathering and then shaving while riding on horseback in moonlight.

This article appeared in Knife World April, 1985.

Heinr Boker & Co.

by Kurt Moe

The manufacturing firm Heinr. Boker & Co. Baumwerk, Solingen, Germany was founded in 1869 by Heinrich Boker and master cutler Hermann Heuser. Mr. Boker saw the advantage of making quality cutlery for his export business based in Remscheid, Germany. Heinrich Boker had kept an office in Solingen to obtain cutlery from different makers for his export firm. Sometimes the quality of the cutlery available was not up to Mr. Boker's standard. Different sources of product also made it difficult to obtain uniformity of the cutlery.

The firm manufactured only a few patterns of scissors and pocket knives at first. A catalog illustration of the Works in 1869 shows that it was a small group of buildings.

Heinrich Boker died in 1873 and one of his sons, Justus Boker, was admitted to the partnership.

Another catalog illustration of the Works in 1876 shows that the facilities had become greatly enlarged. Where there had been one smokestack there were now two additional stacks much larger than the first.

Early in the 1880's the manufacture of razors was started. The shank stamping of H. BOKER & CO. in an arch over a tree trademark appears to be one of the earliest razor marks used by the firm. One razor has a blade etching of a number of buildings identified as WORLD'S COLUMBIAN EXPOSITION CHICAGO 1893. Dates 1492 and 1892 are included in the etching. Attractions included at this

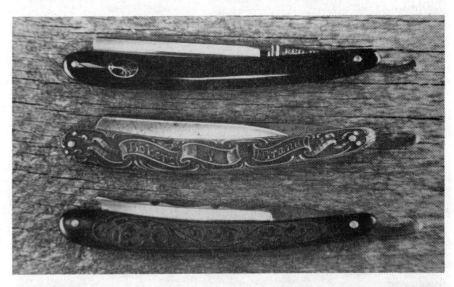

H. Boker & Co. razors. Top: Black handle with metal tree inlay. Center: Celluloid handle with pattern shown in 1897 Sears, Roebuck & Co. catalog. Tree trademark shown in center of handle. Bottom: Handle with leaves and a ladies head.

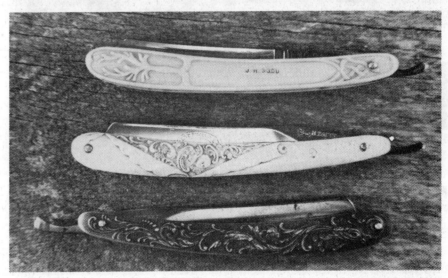

H. Boker & Co. razors with molded celluloid handles. Top: Embossed pattern including tree. Center: Center portion of handle appears to be rolled back exposing design. Bottom: Back side of pattern shown in 1897 Sears, Roebuck & Co. catalog.

World's Fair were a ferris wheel, Buffalo Bill's Wild West Show and an exhibit of the electric light bulb. The commemorative razor likely dates from within a few years of 1893. Its black handle has a metal spacer and small brass pins and collars.

A similarly shaped blade is etched with an illustration of an early steam ship identified as AMERICAN LINE, S.S. ST. LOUIS.

H. Boker & Co. catalog shows this illustration of their factory in 1913.

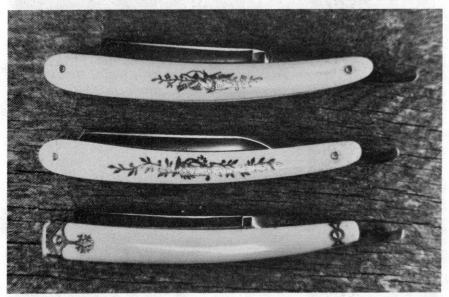

H. Boker & Co. razors with metal inlays. Top: Two birds and vines. Center: Vines and harp. Bottom: Tree inlay in handle.

Still another razor with the same shank marking is etched UNRIVALLED SAFETY RAZOR. The blade of another razor is marked DAMASCUS MAGNETIC STEEL.

Sears Roebuck & Co. catalogs had H. Boker razors shown. The catalog from 1897 shows black hard rubber handles with embossed trees in the center. This pattern of Tree Razor was continued for decades and seems to be the most common of H. Boker razors.

A fancy celluloid H. Boker razor was also offered in the 1897 Sears Roebuck & Co. catalog. The front of a similar handle is molded with a ribbon from one end to the other. Wording in the ribbon reads, BOKER'S BRAND with a tree illustration between the words. The razor's fancy black handle is molded in a leafy scroll. The H. BOKER & CO. stamping is in an arch over a tree trademark.

Hermann Heuser, who had functioned as the factory manager, died in 1898. His son Adolf Heuser, became a partner of the firm.

When Justus Boker died in 1907, his eldest son, Wilhelm Boker entered the firm.

By 1913 a catalog illustration shows that the Works had the look of a large manufacturing complex. Illustrations of the factory's interior show that individual machines obtained their power by a belt from a rotating overhead shaft. Different sizes of pulleys on the overhead shaft and on machines allowed various speeds to be supplied for different work operations.

The illustrations show areas in which blades were forged, hardened and ground. Other working areas included the etching room, box making room, and areas to sharpen blades, clean blades, and for inspection and packing.

The H. Boker firm continued under the leadership of Adolf Heuser and Wilhelm Boker. First quality steel was prepared especially for its final use depending on whether it was used to make razors, scissors, table cutlery, carvers, or daggers. For pocket knives, only the best quality steel for the purpose was used. Differences in price were due to labor required and the finish of the final product. In razors the concave grinding was said to contribute greatly to the value and quality of the H. Boker & Co. product.

The catalog listed direct agencies through which Tree Brand cutlery was sold around the world. Agencies were shown for France, Chile, South America, Mexico, Cuba, Canada, and for the United States. The U.S. agency was Hermann Boker & Co. New York.

The history of H. Boker & Co. to this point in the article was taken from an old catalog. The most recent date mentioned in the catalog was 1913. Heinr. Boker & Co. generously supplied photocopies of this material and other information about their firm.

It was common for hardware distributors in the U.S. to have razor made for them in Germany with their own house marking on the shank. Many razors can be found marked with a hardware company name on the shank and H.B. & Co. GERMANY with a tree trademark on the shank back. These hardware firms probably had the razors or at least the blades made to their specifications and marked with their own name.

Some examples of such razors with celluloid handles include a bamboo pattern razor with WM FRANKFURT HDWRE CO. marking, and a rope pattern razor marked C.W. HACKETT HARDWARE CO. with its blade etched BARERS OWN. Two mottled yellow handled razor are marked MARSHALL WELLS HDWE CO. and have blades etched ZENITH SPECIAL and TONSORIAL GEM. These examples all show H.B. & CO. GERMANY and the tree trademark on the back of the shank.

Wholesale distributors of hardware like LOGAN GREGG HARDWARE CO. of Pittsburg, Pennsylvania handled H. Boker & Co. products. The 1925 Logan Gregg catalog shows many pocket knives. Most are marked on the master blade TREE BRAND with the tree trademark. The catalog also included several types of H. Boker marked shears and scissors.

All razors illustrated in the 1925 catalog are H. Boker & Co. razors. Some of the blade etchings include OUR OWN SHAVER'S DELIGHT.

One razor shown has an imitation ivory celluloid handle molded in a scroll pattern at the ends with small beads along both sides of the razor handle. The etching on this razor's blade is the letter B inside a wreath.

Another razor shown has its blade etched GOOD AS GOLD. The handle is molded to look like the center portion was rolled back to expose a feather like design. This handle pattern can be found in both imitation ivory and black celluloid.

The RED INJUN marking is used on some of these razors. A very pretty razor shown with an imitation ivory celluloid handle has what appears to be a nickel silver leaf and vine inlay covering

H. Boker & Co. razors with etched blades. From the top: "Good as Gold," "World's Columbian Exposition Chicago 1893," "American Line, S.S. St. Louis," "Damascus Magnetic Steel," and "Corn Razor."

the center two thirds of the front handle. The design includes a harp shaped object. This pattern of razor has been seen offered at antique shows for up to $150. My feeling is that a $25 to $35 value is more realistic. Perhaps the dealers mistake the nickel silver and celluloid for a sterling inlay in a real ivory handle.

Greer & Laing of Wheeling, West Virginia also had a catalog showing many of the same H. Boker & Co. razors as shown by Logan-Gregg.

It was also about this time that H. Boker & Co. added stainless steel and silver plated tableware to its cutlery line.

The Heinr. Boker & Co. of Solingen furnished photo copies of razor catalog pages marked H. BOKER & CO. 101 DUANE STREET, NEW YORK, N.Y. This catalog probably dates from about 1928. The catalog indicates that H. Boker & Co. of New York City was established in 1837.

A page preceding the razor illustrations indicates that a very high carbon English Bar Steel was used. All razor blades were hand ground on a narrow wheel. The strain of such grinding was said to show any possible defect in the material. The razor could then be rejected at the factory instead of by the ultimate user. All razors were hand honed so that they could be used immediately for shaving without additional honing or stropping.

Blade etchings of razors in this catalog include, EDELWEISS, FINEST INDIA STEEL, and KING CUTTER. Razors with PEARL and WALDORF etchings have pearl scale tangs. Either arched or straight line H. BOKER & CO. stampings are on the shanks of razors in this catalog.

Small display cases containing a half dozen assortment of razors could be ordered.

A cased SEVEN DAY RAZOR SET is shown. The case slots are marked SUN through SAT on the left and the razor blades are etched in gold on their backs SUNDAY through SATURDAY. The Morocco case with silk and velvet lining could be made up with any of the H. Boker razors.

One razor has its handle reinforced at the hinge pin and has a metal inlay of a tree with the words TREE BRAND at the large end of the razor. This pattern was available in imitation ivory (No.3076) and black handles (No.3071). The blade was etched in gold THE OAK.

The blade etching referring to an oak tree can be confusing. While there were two different trees associated with H. Boker & Co. neither one was an oak tree.

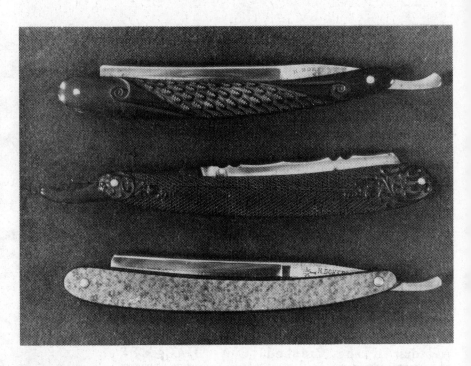

H. Boker & Co. razors. Top & Center: Patterns of handles shown in 1925 Logan-Gregg catalog. Bottom: Imitation wood grain handle.

The origin of the H. Boker Tree Brand trademark is that it is representative of the Boker family's beech tree coat of arms. Also, a huge chestnut tree stood in front of the Remscheid export offices. This very old tree was well known and may have aided the recognition of the firm's tree trademark. The tree was said to be hundreds of years old when a thunderstorm brought it down in 1926.

The RED INJUN 301 had an imitation ivory handle molded with the shape of a tree at the large end and a braided design at the hinge pin. Another razor handle pattern is very similar but has a bunch of leaves with berries instead of the tree.

A Travellers Razor has a handle which fits into a white celluloid fitted case.

Nearly all H. Boker & Co. razors are marked GERMANY. This even includes razors with blade etchings such as FINEST ENGLISH CAST STEEL. One of the few such razors not marked GERMANY has its blade etched SILVER KING with an illustration of a crown. The imitation ivory celluloid handle has a nickel silver inlay of two birds and a vine with leaves and flowers.

Other razors not shown in these catalogs deserve mentioning. A razor has an imitation ivory handle that is molded to look as if it has been rolled back from the central area. The area has much scroll detail including tiny flowers with a small head and wings. This razor blade is etched EACH BLADE FULLY WARRANTED FINEST ENGLISH STEEL.

Two H. Boker & Co. razors deserve special mention because of their rare and beautiful pearl handles. The first razor has four pieces of pearl on each side separated by three pieces of abalone pinned to a thin bone backing. There is a black plastic spacer between the handles. The shank is marked H. BOKER & CO. SOLINGEN. The tree trademark is both on the blade and on the shank.

The second pearl razor has three pieces of pearl on each side pinned to a nickel liner. There are two pieces of nickel silver between the pearl slabs. These pieces of metal are embossed with flowers and are also pinned to the liner. Again the handle is separated by a black plastic spacer. The shank is marked RED INJUN on the front and H. BOKER & CO. GERMANY on the back with a tree trademark.

In recent years H. Boker & Co. has concentrated on lines of pocket knives, hunting knives and scissors. Handle designs have included materials such as mother of pearl, stag horn, and bone. Etching of main blades has been continued using various techniques. Certain knife editions are manufactured for the American collector market.

The destruction of the Solingen facilities in 1945 has made it difficult to obtain information of operations before that time. Thank you to Heinr. Boker & Co. for sharing this information on their razors and on the history of their firm with us.

One observation that I would like to make, is that there are collectors who will go the extra mile to obtain a H. Boker & Co. knife. Some years ago a large farm auction near my home listed pocket knives in the inventory of items to be sold in addition to such items as early tractors and motorcycles. The walk from where

Illustrations from an old H. Boker & Co. catalog showing the founders of that Solingen manufacturing firm. Left: Master cutler Hermann Heuser and Right: Heinrich Boker.

H. Boker & Co. razors with mother of pearl handles. Top: Three pieces of pearl and embossed metal bands pinned to nickel silver liners. "Red Injun" marked on the shank. Bottom: Four pieces of pearl separated by smaller pieces of abalone.

I parked my pickup truck to where the bidding was taking place must have been nearly a mile. The buyer of most of the pocketknives had come much farther. He had invested in a long distance phone call to get more information on the knives and then drove over a hundred miles to bid on them. If you guessed that one of the few knives the collector chose to show me after the bidding was over was marked H. BOKER & CO., you are right!

This article appeared in Knife World September, 1985.

Imperial Razor

Kurt Moe

Imperial Razor is a company that seems to have put a great deal of marketing emphasis on deeply etched blades. Unfortunately little is known about the firm itself. Some sources do indicate that Imperial Razor was a brand name of the importing firm Adolf Kastor, New York City. The Goins' *Encyclopedia of Cutlery Markings* shows an 1886 beginning date for Imperial Razor and also shows a folding knife with an Imperial R. Co marking.

The oldest Imperial Razor that I remember seeing has a shank that reads "Imperial Razor, Warranted, Registered No.20507." The back of the shank isn't clear but appears to read "Sheffield Steel, Ground in Germany." The blade is deeply etched "World's Fair" with a globe and the date "1893" in the center. The World's Columbian Exposition in Chicago is the event being commemorated by the razor. The date 1893 is probably the approximate time the razor was manufactured.

The more usual Imperial Razor shank stamping has much the same information but has four lines on the front of he shank. This stamping reads, "Imperial Razor, Warranted, Registered 20507, Germany." The usual handle is plain black with a white spacer between the handle halves. Most fancy etched blades by any maker have plain handles. The collars and pins are small. The handle style and the choice of etching subjects often indicate that the razors date from about 1900. Of course, the "Germany" marking

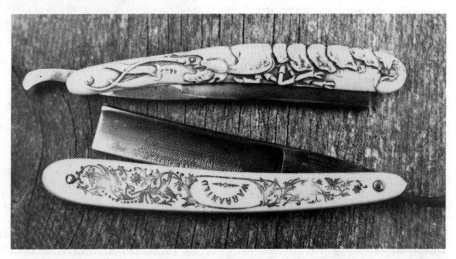

Top: Rare lobster pattern in molded celluloid handle. Bottom: Unusual handle pattern with St. Louis Exposition 1904 etched blade.

A detailed & desirable Imperial etched bicycle scene & larger version of early auto.

tells us the razors were made in that country. Automobiles, bicycles, eagles, and horses could have been etched on razors manufactured for sale anywhere in the world. Some etching subjects, however, seem to be meant especially for market in the United States. The Chicago and St. Louis Expositions; The Indiana, New York, and Oregon warships; the Army & Navy etching; and the Roosevelt etching are all subjects that fit the U.S. market well.

One example of etching shows an early automobile carrying two passengers. The box the razor came in has a matching imprint of the auto and carries the price of $3.00. Other Imperial Razor boxes carry this $3.00 price as well. The boxes are also marked "Germany." The automobile etching can also be found in a larger version that is very similar.

Other etching examples are of U.S. fighting ships from the Spanish American War era. One etching shows the "U.S. Battleship Indiana," another the "New York," still another the "Oregon." These ships served well in the waters near Cuba in 1898 during our war with Spain. The ships were painted a lead color which did not stand out against water background. This helped make them difficult targets and kept Spanish gunners guessing as to correct range. These ships were the pride of the U.S. Navy and were some of the best in the world. Eight inch main guns of the New York threw projectiles of 250 lbs. each. Secondary rapid-fire guns included four Gatling guns. The Indiana and Oregon were even more formidable. Their main batteries included 13 inch guns firing cast iron shells weighing 1100 lbs. each.

An etching "Army and Navy, Registered" shows a mounted cavalryman with saber on one end and a sailor holding the stars and stripes at the other end. The sailor is also holding what appears to be a cutlass. This razor could date from the same time as the ship etchings.

Another razor shows two riders and four horses. Someone with an active imagination could think the

Etchings of US Battleship Indiana and horse & rider group found on Imperial Razors. Below: Imperial Razor Co. World's Fair razor probably dates from 1893. Blade is badly ground out of shape.

horse and rider etching was meant to honor T. Roosevelt's Rough Riders. The Rough Riders were known for their feats in action in Cuba during the Spanish American War.

Other etchings are of bicycles. Razor manufacturers such as H. Boker had nicely done etchings of bicycles as well during this time. Bicycles were regarded as symbols of modernization or of progress. The two wheel bicycle as we know it today was also associated with safety. So wide spread was this bicycle symbolism that even the familiar John Deere Company's running deer was pedaling a bicycle in their 1896 trademark.

Imperial Razor's versions of bicycle etchings include a detailed scene of a person pedaling a bicycle over a bridge with his dog behind and birds ahead. The words "Safety" and "Registered" are included in the etching. Detailed scenes such as this one cover nearly the whole razor blade. They are generally more desirable than a small figure of the same subject etched in the center of the blade as the next razor has.

This smaller, less detailed etching has two people riding a tandem bicycle. The razor's handle is a celluloid imitation ivory. The blade catches on the handle as it seems to be too long and bulky for the handle. Grind marks at the pivot pin on the back

Etchings of auto, eagle and tandem bicycle.

place in someone's collection. It should not, however, command the price equal to a similar razor in original condition.

A slightly different Imperial Razor has a light etching of Theodore Roosevelt. The etching probably included a gold wash on the design. A caution, most cleaners used to polish razor and knife blades are too harsh to be used on the delicate thinly gold washed designs without losing the gold completely.

The Roosevelt razor etching includes the date 14-9-1901. I had to research the date. Of course, you knew that T. Roosevelt was Vice-President at the time William McKinley was assassinated. The 14th of September 1901 is both the date that McKinley died and that Roosevelt was sworn in as President of the United States. I believe the date 1901 approximates the date of the razor's manufacture.

Another etching found in the usual black handles is an etching with an eagle holding arrows and marked "The Improved Eagle Razor."

Another etched scene is of the "St. Louis Exhibition 1904" and shows a group of buildings. Though the date is extremely hard to see, The Louisiana Purchase Exposition in St. Louis was held in 1904. A variation of this etching is marked "Horticulture Building."

The back handle of the Exhibition razor has

side of the handle confirms to me that the razor was repinned. The blade was probably originally in a black hard rubber handle. Is there any other reason for grind marks other than a way to remove the old pin as a step in repinning the blade to a new handle?

My feeling is that repinning can lower the value of a razor considerably. It would seem fair to subtract from 20% to 50% from the value of the razor had it been in excellent original condition. Many factors affect the value, however. Was the blade placed in a handle from the same time period or perhaps even from the same manufacturer? Was a neat job of repinning done without removing any of the detail from the handle and without leaving grind marks? Does the length and size of the blade match that of the handle? Does the pivot pin and collar match the pin found on the other end of the razor?

This is not to mean that repinned razors are not collectable. If the handle is unusual or if there is a nice etching certainly the razor can still find a

Belt buckle showing the John Deere company's 1896 bicycling deer trademark.

faint marks on its ivory colored celluloid handle. It may not be original to the blade. The handle does show the word "Warranted" as does the blade's shank and is of an unusual design. The handle is embossed with gold scroll, vines, and birds. The handle could easily date from this time because of its lead like metal spacer between the handle halves.

Imperial Razor seems at some point to have added a line of fancy handled razors to their usual etched blade line of products. I have seen an Imperial Razor blade in the molded celluloid handle of the traditional bamboo pattern. That razor did not have an etched scene but was simply etched "Extra Hollow Ground, Fully Warranted." The shank was stamped with the words "New York" as well as "Germany."

Finally, a super pattern, a hard to find razor with a molded handle in the design of a lobster. Being from Minnesota with little experience in sea life, at least I think it's a lobster. It has claws, little legs, feelers, and a shell. If you've been reading along about Imperial Razor you might say these last two razors should have

Top: U.S. Battleship Oregon. Imperial razor owned by Mark Zalesky and displayed at Minnesota Tri-State Knife Show.

Bottom: Imperial Army & Navy etching showing a cavalryman and a sailor.

black handles. You may be right. However, there isn't even the slightest grind mark visible by the pivot pins. These two razors are also different from the other Imperial razors with etchings and black handles in one important factor. These razors have no etched scene on their blades as do the razors with plain black handles. Even if the razor could have its blade repinned in a handle not original to the blade, or even if the pattern is of a crab instead of a lobster, this last razor has a place in most anyone's collection.

This article appeared in Knife World October, 1989.

J.A. Henckels

by Kurt Moe

The cutlery manufacturing firm, J.A. Henckels, traces its Zwilling trademark to the year 1731. In that year Johann Peter Henckels registered his trademark with the Solingen Cutler's Guild. The initials J.A. in the firm's name came some years later from Johann Abraham Henckels.

The year 1853 brought the first steam engine to the Solingen factory. Over the years production increased and sales expanded internationally. In 1906 the master sales catalog was published in four languages. Several products made then continued to be made for decades. These products include scissors, kitchen knives, pocketknives and straight razors.

Some recent Henckels literature contains pictures of presentation and display pieces that are examples of nearly all craftsmanship and ornamentation possible by turn of the century cutlers. A beautiful mother of pearl razor made by Henckels for display would be a center piece of any collection. Its 3/4 yard length would make it hard to overlook. In addition to photographs of ordinary sized presentation quality swords, carving sets, and scissors, there are larger display items shown. A giant pair of Gothic scissors made in 1900 and a kitchen knife made in 1912 are taller than the young ladies holding them.

The Henckels firm did not limit beauty to only nonfunctional display pieces. One can hope to find a Henckels marked razor with genuine carved pearl handles. The

Henckels 7 day set of razors with ivory handles and tangs.

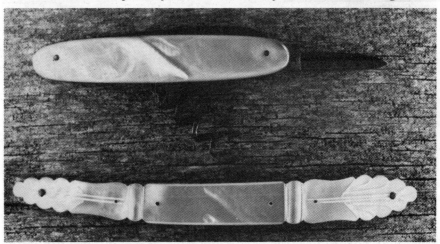

Pearl handled pocketknife with corkscrew. Each blade is marked "J.A. Henckels, Solingen" with the Twin trademark. Bottom: Genuine carved pearl razor handle.

handle is composed of three pieces of pearl on each side pinned to a nickel silver liner. The center section is plain but both ends of the handle are carved with even the perimeter or outside edge of the handle shaped.

The spacer between the handle parts is a lead-like metal. Unfortunately these pearl handles are easily broken. It is a great day for today's razor collector to locate an example of this beautiful handle pattern without cracks or chips. It was my luck to find two

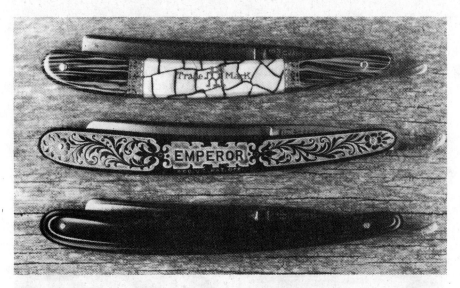

Henckels razors. Top: Razor with fancy celluloid handle has metal inlay of Henckels Twin Trademark. Center Black celluloid handle has white added for this photo to show ornate design of the Emperor pattern. Bottom: Black handle with ridge bordering edge of handle.

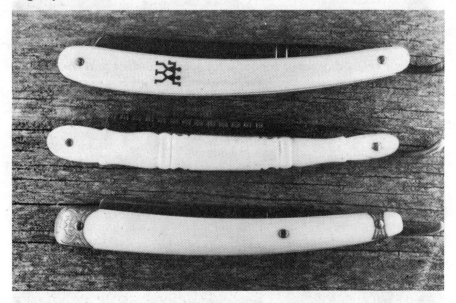

Henckels razors. Center razor has a carved bone handle with worked blade back. Top and bottom razors show Twin trademarks in metal inlay or cut from fancy metal end cap.

razors of this pattern but both with broken handles. Each handle was noted to be a different size to accommodate blades of different widths.

Henckels made some ornate celluloid handle patterns. One such razor has its black handle molded in a detailed pattern on the front side only. A little dried shaving soap would make the design stand out well. The handle front is marked "EMPEROR REG. U.S. PAT. OFF."

The Henckels firm indicates that in 1914 there were 135 different razor stock numbers. Variation in blade widths, etchings, and handle materials would account for such a large number of different razors.

Some Henckels blades have worked backs. One such blade has the Twins trademark and a row of flowers deeply etched into it. The blade is found in a carved handle which is probably bone in spite of its very white and smooth appearance. Most carved bone handles by other firms are very simple in design having straight lines or perhaps a border carved along the edge of the handle. The Henckels carved bone razor is more complex than most by having even the outline of the handle changed. The back side of the shank of this razor is stamped "GRAFF/ SCHMIDT." A scissors box indicates that the firm was for a time sole agents in the United States for J.A. Henckels razors.

A Henckels pocketknife has ivory scales with a hole extending completely through the sides of the knife. The blades include a corkscrew and a blade to cut wire. The master blade normally sets high. The blade is then used as a cigar cutter when the end of a cigar is put into the hole.

A 1926 Henckels catalog includes a variety of strops including those that look like cushioned paddles, the more common wide belt type and even a mechanical style for use with safety razor blades.

Most handles shown in the catalog were of flat ivory, bone, or rubber.

Several models of razors show shank and tang covered with one piece of ivory. Usual treatment by most other razor manufacturers was to pin a piece of ivory to each size of the shank and tang. Looking at the razor from the top showed that there were gaps between the layers of ivory, metal, and ivory. Sixty years later, today's collector notices unsightly rust in those small gaps. Henckels' version of the ivory shank and tang seems to have been to cut a groove in one piece of ivory for the razor shank to fit into. In fact the metal usually ends just past the hinge pin leaving the tang nearly all ivory. From the top and sides the shank and tang show only ivory. The shank shows an ivory, metal, ivory sandwich from the bottom only.

A complete set of seven Henckels razors has each blade marked on the back with one of the days of the week in English. The ivory handles have stylish pointed ends. The handles are separated by an amber colored spacer. The shanks and tangs are covered in the Henckels' style with ivory also. This very desirable set was put up in an oak case lined in purple velvet and satin.

A stag handled Henckels knife seems to be a combination horseman and bartender knife. A stone hook has a file on the inside edge. There is a punch for cutting small round holes in a harness. A gimlet for drilling holes and a saw with sharpened set teeth is included with two more ordinary knife blades. Throw in the corkscrew and wire cutter or Champagne hook and our young horseman was all set for a carriage ride into the country and to have a leisurely bottle of wine under some shade tree. Just think how well he would impress a lady friend by having this one knife in his pocket that could solve so many problems and have so many uses.

J.A. Henckels had a safety razor. It held thick hollow ground blades marked "RAPIDE." There

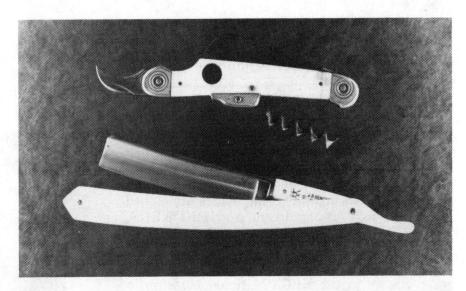

(Above) Henckels pocketknife with corkscrew and wire cutting blade. When master blade is depressed past hole in the ivory handles, the knife is also a cigar clipper. Razor is part of 7 day set. It has ivory handles and one piece ivory shank and tang.

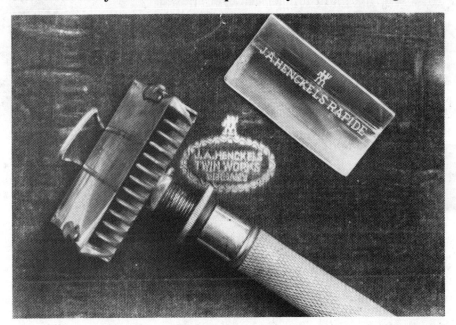

Henckels safety razor. A much larger version of this razor was seen at the NKCA museum in Chattanooga.

was a handle used especially to hold the blade for stropping. The leather box holding the razor was lined in red velvet and included slots for extra blades.

Later Henckels straight razors have flat celluloid handles. Some handles are grained to look like ivory, others to look like woodgrain. Sometimes there is a metal inlay of the Twin trademark. Sometimes the fancy metal end cap has the metal cut out in the shape of the Twin trademark.

The firm continues to offer straight razors. Instead of the 4/8,

5/8 and 6/8 inch blade widths offered in 1926, however, the blade widths are now 17 and 20mm which are the corresponding metric measurements.

The handles are of two styles. The first is a 3 pin version in white plastic material with a red and white Twin trademark. The second version is an ivory colored plastic with the Twin trademark and the word, "FRIODUR" in black. The blades are of a high carbon not stainless steel. The process invented in 1939. Some blades are etched in red, black, and gold, "J.A. HENCKELS, SOLINGEN" with the Twin trademark.

The largest Henckels razor that I have personally seen was a display model of their safety razor. Shown at the NKCA National Museum in Chattanooga, Tennessee, the razor was several feet long. This razor was large enough to have been used by Minnesota's mythical Paul Bunyan. That is, if that giant lumberjack ever shaved.

To those of you unfamiliar with Paul Bunyan, his tools and his giant blue ox were the largest and his feats most extra ordinary. One tale of his tracking ability as told by the lumberjacks was that Paul, coming upon a bull moose that had died of old age, decided to backtrack its trail. All the footprints the poor animal ever made throughout its life were traced until finally Paul had tracked the moose back to the place where it had been born.

I'd like to thank Henckels for providing information on their history and products.

This article appeared in Knife World March, 1987.

Label from Henckels scissors box. Shows Twins trademark and states Graef & Schmidt firm was sole agent in the United States.

Lakeside Cutlery Co.

by Kurt Moe

The Montgomery Ward & Co. of Chicago, Illinois offered cutlery for sale marked "Lakeside." The same 1925 catalog that shows Lakeside Cutlery also offers the more well known brand of Riverside Tires. The catalog contains a statement by the firm's president, Theodore Merseles, that sometimes M.W. & Co. would take a manufacturer's entire output or even arrange the building of a factory. This could be the case with Lakeside Cutlery products.

Aaron Montgomery Ward and George R. Thorne established their business in 1872. By 1925 there were large Montgomery Ward & Co. buildings in Chicago, St. Paul, Oakland, Kansas City, Ft. Worth, and Portland. Mail order catalogs from this company reached a large segment of the population that otherwise would not have had access to such a variety of goods. Recent news clippings indicate that the Montgomery Ward & Co. mail order business may be discontinued by the end of 1986. Knife illustrations in the 1925 catalog don't show readable Lakeside tang stampings. Two of the illustrations, however, show the knife master blade to be etched "Lakeside." There are also Lakeside butcher's knives, cleavers, razor strops, razors, and razor blades. Single edge razor blades marked Lakeside were available to fit Gem, Ever-Ready, King, Superior, Wiss, and Clauss safety razors.

The catalog shows a straight edge razor with its blade marked "Army and Navy" between kneeling figures of a soldier and a sailor. The catalog says that this razor is a duplicate of the razor made for the United States Army and Navy. The blade was said to be genuine English steel. The shank marking is "Lakeside." The razor has an oval shaped black hard rubber handle. Similar razors have been seen marked "Lakeside Cutlery Co., Chicago, Ill."

Another razor shown in the catalog is etched "Silver Steel." The handle is a celluloid reproduction of smoked pearl. This razor's shank is marked "Lakeside." Two styles of razors have the option of having the owner's name stamped in gold on the white celluloid handles.

This Montgomery Ward catalog had H. Boker,

"Lakeside" and "M.W. & Co." markings are on this safety razor and blade. Marked patents are from 1901 and 1902. Blade holder at the bottom can be used for stropping and honing.

Genco, and Wade & Butcher straight razors. Many brands of safety razors were shown as well as Wade & Butcher, and Marble hunting knives. Products such as shaving cream and Bay Rum were marked with the name "Wardgrade."

Some items have been found to be marked both with the Lakeside and the Montgomery Ward & Co. names. One such piece was the Lakeside Safety Razor. Both the safety razor and the thick hollow-ground blade are marked "Lakeside" and

"M.W. & Co." The tissue paper instruction sheet with the razor is signed "Montgomery Ward & Co."

The safety razor is also marked "Patents Dec. 31, 1901" and "Apr. 29, 1902." There are five square projections that are used to adjust the comb guard, the blade, and spring tension. The end of the razor handle has a small square hole. This hole allows the handle to function as a wrench.

There is a blade holding section of handle. The blade can be removed from the razor and slid into this holder. A part of the razor handle slides over the holder section. A second part of the razor handle can be screwed to the first part. These two pieces have a double purpose and can be used to lengthen the blade holder for easier stropping or can be used as the razor handle.

New blades for the safety razor were 75 cents each. A blade could be honed for 25 cents each.

Joseph Turner of Massachusetts was the inventor of record for the patents shown on the Lakeside Safety Razor. The patents 690,380 and 698,763 refer to the adjustment features of the safety guard and the blade of the razor. The patent information did not make reference to either Lakeside Cutlery Co. or to Montgomery Ward & Co.

Several attempts were made to locate more information about Lakeside Cutlery Co. Because the firm may have been located in Chicago, the Chicago Public Library was contacted. They replied that an attempt should be made somewhere else, such as at our local library. My primitive feelings were that the small town of Springfield, Minnesota was not the place to pursue information on Lakeside Cutlery. The local librarian after laughing at the

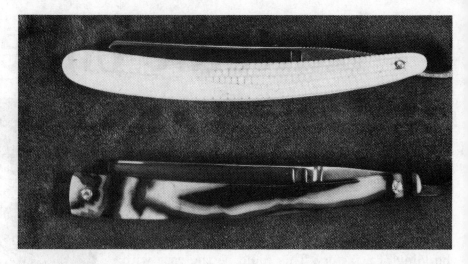

Top: "Montgomery Ward" is marked on this razor's shank and "Lakeside" is etched on the blade. Celluloid handle is the popular "ear of corn" pattern. Bottom: Mottled tan and brown celluloid handle with waterfall effect. Shank reads "Lakeside Cutlery Co."

Illustration from 1925 catalog of A. Montgomery Ward and George Thorne as shown with the building where their mail order business started in 1872.

response received from Chicago agreed to pass my request to another part of the library system.

Another attempt to obtain more information was made at the large Minneapolis, Minnesota library. Their information before 1940 was said to be very limited. Since a 1935 Montgomery Ward & Co. catalog no longer shows the Lakeside trademark, this source is not promising. The research staff at this library charges a fee of $40 per hour. According to the individual that we approached for help, this fee was charged whether or not any information was located.

That $40 per hour charge would represent a whole week's worth of my earnings as a farmer. Perhaps identifying the mysterious Lakeside Cutlery Co. should be left to someone better connected with the library system or to someone who can better afford research costs.

Two more Lakeside Cutlery Co. razors were discovered at a recent flea market. The first was blade etched "Select" and has handles with a waterfall effect in shades of brown and tan.

The second razor had plain black handles but was blade etched "Hygienic Razor." There were felt pads touching the blade when the razor was closed.

A very desirable handle pattern is one that is shaped like an ear of corn. This pattern in ivory colored celluloid has rows of corn kernels and a few small husks covering the whole razor handle. The blade of this razor has its shank stamped "Montgomery Ward & Co., Chicago." The blade is etched "Lakeside."

In spite of the apparent large number of catalogs printed over the years, it is difficult today to find old examples that still survive. Kids sometimes took catalog pages behind the barn to roll their own corn silk cigars. The pages were often used to start fires in wood or coal burning stoves. Perhaps the most universal use of outdated catalogs was when they were finally placed in the outhouse.

If you have a pre 1935 Montgomery Ward & Co. catalog, treat it with respect. It may be one of the few remaining sources of information about Lakeside products.

This article appeared in Knife World December, 1985.

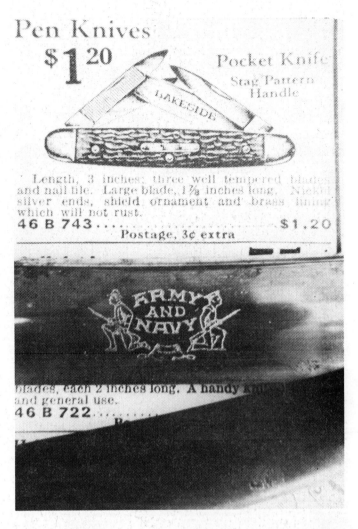

A Lakeside razor with "Army and Navy" etching.

93

Robeson Cutlery Razors

by Kurt Moe

"Ask the man who uses a Robeson ShurEdge Razor" was the lettering on a display case that I saw several years ago. More recently, I had the opportunity to see a fine collection of Robeson razors owned and displayed by Lew Angell in the same case.

Inside the case's glass window is a drawer with cutouts for 18 razors. The cutouts allow each razor to have its blade displayed partially open. Such a display allows the style of blade point and any etching to be evident. Wire clips keep the razors from falling out. Each razor has a brass oval price disc under it. The $2.50 prices are displayed in the center while $2.00 and $1.50 prices are displayed closer to the ends of the cabinet. There are eyescrews which enabled the whole display to be suspended. There is a pair of handles on the bottom of the cabinet which secure the drawer of razors.

The case itself is a nice piece and with ordinary razors inside would make a good display. The "Robeson" razors inside were not ordinary, however! Some of the handle patterns included celluloid molded with wreath and vines, as well as rope and bamboo patterns. Some handles were colorful mottled oranges and greens. One was even a bright speckled gold color.

Two razors must have been extremely difficult to obtain for the Robeson display. One has beautiful one piece genuine mother of pearl handles. The other one I thought might be stag but am informed is really pick bone.

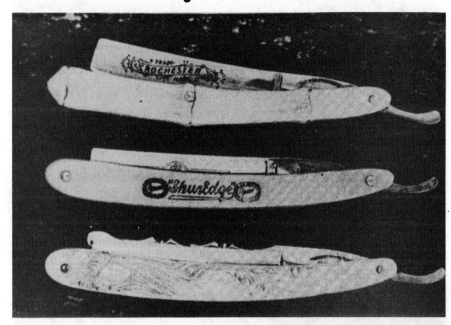

Top: Robeson razor with bamboo pattern celluloid handle holds blade with Rochester trademark. Center: ShurEdge handle with a pattern also found in black. Bottom: Art nouveau style goddess head with long flowing hair. Blade back worked.

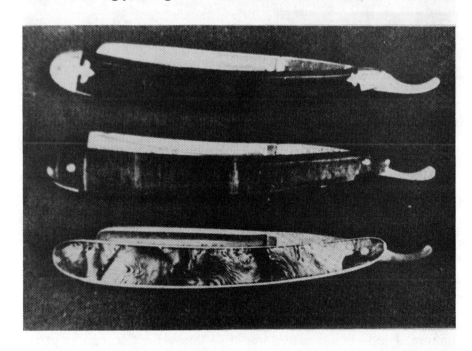

Top: Typical "Razor that fits your face." This one is numbered 36 M-400. Center: Red and black mottled handles that appear to be hard rubber. Bottom: Mottled green handles with blade etched "Nubak the razor that does not cut the strop."

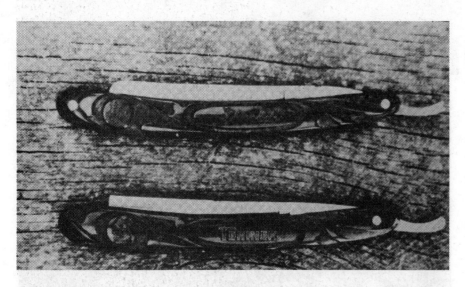

Similar patterns in black plastic handles. Top: Robeson ShurEdge marking on handle and shank. Bottom: Terrier marking on handle and shank.

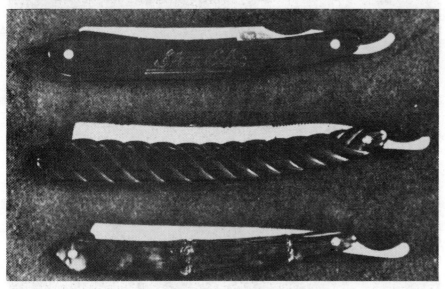

The handles are thought to be original to the Robeson blades they hold.

The razors in the display probably cover a time period beginning many years before the manufacture of the case and ending years after the case itself was obsolete. Mr. Angell has what appears to be the fanciest and most sought after razors from several decades in the one display case. The shank stampings cover a time range from "Premier" to "ShurEdge." I'm told that one of the shanks has a "Boker" tree mark as well as a "Robeson" stamping.

Taped to the back of the Robeson display case is a certificate for honing. The Robeson razors would be honed for the regular price of 25 cents or for one of the four 25 cent coupons perforated like stamps on the right edge of the certificate. The certificate also guaranteed the razor to be made from S & C Wardlaw's Bar Razor Steel free from flaws and properly tempered.

Mr. Angell's show exhibit also included a pair of hand barber clippers and a seven day set of razors among other Robeson items. The box holding the seven Robeson razors is of a celluloid grained to look like ivory. The days of the week, SUN through SAT are stamped along the side of the box. The inside lid of the box is embossed "ShurEdge."

Visitors to the NKCA museum in Chattanooga, Tennessee this past summer were also able to view this quality razor exhibit. Any one visiting that part of the country should make every effort to visit this fine museum to see the many fine cutlery displays.

Robeson had a slogan for a time, "The Razor that Fits your Face." This phrase can be found etched on the blade of many Robeson razors. Such a razor is likely to have a plain handle in one of several colors. Sometimes nickel silver end caps are on such razors also. The razors are likely to have hand hammered tangs and shanks with Robeson ShurEdge stamped into it. There is likely a number such as 36 M-400 stamped into the tang as well. That particular number identifies a razor that was ground and honed for a tough wiry beard and skin exposed to the weather.

Another feature of the Robeson razors is that they often are found in a brown rust proof woolen bag with a label saying "The Razor that fits your face, Robeson ShurEdge." As might be expected, it is difficult to find a case in good condition. Over the years, the moths usually eat holes in the woolen cases.

A booklet titled "What kind of a beard have you?" was expected to help a man choose his razor. Robeson felt that it was unreasonable to expect the same razor to shave a tough wiry beard on weather skin or to shave a light beard on tender skin and give satisfaction to both users. The booklet goes on to say that the edge of a razor when magnified resembles the teeth of a saw. A razor with fine teeth was best suited for a fine or medium beard, while a razor with coarse teeth was better for a tough, wiry beard. The blade width and degree of concave of a razor are also elements in properly fitting a razor to a man's beard and skin.

Another display case is apparently from the same time period as the booklet and plainer razors. The decal below each razor lists stock numbers and comments concerning the type of beard and skin for which the razor was best suited. The gold lettering on this case reads, "The Razor that fits your face," on top and on the front of the case reads, "Robeson ShurEdge," "A better quality razor," "Ground and Honed for your own particular Beard." The locking back of this case folds down to reveal a storage space for additional stock.

The glass covering the display is a replacement as is the green felt and the screws holding the glass. Pieces of the previous felt were faded but appeared to be a brighter lime tinted green than the felt commonly available in stores now. Every effort was made to keep the case as near to the original appearance as possible. The glass thickness and dimensions were obtained from the owner of similar cases. The holding screws were positioned in existing holes in the wood. The finish of the case was not redone but left in original condition showing its age. Only in situations where the piece is in the worst of condition, do I feel one is justified

Another Robeson display case holding razors of several other brands. Glass and fasteners are replacements. Back folds down to hold extra stock.

in refinishing such an item. Refinishing can alter the original appearance and destroy the character an item acquires with age.

Robeson also sold a few razors with fancier handles. One such razor has an etching NUBAK. "The razor that does not cut the strop." The flat handles are a white plastic-like material with a mottled green material laminated on it. Robeson catalogs often referred to white, black and colored plastic like material used on knife handles as Pyralin.

Another razor has a molded handle in an art nouveau style showing a goddess head with flowing hair. The blade has a fancy back. The shank is stamped "The Robeson Cutlery Co." in an arc over "Rochester N.Y." The shank back is stamped 2547.

Two razors have red and black handles. One has ShurEdge Warranted etched on the blade and large rounded mottled handles. The material appears to be a hard rubber rather than plastic, celluloid, or Pyralin. The other razor has celluloid handles that have the red and black patterned to look like wood grain.

Two more razors have an unusually small size. One has black plastic handles embossed ShurEdge. The shank is curved on the top for a finger hold. The tang back is marked "Pat No. 730360." There is a third pin which does not show from the outside but keeps the blade from falling through the handles. The spacer between the handle sides is ivory grained celluloid.

The second small sized razor has imitation tortoise shell handles in the bamboo pattern. The shank is stamped 2417 on the back side.

The next pattern in black plastic could be unique to Robeson Cutlery. The ShurEdge trademark is embossed in the handle center. Two men and a coat of arms are in a circle on the left. A kind of pebbling effect is in the background. A red stain is often in the embossing. On the tang is 3585.

A variation exists of this pattern with the trademark and men raised instead of being embossed into the handle. The tang on this razor was numbered 1585.

A similar razor has the same basic pattern with pebble background in black plastic. Inside the oval, however, the embossing reads TERRIER in red. Inside the circle is an illustration of a terrier. The shank is stamped "Terrier Cutlery Rochester, N.Y." The shank back has another terrier illustration stamped. The similarity of the pattern and the Rochester N.Y. stamping on both razors must be more than coincidence!

Another pair of razors has similar markings on their handles. The first has "White King" etched on its blade and 1601 on its tang. The ivory grained celluloid handle has the word "ShurEdge" embossed on it. At each end of the word is a wreath. The left wreath has the word "Robeson" inside and the right wreath has the word Razor inside it. All embossing is stained red.

The second razor of this pair has the same pattern but in black plastic. The blade is etched "New Science Concave" with fingers pointing down to the double concave ridge on the blade. The tang is marked 1660.

An ivory colored handle molded in the shape of bamboo has a blade etched "Rochester" in a ribbon and the words "TradeMark." The tang is stamped 1518 on the back.

One of the difficulties faced by collectors is the problem of finding information on a particular cutlery company. One of the books often mentioned as a good source of information on the Robeson Company and its cutlery is the pictorial price guide, "Romance of Collecting Cattaraugus, Robeson, Russell, Queen, Knives," by Mrs. Dewey P. (Lavona) Ferguson. This book includes illustrations of stamping variations and the dates they were used as well as pages of pocketknife patterns. A history of the company founded by M.F. Robeson also in the book makes good reading whether your interest is Robeson pocketknives or razors.

This article appeared in Knife World December, 1982.

Shapleigh Hardware

by Kurt Moe

The Shapleigh Hardware Company of St. Louis Missouri handled many razors marked with its own name. Shapleigh also stocked razors marked with other names of high quality and a few razors competitive in price only. Of course, knives and razors marked with the Shapleigh name or the "Diamond Edge" trademark are sought by machairologists. Other items such as tools, displays, and advertising of this firm are sought as well by an increasing group of collectors.

A General Hardware catalog marked 1915-1916 yields much information about Shapleigh Hardware at that time. A.F. Shapleigh is pictured and according to that page he was born January 9, 1810, and died February 27, 1902. The page says that he established the business in St. Louis in 1843. Three buildings are pictured in the catalog. The descriptions with those pictures indicate the main store at Fourth Street and Washington Avenue and the Ashley Warehouse each covered an entire city block. A smaller Locust Street Warehouse is also pictured. The company name is shown on the buildings and on the catalog as "Shapleigh Hardware Co."

E.C. Simmons was a competitor in the hardware trade and operated out of St. Louis as well. E. C. Simmons apparently retired at about the same time as A.F. Shapleigh died. Management of both companies as a result were under going changes. It was about this time that Saunders Norvell

Shapleigh Hardware Co. store as shown in the 1915-1916 catalog.

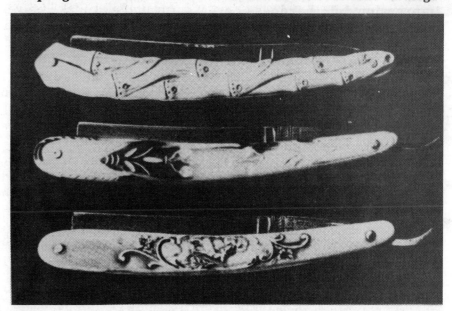

Top: A.F. Shapleigh razor with celluloid handle that looks like twisted bamboo. Middle: Norvell Shapleigh razor handle has the coloring of real bamboo but is molded or carved celluloid. Bottom: Norvell Shapleigh razor handle with raised deer. Handle is celluloid stained bright red.

might have become unhappy with the new generation of management at Simmons Hardware and became associated with the Shapleigh firm. Sometime after that, "Norvell-Shapleigh

99

Hardware Company" was the name used on many products. I could find no mention of Norvell by name in this 1915-1916 catalog. The catalog does list A.L. Shapleigh as Chairman of the Board and Treasurer. It lists R.W. Shapleigh as President and nine other names as directors. The other names include W.G. Yantis, W.L. Clarke, L. Matthews Jr., W.B. Willis, H.M. Owsley, G.T. Sprake, E.L. Johnson, J.C. Reed and F.E. Smith.

There are a number of products in the catalog, however, that indicate Norvell having been there. The brand name "Norleigh Diamond" appears on such products as door locks, roof paint, shaving brushes, shampoo, talcum powder, spark plugs and rubber roofing. The "Diamond" was probably to give an impression of hardness or sharpness of the product. That could be a reason that the toilet paper was branded only "Norleigh" without the "Diamond!" The catalog also shows a "Norshap" Silex roofing and had "Norshap" lines of butcher knives and kitchen knives.

Both the names "Norshap" and "Norleigh" probably used the first syllable of Nor-ell and either the first or last syllable of Shap-leigh. Certainly the "Norvell-Shapleigh Hardware Company" stamping could use some shortening!

Some examples of the Norvell-Shapleigh marking I believe were used in the early 1900's follow. One example is an aluminum hone box marked "Diamond King Razor Hone," "Norvell-Shapleigh Hardware Co, St. Louis." A brightly colored paper inside the lid is printed exactly as the lid is embossed. The detail in the diamond looks like a sparkling

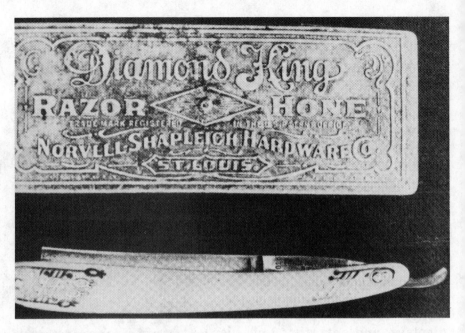

Aluminum Diamond King razor hone box and unusual nickel silver inlay razor handle. Both box and razor are marked "Norvell-Shapleigh Hardware Co. St. Louis."

gem. The hone itself is embossed "The Diamond King Razor Hone," in a diamond shape.

An unusual nickel silver inlay is in the celluloid handle of another "Norvell-Shapleigh Hardware Co." marked piece. This razor is stamped "015" and "St. Louis." The shank back reads, "Made in Germany."

A second unusual razor is marked "Norvell-Shapleigh Hdwe Co. St. Louis" and "118" on the shank. The shank back reads, "Made in Germany." The celluloid handles look the varied coloring of bamboo. Designs were either molded or cut into the front handle only.

Two more razors with bright red stained handles have a deer, tree, and cloud scene framed in the center. One shank is stamped "126 Norvell-Shapleigh Hdwe Co. St. Louis." On the shank back is, "Made in Germany." The similar razor shank is stamped "no. 110R." On this shank's reverse side is "Norvell-Shapleigh Hardware Co St. Louis" "Made in Germany."

According to the 1915-1916 catalog, the "Diamond Edge" trademark was registered September 25, 1888. A statement claims that the trademark had been used continuously since the month of May 1864. The company was proud of its trademark. Generally it was the top quality knives, razors, and edge tools that were stamped, stenciled, or labeled with the "Diamond Edge" mark. The catalog itself has the slogan "Diamond Edge is a Quality Pledge" over a dozen times on its covers. The same slogan is repeated on nearly every one of the almost 2000 pages in the catalog.

The company was also proud of an axe handling plant. Four different brands are shown with a picture of workers putting handles on axes and packaging them for shipment. Those names

100

sometimes show up on cutlery also and are "Diamond Edge," "Black Prince," "Bridge," and "Mound City." If you thought one axe is just like another, you should see the fourteen patterns of double edge axe heads and the twenty eight patterns of single edge axes shown.

An exclusive wedge used by Shapleigh Hardware to bind the handle to the axe head is described in detail with several illustrations. Two round slivers were cut in the process of driving the wedge into the handle and these slivers become twisted in a manner designed to prevent the handle from loosening.

The Shapleigh catalog is marked "No.200." Perhaps some catalogs were merely supplements and not full sized as the 1915-1916 book was. The prices in this catalog were not firm but were subject to change. I doubt, however, that their prices were subject to the frequent and large increases we often see today.

Shapleigh Hardware published a trade periodical titled, "Gimlet." A cover of the June 15, 1915, issue is shown picturing a gimlet tool. The gimlet itself is a boring tool usually with a cross head handle. The magazine cover states: "The gimlet is a small instrument with a point." Besides being a broad description of the tool this appears to have a second meaning when applied to the small magazine making points about the hardware business.

The magazine was apparently full of working man's humor. With this in mind, the pricing statement comes as no surprise, "Damages 5 cents a copy or 25 cents a year."

The 1915-1916 catalog had a Motor Outfit that contained a gimlet and eight other useful tools which fit firmly into a pocket knife handle. A leather case held all the parts.

The Anglo-Saxon pattern walnut handle was 3-7/8 inches long. There was one spear blade and removable claw hammer, file, gimlet, chisel, reamer, screwdriver, can opener and saw. The saw had a guard graduated on one side in inches and on the other side in millimeters.

The General Hardware Catalog included accessories used to help stores merchandise the Shapleigh products. I'd like to be able to order some of the display and show cases. Beveled plate glass, green felt billiard cloth, mirror lined sliding doors, white riverside marble, and etched glass were some of the features available on golden finished oak cases. Many sizes of the cases including outside display cases as well as counter or floor showcases of the store could be ordered.

Display corks in the shape of spheres, hemispheres, flat ovals, squares, and of course the trademark diamond shape were available. These cork shapes were especially intended for display of pocketknives and other cutlery. The cork could be covered with plush cloth or aluminum paint. Pocketknives, for instance, could have their blades half or

A.F. Shapleigh as pictured in 1915-1916 catalog. Born January 9, 1810, and died February 27, 1902.

fully open and stood up with one blade stuck in the cork. This would give a more attractive display than seeing only the top side of a closed knife in a box.

Boxes were available in various sizes, most to hold about a dozen pieces. Samples could be shown in a plush lined tray on top. The remainder of the stock could be stored in the large part of the box below. The boxes were furnished in a black seal grain leatherette and in shapes for razors, scissors, or pocketknives. The company spent a lot of effort to ensure exposure of the cutlery and company name. Shapleigh Hardware felt that their cutlery was some of the best advertising a merchant could have for his edged tool line.

Often price tags were tied to stock to show the selling price. This catalog shows two additional pricing systems for cutlery. David's Cutlery Marking Ink was sold for pricing. A rubber eraser could be used to remove grease, then a clean pen used to mark the prices on blades. The ink was not supposed to rust even the finest polished steel.

The second system was to use preprinted tacks stuck next to a sample. The buttons in this catalog were of white celluloid and had a metal base 5/8 inch in diameter and had a 1/2 inch steel pin. These buttons were offered free with cutlery orders. They were in fifteen denominations from 25 cents to $3.00. The buttons when stuck into a box indicated the price for that sample and stock inside.

There are many "Diamond Edge" razors shown in the catalog. The square, round and hollow point blades were offered. The blades were described as hand forged from the best English Crucible Cast Steel and ground in Hamburg. If the English steel was ground in Germany and sold in the United States the blade certainly had a lot of miles on it before it even touched a face. The blades were further claimed to be unsurpassed for both barber and private use.

Most razors shown were marked with stock number and the words "Diamond Edge" on the shank. The stock numbers are not consecutive as there are many numbers missing. A large variety of handle materials were offered.

Genuine ivory flat handles were on the razor with stock No.2. A black rubber oval handle was on a blade marked No.4. This was one of the least expensive "Diamond Edge" razors at $24.00 per dozen. This handle was offered on blades 3/8, 1/2, 5/8 and 3/4 inches wide and on blades of all three point shapes.

A flat celluloid imitation tortoise shell handle was stock No.12. A heavy pearl scale tang probably was the cause of this razor being $48.00 per dozen.

A very desirable razor today would be No.14 with a pieced abalone pearl handle. Each handle side had four pieces of pearl separated by three smaller bands of darker abalone. "Diamond Edge" was etched in gold on the blade. The razor was only offered in 5/8 inch width and square point blade at $72.00 per dozen.

Other handle materials offered included a mottled red rubber with nickel silver end caps, pearl gray pyrolin (plastic like), bright red pyrolin, and light amber pyrolin.

"No.11 Black Prince" was stamped on the shank of a black rubber handled razor. The ends of the handles were shaped to look something like tree buds.

"No. 76" had "Country Club" embossed on the flat rubber handle and imprinted on the shank. The blade was etched with a horse and rider leaping a fence. I have a razor that matches the catalog illustration of No.76. On the reverse side of the shank it is marked "Shapleigh Hdw Co. St. Louis USA." Some of the rest of the razors in the catalog are quite likely marked the same.

The "Diamond King," "Gypsy," and "White House" were three more razors with names.

Three fancy celluloid handled razors were marked on the shank with their stock number and "Shapleigh Hardware Co. St. Louis." "No.70" had "Beauty" etched in gold on the blade. A raised peacock design was stained in natural colors.

"No.80" had "Art" etched in gold on the blade. The handles have a raised lady wearing nothing but her long hair. There are some flowers and stems and the description says it is stained in exquisite colors.

"No.90" had "Nonpareil" etched in gold on the blade. A crane design is raised on the handles and stained in natural colors.

What is surprising to me is the relatively low cost of these razors with the gold etching and the fancy celluloid handles at $24.00 per dozen. It might be that some high quality blades were coupled with plain, functional handles to demand top prices because of their shaving qualities. Other fancy celluloid handles coupled with lower quality blades etched in gold could be inexpensive as in the 1915-1916 catalog.

Razor No.777 had a highly magnetized blade that was described as "Famous for its Curative Qualities." It was stamped on the shank "Magnetic 777." The description doesn't even insist that you must shave with it to enjoy the curative qualities. Perhaps putting it under your bed before going to sleep will do just as much good.

Other brands of razors are also shown in the catalog. The all metal gunstock style of razor was called the "ERN Junior Razor." Three finishes were offered, gunmetal, silver and gold at $40.00 per dozen.

A less expensive "Bridge" trademark razor was offered. It had a plain handle with the blade etched in gold, "Bridge" and marked on the shank, "Bridge Cutlery Co. No. 20 St. Louis."

A "Wade & Butcher Special" was described as made exclusively for Shapleigh Hardware.

"Joseph Rogers & Sons, Sheffield" also was

represented with a plain razor in the catalog.

"Geo. Wostenholm & Son" had fourteen "IXL" and "Pipe" razors on the pages. They ranged from $9.00 per dozen to $44.00 per dozen for a razor with pearl scale tang and another with genuine flat ivory handles.

Several "Mizzoo Cutlery Co." razors are shown. This is interesting because the "Mizzoo" brand appears many places in the catalog on such diverse products as rubber water hose, shoe heels, pencils, and toilet paper. The razors are marked "mizzoo" on the shank along with the "M-1" through "6" stock numbers. The prices range from $8.00 to $15 per dozen. The blades were described as made of English steel ground in Germany. The "M4" had a fancy celluloid handle with a raised bug crawling among oak leaves and acorns. I'm not sure how the lady of the house received that design.

There were many shaving items shown such as the "Norleigh Diamond (Demulcent) shaving Tick." The word demulcent implied a soothing nature of the soap. Each stick was in an embossed nickel plated metal cylinder box with telescoping cover. Instructions were to wet face with a brush then rub stick on the face. Then use a wet brush again to make a lather on the face. This method of making lather was claimed to be cleaner and more economical than the old fashioned mug.

Two seven day razor cases were offered. One was a Russet Pig skin roll with flaps to keep razors from falling out. Days of the week were printed in gold. A leather strap with a brass buckle secured the roll.

The second seven day razor case was a wood box covered with Black Morocco leather. Razors fit in partitions marked with the days of the week in gold. The lining was red velvet. Two glove fasteners (snaps) held the cover down. Either style of case was $48.00 per dozen.

A small wood case covered in Black Morocco leather and lined with purple silk and velvet was for two razors. A similar case for four razors had green silk and velvet lining.

There was no mention of blades etched with the day of the week. Apparently one selected whatever razors he wanted from stock offered and could then place them in a case. The days of the week stamped in gold along side each razor allowed the user to keep track of which razors needed stropping.

"Gillette," "EverReady," and "Diamond Edge" safety razors are shown in the catalog. The more cumbersome appearing "Star" and the "Gem" packaged in a lithographed tin can are also shown. A folding "Durham Demonstrator" with black fiber handles, one Norwegian steel double edge blade and a stick of soap was 50 cents. The "Diamond Edge" blades were sold in sets of five for 36 cents and were wrapped in an oil paper and in a sealed envelope with trademark.

The following two "Diamond Edge" blades are packaged in bright red paper with gold trim and black and white letters. The "Diamond Edge" trademark and pledge is shown. The back is stamped, "Sample, not to be sold."

A double edge blade is also packaged in bright red paper but with blue trim. The trademark and pledge is similar to the other blade. On the back is the admonishment, "no stropping, no honing."

The third blade is packaged exactly as the E.C. Simmons Hardware Co. sold it except the name is "Shapleigh Hardware Co." Most sources indicate that Shapleigh Hardware bought out their rival in 1940 along with the red Keen Kutter trademark shown on this orange and green blade wrapper. Before you conclude that the name E.C. Simmons was no longer used with the trademark, look at the label on this sprouting hoe shown without its handle. Note the Keen Kutter trademark imprint as well as both names, Simmons and Shapleigh, on the label.

Some visitors to the excellent Gator Cutlery Club Knife Show January, 1982, in Tampa, Florida were able to see Lawrence Bireline's exceptional "Diamond Edge" razor. Its handle was an unusual gunstock shape made of a pretty mottled orange and cream like material. The detailed "Diamond Edge" trademark was a nickel silver inlay. The shank was stamped "DE17" "Shapleigh Hdw Co. St. Louis USA" "Germany."

A second unusual feature of this razor are the letters SHAPLEIGH in relief on both sides of the blade's back. The blade was also etched with a diamond trademark.

It is a razor that I as a collector find difficult to live without, but it wasn't for sale. But maybe there's hope after all? If I could only come up with the right antique watch to trade!

This article appeared in Knife World June, 1982.

Slayton Razor and Knife

by Kurt Moe

Nelson B. Slayton of Rochester, New York was holder of several patents. These patents even included some involving a process for metallic fillings in teeth and improvements in gloves. Here we are most interested in his patents for improvements in razors and knives.

Patent #220,438 was issued on October 7, 1879. The object of this invention was to provide a razor that could be closed and safely carried in the pocket without the need for a protective case. Knives, especially fruit knives, were also mentioned in the patent specifications. These knives could have their open blades held firmly in place without requiring a backspring.

An example of a Slayton Razor and Knife that resembles patent #220,438 drawings and specifications is marked "SLAYTON" on one side of its handle and "PAT APL'D FOR" on the other side. The handle of the example, however is more ornate than that shown in the patent drawings. Its design is a pattern similar to engraving but appears to be stamped in a thin brass material which was then nickel plated. The razor is about 3-1/4 inches closed. The pivot pin of the razor is allowed to move in a slot. The blade can be pushed out, pivoted, and then its other end pushed back into the handle ready for use.

Another difference between the patent drawings and the actual razor is that the drawings show a pin to help hold the blade closed. The razor itself relies on a friction

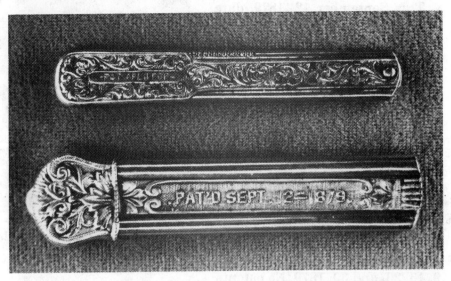

Two Slayton marked razors in closed position. Designs are pressed in brass then nickel plated. Top: Handle marked "Pat Apl'd For." Bottom: Handle marked "Pat'd Sept 12-1879."

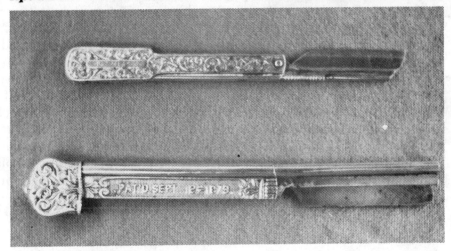

Both Slayton razors shown in locked open position.

fit in the handle to hold the blade closed.

The Phillip Krumholz book, *A History of Shaving and Razors*, has a listing for the Slayton straight razor-knife. The illustration shown there is that with a different handle design. Part of the design includes a ribbon with what appears to be the patent date of Oct. 7, 1879, written on it.

Another example of the Slayton razor is 1/4 inch longer than the first example mentioned and is wider as well. Its construction and operation is very similar to both the first example and patent #220,438 specifications. The razor like blade is easily removable. This piece's variation of handle design has the words "SLAYTON

RAZOR" pressed in one side of the handle. The words pressed into the other side of the handle are "PAT'D SEPT 12, 1879."

This September 12, 1879, date is a great puzzle to me. It is not the date the patent was applied for. That date was June 16, 1879. The 1879 alphabetical list of patentees was consulted for a Slayton listing. The alphabetical list of inventions was checked. The search did not locate a design patent or trademark issued to Slayton in 1879 either. This search of the 1879 patent records did not show any patent granted to Nelson Slayton on the September 12 date. In fact, it appears that patents were issued only on September 2, 9, 16, 23, and 30, 1879. No patents were found issued to anyone on September 12, 1879.

Considerable time was spent trying to solve this mystery but perhaps something was missed. The print in these records is very small. If anyone can offer an explanation of the significance of the September 12, 1879, date embossed on the Slayton razor-knife handle, please, share it with us.

The search for information did uncover other related patents issued to Nelson B. Slayton now

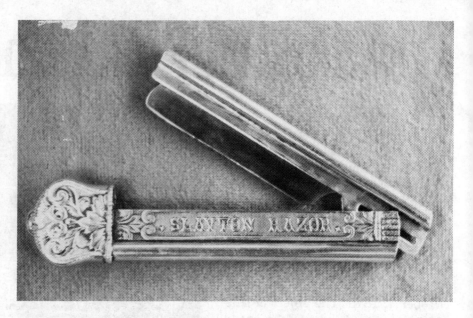

Slayton razor-knife with blade partially open. Notice slot that pivot pin can slide along.

shown to be of Alfred Centre, New York. Patent #230,443 issued on July 27, 1880 shows a handle very nearly like that of the razor-knives. This handle, however, was used to hold a comb instead of a blade.

Patent #234,731 issued November 23, 1880, shows a pocket knife design especially suited for use as a fruit knife or nut pick.

Patent #237,138 issued on February 1, 1881, has a variation of the razor-knife that uses several blades. The drawings show three instruments in the handle including a razor, a comb, and a nail file. Another patent, #239,068 also issued in 1881 shows a pocket cutlery piece with a combination knife and fork.

Certainly we must make the observation that if the Slayton razor-knife with its single blade was good, of course, the Slayton handles holding two or more tools were more useful and even better!

This article appeared in Knife World February, 1991.

Torrey Razor Co.

by Kurt Moe

Most sources show that the J.R. Torrey Co. produced razor strops as early as 1858 and in its early years dealt in razors imported from England and Sweden.

The American Cutlery magazine frequently featured "Men Who Are Making Our Cutlery Industry." One such article tells of an important man in the history of the J.R. Torrey Company. Joseph Turner arrived in this country from Sheffield, England in 1870 and soon began manufacturing razors in Meriden, Connecticut. Later in 1880, Joseph Turner and J.R. Torrey formed the J.R. Torrey Razor Co. and manufactured razors under that name in Worcester, Massachusetts. An early catalog shows that Joseph Turner was president of the firm while J.R. Torrey was the treasurer of the company bearing his name.

Joseph Turner's son William had received experience in Meriden and moved to the J.R. Torrey Co. with his father. In 1886, upon reaching his 21st birthday, William was made superintendent of the factory.

An unusual and perhaps early marking for Torrey razors is THE TORREY RAZOR CO./ WORCESTER, MASS/ USA. in three straight lines. Notice the word RAZOR in the marking.

A Torrey catalog from about 1895 shows the usual Torrey marking. This is THE J.R. TORREY CO. in an arc over a U.S. and arrow trademark and WORCESTER, MASS. under the trademark.

In addition there was a "whip line" of razors with a buggy whip as the trademark. This razor line

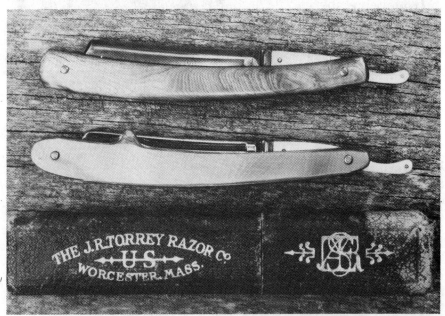

Imitation wood grain Torrey razors with pearl tangs. Center razor has Aug. 1, 1905, patented blade holder. Razor case shows marking much like that usually stamped on Torrey razor shanks.

Razor shank shows Torrey's Whip Line trademark. A low priced line of razors from about 1895.

was made to meet the demand for a medium priced razor. The blades were made of the same steel as the finer grades of razors,

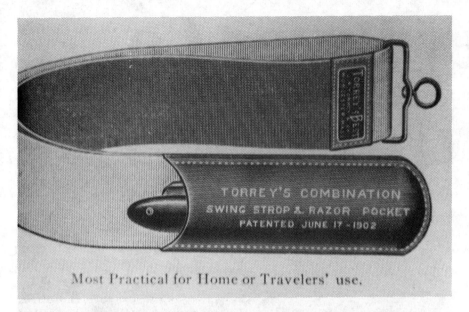

Catalog illustration of Torrey's Combination Swing Strop and Razor Pocket.

Torrey Safety Razor with separate blade for each day of the week as illustrated in catalog.

but not as much time was spent on their finish. In fact, one model of the line was plain ground, not the more expensive hollow grind of most razors of the day.

Corn razors were offered with ivory or stag handles. Later catalogs had corn razors with fancy celluloid handles such as those with the rope pattern. Other products marked Torrey's included strop dressings, scissors and shears.

One strop had a small pocket in the end to hold a razor. The Torrey's Combination Swing strop and razor pocket was said to be

patented June 17, 1902.

Patent No.795,996 was granted to S.W. Marvin for a razor handle with projections to hold the blade. Torrey has razors using this patent. They are usually a mottled green wood grain celluloid handle with the patent date Aug. 1, 1905, stamped into the back of the handle. The projections were said to guide the blade to its closed position thus preventing the blade from nicking the handle and dulling or damaging the cutting edge. The projection also locked the blade in a closed position and prevents the blade from accidentally opening.

When Joseph Turner died in 1907, William Turner was made president of the J.R. Torrey Razor Company. John J. Turner, Joseph Turner and Louis H. Torrey were all involved with the firm too.

J.R. Torrey is known as a manufacturer of razors and strops and as an importer of fine razor hones. Surprisingly several TORREY'S BEST pocketknives are illustrated in one of the firm's catalogs. The tang markings are not shown, but the phrase "Torrey's Best" is used as a master blade etching. Eleven styles of pocket knives are described. These include knives with pearl handles and aluminum or German Silver bolsters and stag, ivory, ebony, coca, or all aluminum handles.

A folding safety razor with removable and reversible guard enabled the timid or blind to use the razor with perfect confidence. This razor's guard lacked the comb or teeth of most guards of the time.

Celluloid handles were offered on most razors and were available for 50 cents more than black rubber handles. Several patterns of the so called "carved" handles were shown. These molded celluloid patterns included the ear of corn

Back cover of Torrey catalog. Little figure seems to be dripping blood on a large razor.

pattern and other designs. Genuine ivory handles were $1.00 more than the standard flat black rubber models.

The Torrey Co. had a Design Patent dated June 21, 1892, on the "ear of corn" handle pattern. This is interesting because many ear of corn handles are found with Lakeside Cutlery blades. Lakeside Cutlery you will recall was a brand of cutlery sold in Montgomery Ward catalogs. Early Montgomery Ward catalogs from about 1895 do carry a lot of Torrey razors. Add to these facts the similarity of the Torrey and Lakeside safety razors and one could begin to think that the same plant was the source of both the Lakeside and Torrey marked products.

The new Torrey Safety Razor was shown in one of the Torrey catalogs. One razor with one blade in a nickel plated can sold for $2.00. Razors in boxes containing 2,3,4 or even 7 blades were also offered. The safety razor handle could be removed from the razor and screwed into a blade holder. The thick, hollow ground blade held in this manner could then be honed or stropped like an ordinary straight razor blade. Lithographed blade boxes were shown and described as useful when mailing blades to the factory for repair.

The Torrey Safety Razor is very similar to the Lakeside Cutlery model right down to the two four leaf clover cut outs in the razor head. The patents shown on the Lakeside razor belong to Joseph Turner of Worcester, Massachusetts.

A coupon worth 10 cents off was included with some Torrey material. This coupon was a sort of bounty paid for a potential new customer. The coupon was valid if the name and address of another razor user was furnished. A related special offer was also made.

For the names and addresses of 2,3 or 4 people who were self shavers, Torrey would send articles such as pocket knives, shears, or scissors at reduced prices. The reduced price was roughly 60 percent of the usual retail price.

A 1925 United Cigar Store's Premium Catalog shows that Torrey razors could be obtained as premiums. A full concave blade with flat white handle was 125 certificates. The catalog offered The Gillette Safety razor with blades for 275 certificates, as well as a cheaper half concave Torrey razor for 75 certificates. The catalog featured the Gillette products a second time in color on the catalogs' back cover. Perhaps this shows that the safety razor was already replacing the straight razor in popularity.

Many manufacturers included coupons with their products. Wrigley's Chewing Gum, Swift's soap products, Barker's Lice Powder and Worcester Salt products are a few of the items that offered profit sharing United Coupons. The premiums could be obtained through the U.S. mail or at one of United Cigar Store Premium stations.

A product from about 1895 that I failed to mention earlier was "Torrey's Strop Dressing for Razors and Surgical Instruments." The small round metal box was divided in half with one side holding coarse dressing and the other side holding fine dressing. A second product was a cushioned strop with a Genuine 5" Italian Rock hone especially for surgeons.

The sound of a butcher knife sharpening on a steel and the sound of a barber using his strop have always given me a sense of foreboding. The hair on the back of my neck stands up. I don't care to even imagine my feeling if I were to hear my surgeon honing or stropping his scalpel!

This article appeared in Knife World July, 1988.

110

Van Camp Hardware

by Kurt Moe

A publication from 1897 called "Hyman's Handbook of Indianapolis" states that a partnership formed in 1876 grew into the Van Camp Hardware & Iron Company which was incorporated in 1884. Cortland Van Camp was shown as the president and David C. Bergundthal was shown as secretary & treasurer. The trade area of the general hardware business in 1897 included Indiana, Illinois, Michigan, Kentucky, Iowa, and Missouri. Twenty one people traveled for the company and about 80 more were employed in Indianapolis. The stock carried by the company included a line of light and heavy hardware and an extensive bicycle and gun department. Carriage and wagonmaker's materials and a tin ware manufacturing plant employing another 15 to 20 hands made this hardware supplier different from some of the others of the time. Two buildings are mentioned, one on South Illinois Street, and another on West Chesapeake Street. A thank you to the Indiana Historical Society Library for furnishing the information on this Indianapolis, Indiana firm, Van Camp Hardware & Iron Co.

John Goins in his book "Pocketknives" indicates that Van Camp Hardware & Iron Company had its own cutlery factory from about 1904 to 1948. He goes on to say that the company, Capitol Cutlery Company of Indianapolis, Indiana, made both Van Camp Hardware and Capitol marked knives.

Some very unusual razors are marked "Van Camp Hdwe & Iron Co. Indianapolis Ind." These razors are all marked "Germany" and were probably made there in large quantities for Van Camp Hdwe.

An unusual razor pattern with an Indian and a swastika included in it may have been exclusively Van Camp Hardware & Iron Company's pattern. The examples of this pattern that I've seen have all had handles molded in black celluloid and have all held blades marked with the Van Camp Hdwe & Iron Co. name.

The handle is molded on the front side only with a standing Indian holding a bow and tomahawk. The Indian is quite detailed including fringe on his garment and feathers in his headdress. This razor is one that looks better after some use. Then it has

Van Camp Hdwe & Iron Co. razors with black celluloid handles. Left: Nickel silver flower inlay. Center: Design with Indian and swastika combination. White stain was used to antique the scene for this picture. Right: Real pearl shank and tang.

accumulated some soap residue to define the design. A white, water base stain was added to this razor so that the detail of the molded scene would photograph better.

Under the Indian figure molded into the handle

Ben Hur racing chariot scene etched on blade and molded in celluloid handle. Color was also used to antique this scene for the photograph.

is a metal inlaid swastika. One might think that this razor more properly belongs in a World War II collection. This swastika symbol, however, has existed long before Nazi Germany used it. Both early Christians and American Indians are said to have made use of the symbol.

The next object has no relationship to Van Camp Hdwe & Iron Co. but does show an Indian and the swastika together. The silver plated brass hand mirror has an Indian on horseback pursuing a buffalo. There are four swastikas arranged around the hunting scene.

The mirror frame has a stamping which reads "Pat. June 13, 1905." A 16 power magnifying glass was very helpful to determine the actual date shown in the stamping. There is a patent issued on that date referring to the construction of the frame, handle, and body of a hand mirror. The mirror was probably made after the June, 1905, patent date and during the life of the patent. If the mirror was made in the 1905 to 1922 period, it would seem to predate the usual swastika marked Nazi Germany articles. In any case, the mirror serves as another examples of a design using an Indian and swastika combination.

Two more Van Camp razors have black celluloid with the same stamping as the swastika razor. One of the razors have a nickel silver inlay in the shape of flowers and vines. This particular design is not very common. The black celluloid background gives enough contrast to make the design stand out well.

The other razor handle is very plain but has pieces of mother of pearl pinned to the shank and tang. There is a circular trademark etched on the blade using the firm's name.

A razor with ivory colored celluloid handles has an unusual scene molded into the handle. There are four horses pulling a chariot on the handle front only. The arches and pillars of an arena show in the background. The flying manes and tails as well as harness and whip detail are included in the scene. For the photograph a water based stain was used to antique the scene and better show the detail.

The blade shows faint traces of the same chariot scene as is molded into the handle. The scene is etched between the words, "Ben Hur." "Ben Hur, A Tale of the Christ," was a novel published in 1880. Over the years the novel was dramatized for stage and screen. One film dates from about 1926. John Goins indicates that Van Camp used the trademark "Ben Hur" from about 1928 to 1954.

There does seem to be two unusual features of the swastika and Ben Hur razor patterns. One feature is that the razors have a blade etching of the words "swastika" or "Ben Hur" to match the handle pattern. The other feature is that handles I have seen with these patterns have been used only with Van Camp Hdwe & Iron Co. razors. If someone has these razor patterns with what appears to be original blades marked with other makers or distributors, let us hear from you.

This article appeared in Knife World July, 1985.

Vom Cleff & Co., Inc.

by Kurt Moe

An advertisement for Vom Cleff & Co., Inc. razors in the May, 1925 *Barber's Journal* offers some information about the firm. "On the market since 1885" is a phrase used in the ad. If Vom Cleff was founded or started business in 1885, why doesn't the ad say exactly that? The phrase used could mean that Diamondine razors were sold since 1885 but at first by another firm. More than one reference source shows an 1887 beginning date for Vom Cleff & Co. The firm is said to take its name from its owner, Robert Vom Cleff.

The razors that I've seen having the Vom Cleff stamping have all been marked as manufactured in Germany. Most sources describe the firm as an importer of knives, razors, and corn razors. The placement of the ad in the *Barbers' Journal* certainly indicates that they were after sales to the professional barber trade. The words, "all handles- all sizes" suggests that various combinations of different blade widths and handles were available.

The firm's office locations are listed in the ad as 105 Duane Street, New York City and as 190 N. State Street, Chicago.

One of the firm's older razors has metal ends reinforcing the handle. The pins have no collars. Metal ends are often found on celluloid handles. The handles on this Vom Cleff razor, however, are of mottled horn. Razors with handles in this pattern and manufactured from natural materials instead of celluloid are

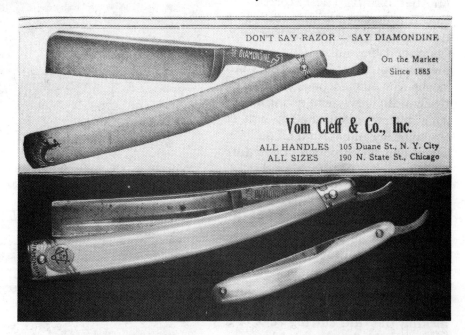

Top: Advertisement from 1925 showing Vom Cleff's Diamondine razor. Middle: Model 1006 Diamondine razor. Bottom: Bone handled corn razor.

not often found. Certainly it was less costly and easier to manufacture the same handle in celluloid when the new man made material became routinely available. I suspect that this razor dates from the late 19th century.

The markings on the razor's shank include, "Vom Cleff & Co." "New York" and "Made in Germany."

Another razor has a handle in the same pattern but of celluloid made to look like a burl wood grain in brown. This and the following razors have collars with the pins. The shank back reads much like the previous razor. The front reads, "1005 Diamondine" and has a trade mark figure that is half horse with the tail of a fish.

The next razor has a very similarly marked shank except that it says 1006 instead of 1005. Its handle is ivory colored celluloid and has fancy metal ends. The large end has an inlaid design with the intertwined initials "V" and "C" with "& C0." The design is the same on the back side.

There is, of course, the razor pictured in the ad itself. It appears to be the 1007 (not real clear) Diamondine model and has a metal inlay of the interesting horse and fish figure.

A razor with a plain celluloid handle in a sort of butterscotch color has a shank marked "Bull Head."

A small razor was found in a tan sliding box marked, "Vom Cleff & Co. Corn Razor" "Germany." This corn razor has a beautiful tan bone handle.

Finally a Vom Cleff razor that is a real odd ball. I've never seen another like it. The razor can be taken apart without tools. The handles are held together by a fastener type more often seen on old coin purses. When the snap knobs are pushed past each other the handle halves can swing apart. At a certain point the top half of the handle can be lifted off and the blade can be removed. The razor handles are made of brushed steel. The shank is stamped "hand forged steel- Antiseptic Razor." The razor's handle parts and its blade could be taken apart to be cleaned. The all metal razor could survive the heat of sterilization. The blade does carry a nick in its cutting edge. The possibility of nicking the thin cutting edge of a blade on the hard metal handles was always there.

World War I (1914-1918) hostilities between the Allies and Germany would have disrupted the supply of German made cutlery shipped to the U.S. This obviously was not the end of Vom Cleff & Co. operations, however. The ad in the 1925 magazine is proof enough for me that razor sales were still taking place seven years after the end of World War I.

This article appeared in Knife World March, 1990.

View of Antiseptic razor showing handle snaps apart. Rotating the top handle a little further allowed it and the blade to be lifted from the pin for cleaning.

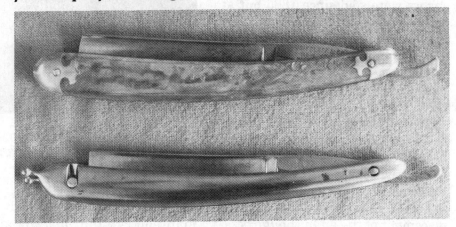

Top: Vom Cleff razor with mottled horn handles and metal reinforced ends. Bottom: Bone handled corn razor.

Wostenholm & Sons Frameback

by Kurt Moe

Seldom does a razor's handle have as much information pressed into it as this "George Wostenholm & Son's" razor. The gold colored print pressed into the dark horn handle goes on to say "Doubly Carbonized I*XL Razor," "Registered Sep. 10, 1850. No.2434." The handle has brass pins and a metal spacer.

The razor's shank is stamped "The I*XL Improved Swiss," "manufactured solely by," "George Wostenholm & Son." No mention is made as to the manufacturer's location. The shank has file cuts on the bottom. The tang is quite short. The back of the blade is thick, about 3/16 inch in diameter. It is even thicker than the shank. A very thin blade is permanently attached to the blade back.

The frameback blade is a completely different blade type than the wedge blade of the same time period or the later hollow ground blade. The heavy frameback gives rigidity to the otherwise thin blade. Yet the blade would be lighter than a similar wedge shaped blade and have a thinner shaving edge.

The gold lettering indicates that the "Wostenholm" firm was extremely proud of the Sept. 10, 1850, date of register. I doubt that 15 or 20 years later, the maker would have been likely to put the 1850 date on a handle. The date suggests to me that this razor was manufactured after Sept 10, 1850, and within perhaps the next dozen years. I do not wish to say that all frameback razors are this old, however. The frameback style continued to be sold for decades

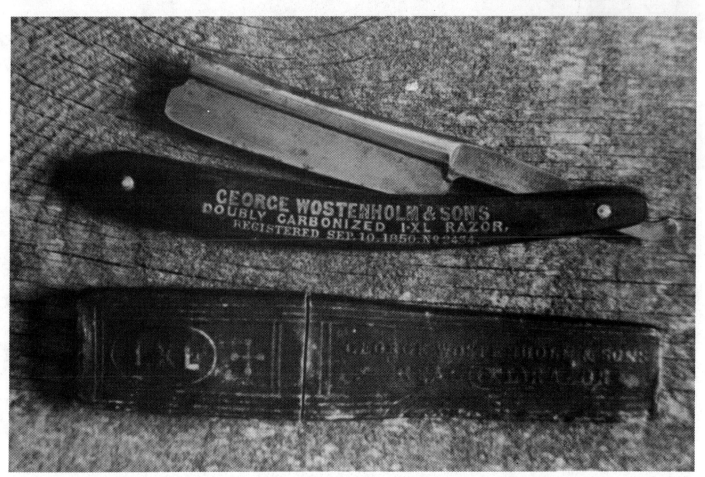

Frameback Geo. Wostenholm razor. "Registered Sep. 10, 1850" is part of the information pressed into its dark horn handle.

though not in great numbers.

The coffin shaped box the razor was found in might be original to the razor. In any case it is marked with the correct manufacturer.

A second similar razor has much the same shape to its black horn handle and frameback blade. It does not, however, have any information on its handle at all.

The frame back portion of this blade is flattened slightly and stamped "Geo. Wostenholm & Son's Doubly Carbonized I*XL razor." The I*XL letters, of course, are pronounced nearly the same as the statement, "I excell."

The frameback and the blade's edge have a curve to them instead of being straight. The curve is about the same as that made by the razor's handle. The shank has a diamond shaped mark and is stamped inside the mark "Registered," "10 Sep.," "1850," "No 2434," "I*XL."

Often older razors have had holes bored in their horn handles by some stage of insect life. Or the horn might be cracked at one of the pins. The blades often have suffered rust damage or show the marks of a coarse grindstone.

These two examples survived what could be as many as 130 years remarkably well. In fact, if I wasn't so squeamish about the sight of my own blood, I might try shaving with one.

This article appeared in Knife World January, 1983.

Geo. Wostenholm & Sons

by Kurt Moe

A full page advertisement in the 1919 Sheffield "Trade Marks Register" indicates the the firm "George Wostenholm & Son Ltd" was the sole manufacturer of the Celebrated I*XL Cutlery Pen & Pocketknives, Table Knives, Carvers, Farriers Knives, Erasers, Razors, Scissors, Bowie Knives, Shoe Knives, Butcher's Knives, and Tea Pruners. The advertisement pictures the firm's "Washington Works" in Sheffield, England.

According to John Goins' *"Pocketknives"* book, the company's history began in 1745 with a Stannington cutler who spelled his name George Wolstenholme. The name was shortened to Wostenholm in about 1815.

A fine example of a pressed horn razor is marked WOSTENH...on its shank. The stamping is deep at the W and becomes lighter at the end of the stamping. The marking "Wostenholm" is listed as one of the marks used by George Wostenholm & Son. The razor is of a style that suggests that it dates from about 1815.

The handle is pressed dark horn with three figures on each side of the handle. The mark side has on the top a figure which is identified as a "Dog." The middle figure is a "Horse." The bottom figure is a "Stag." The back side of the razor handle has the figures of more exotic animals. The first figure is identified as a Kangaroo, the second figure is a Tiger, and the third is a Lion with its kill. There are a few leaves, trees, and some grass included in the pressed animal scenes.

The pins and large collars

Advertisement from 1919 Sheffield Trade Works Register showing George Wostenholm and Son's Washington Works.

*Razors with horn handles and pressed wording and designs. Top: Joseph Wostenholm & Sons razor. Center: George Wostenholm & Son I*XL razor. Bottom: George Wostenholm & Sons razor with Swiss or LeCoultre style of blade.*

appear to be iron. There is no spacer between the square ended and flat handles.

The blade is a wedge shape. The wide tang has been tapered very

117

Top: Geo. Wostenholm razor with imitation horn handles of celluloid. The other razors are very similar to each other but have different makers. Center: Geo. Wostenholm "Original Pipe Razor." Bottom: Joseph Allen "Original Dagger Razor."

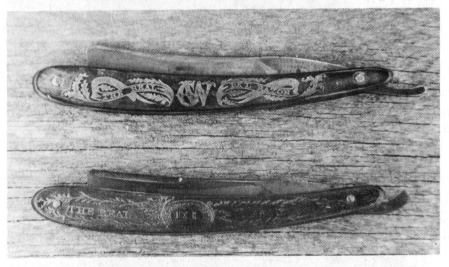

*George Wostenholm razors with horn handles and pressed lettering and designs in gold. Both are marked "The Real I*XL Razor." Designs are similar to those dated 1895.*

thin compared to the shank.

The same figures and words are on a nearly identical razor handle of pressed clear horn instead of dark horn. As is more usual of razors of this time, however, the shank is not marked with any name or trademark. It is marked only "Refined Steel." It is unfortunate that some mark was not used so that the maker of this razor could be known.

The book *"Pocketknives"* goes on to say that in about 1832, grandson George Wostenholm moved the business to the Rockingham Works in Sheffield. In about 1848, the business moved the Washington Works.

A third George Wostenholm was in control of the business in 1875 when the company was registered on December 4 as a Limited Company (Ltd). This reorganization of the company is similar to our U.S. procedure of incorporation. The company was restructured with a board of directors and shareholders. The shareholders as owners have a liability limited to the amount of their investment in the business.

George Wostenholm held the office of chairman of the new organization until his death April 3, 1876. Bernard Wake, a director, became the next chairman.

The annual reports to the stockholders indicate that trade in America was very depressed during these early years of the Limited Company. Most of the firm's product was sold in America so the first years following 1875 were not very profitable. George Wostenholm and later his estate supplied funds to ensure a 10 percent annual dividend to shareholders. This guarantee by Mr. Wostenholm extended for the first five years of the Limited Company's operation. Mrs. Wostenholm made a sizable loan to the company to help it through the years following her husband's death.

The stockholder's reports for the Limited Company contain various items of information. One such item was that razor maker James Bingham died August 18, 1876, after 33 years service to the company. Another item was that the company would exhibit at Sydney and Melbourne. It hoped to open an agency in Australia.

By 1882 the company was enjoying prosperity. The excellence of the goods and their low price was given as the reasons for much higher sales volume than before. The good fortune was shared with workmen and good relations existed between labor and management. A new engine and boilers at the Washington Works facility was expected to increase the comfort of the workmen and contribute to more economical manufacture of goods.

Very little of the company's goods was sold in England. While market expansion was being made in British Columbia, Canada and in Australia, most goods continued to be sold in America. American tariff changes, therefore, had a large effect on Geo. Wostenholm's volume of business. When trade was dull in America, the workmen would concede to reduction in their wages. Goods were made and then stockpiled until market conditions improved.

In about 1885 or shortly after, an illustrated catalog was prepared at a cost of 1000 pounds. The catalog was to assist sales where goods were already known as well as to help acquire new markets.

It is apparently a copy of this first catalog that was reprinted some years ago. Several pages of full size razor illustrations show the blade styles, etchings, and handle materials available at the time. Most of the handles appear to be dark horn. Other handles are identified as ivory or bone.

Blade styles vary even more from wide wedge blades to narrow hollow ground blades. There is a difference between what the catalog calls the "Swiss or LeCoultre" razor.

The blade style new to me is called the Swiss or "LeCoultre" razor. I would have called the razor with a thick back and separate thin blade a FrameBack. The back, shank, and tang appear to be made from the same piece of metal. The blade is attached and is the same thickness throughout.

The catalog illustrations for the Swiss style blades are numbered 0484 and 0488. According to the Pattern Book, 0484 has a back of "Ball's Composition Metal" and "The Best of All Razors" etched on the blade. Number 0488 has a flat steel Back marked "The Best of All Razors."

An example of the FrameBack razor is etched, "The Celebrated I*XL FrameBack Razor." This blade appears to be made of the same piece of metal as the shank and tang. The blade has a surprising wedge shape and its back is strengthened by a separate piece of metal.

Two catalog illustrations for FrameBack razors that look very similar have different pattern numbers 01477 and 01478. The descriptions in the

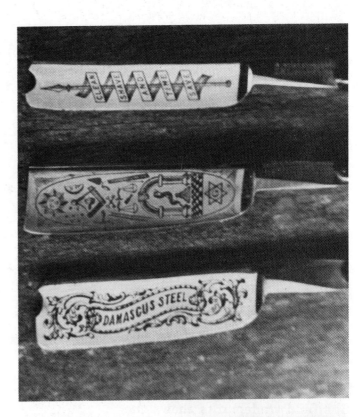

Geo. Wostenholm razors with etched wedge blades. Top: "Clean Shave and Time Save." Center: Masonic symbols. Bottom: "Damascus Steel" blade similar to 1885 catalog pattern.

Pattern Book show that the first has a steel back and the other a (German) silver back.

Most of Geo. Wostenholm & Son's razor blades are marked with one of their pipe or I*XL trademarks. Others have etchings which include a horse and rider, masonic symbols, or have wording such as "Damascus Steel," "Advance Australia," or "Colonial Razor."

In 1887 a system was discussed that would use a small portion of dividends with the object of promoting thrift among the employees and providing for their infirmity or old age. An account was established but the work people apparently had little enthusiasm for thrift. In 1890 the account was closed.

A Washington Works Charity had been established in 1887 also. Mr. Asline Ward transferred two cottages at Ecclesfield with a value of about 200 pounds to a trust. It was hoped that the cottages would benefit some employees who spent their youth keeping up the reputation of Wostenholm knives and razors. Two donations of 200 pounds each by B. Wake and J.C. Wing and some smaller donations by others helped The

Washington Works Benevolence Fund off to a good start.

The Geo. Wostenholm company often filed suit against other firms with similar trademarks. This was costly but deemed necessary to protect their name. One such litigation in 1888 was against a Wm. Woolhouse of Melbourne for the similar trademark of "Non XL." While this action was apparently successful against Woolhouse, Joseph Allen of Sheffield made application to register a similar mark.

A razor with a checkered celluloid handle has a blade etched "Our Best Make" with a sword running through the words. The shank is marked "Non XLL," "Joseph Allen & Sons," "Sheffield, England." The 1919 register of Sheffield trademarks shows the "Non XLL" mark as still used by Joseph Allen & Sons Ltd.

One of the most common Geo. Wostenholm razors has a handle of clear horn pressed in gold, "Original Pipe Razor." The same information is on the blade along with the words, "Medium Hollow Ground." The Pipe trademark is on the blade and on the shank.

A razor marked "Non-XLL Joseph Allen & Sons, Sheffield, England" looks very much like the "Pipe" razor just described. The brass pins, metal spacer, clear horn handle and the gold design are very similar to the Geo. Wostenholm razor. The word, "Dagger" and an illustration of a dagger, however, are substituted for the word "Pipe" and illustration of a pipe.

Also in about 1888 the Wostenholm company appealed the decision of the Sheffield Cutlers Company to register to a new proprietor a pipe trademark with the addition of a dart. Wostenholm claimed this to be an

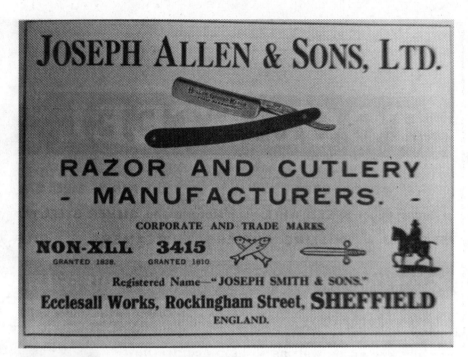

Advertisement from 1919 Trade Marks Register showing Joseph Allen & Sons Ltd. Trade Marks.

infringement because the original user of the mark had long been dead. This mark shows in the 1919 Register as belonging to Geo. Wostenholm & Son Ltd.

"Joseph Wostenholm & Son's," "Corporate Mark EBRO" is the wording pressed in gold on a razor handle. "J. Wostenholm, EBRO, Sheffield," is the mark on the razor's shank. In both cases a Maltese Cross is before and after the word EBRO.

A second razor had rounded clear horn handles mottled black to resemble tortoise shell. It has nearly the same stamping on the shank as the first razor. There is no spacer between the handles on either Joseph Wostenholm razor.

The 1919 Sheffield register lists the EBRO mark as belonging to Adolph Castor.

In about 1906 legal action was started by the Geo. Wostenholm Company "against certain persons styling themselves as Joseph Wostenholm & Sons Limited of Rivington Works, Sheffield" for the manner in which they were using the name of Wostenholm. The 1907 annual report indicated that negotiations were proceeding on the basis of Geo. Wostenholm & Son's claims and costs being allowed.

Some very interesting illustrations are pasted inside the back cover of a Geo. Wostenholm Pattern Book. The illustrations appear to be pencil rubbings of the designs on razor handles. The designs are numbered and are priced per gross. E.D. Fairest is shown as a "manufacturer of every kind of paper razor case and gilder of all descriptions of book covers &c." Because of the design rubbings, the prices quoted are probably for gilding handles with those designs.

E.D. Fairest is shown as a successor to the late A. Fairest. A

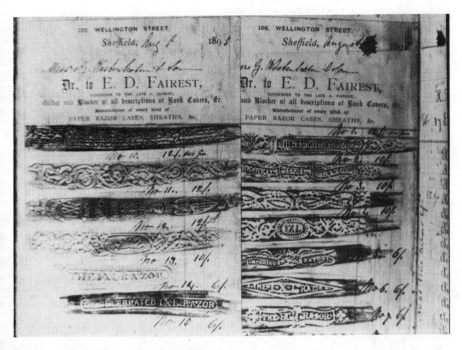

Pencil rubbings of George Wostenholm razor handle designs. E.D. Fairest price list is dated 1895.

later price list has the heading "H. Fairest Gilder." The later list shows some design numbers as being on Vulcanite handles and one design is in silver.

Most of the designs shown in the pencil rubbings make use of phrases like "The Real I*XL Razor" and scroll and ribbons.

There are examples of razors that have designs similar to those shown in the pencil rubbings. One such razor has dark horn handles with a metal spacer and small brass pins and collars. The pressed design includes the words in ribbon, "The Real I*XL Razor" and the initials "GW" in the center. The design still shows some gold. The shank is marked "George Wostenholm & Son's Celebrated I*XL Razor, Washington Works, Sheffield."

The August 1895 date shown on the E.D. Fairest price list tells the approximate age of razors with those designs. The most desirable designs of the group would probably be those with pressed orate decorations completely covering the handle. The pressed horn handles from about 1895 generally have rounded ends and are secured by small brass pins and collars and separated by a metal spacer. There are, of course, many exceptions to this generalization because of the many cutlers.

The older pressed horn razors from about 1820 often have a squared end, no spacer and large iron pins and collars. The razor's tang is shorter as well.

While the older pressed horn razors generally fetch higher prices there is one of the pencil rubbing designs that would be an exceptional find. Its handle is marked "Geo. Wostenholm & Son's I*XL American Razor." There is an eagle sitting on a shield decorated with stars and stripes. A ribbon trails with more wording. Another figure was more difficult to identify, but it is probably a "Liberty Cap" surrounded by shining rays. Though the Liberty Cap is more French in origin, one certainly shouldn't mind finding a razor with that handle design. I wouldn't even mind if the handle turned out to be some unknown composition material instead of pressed horn.

This article appeared in Knife World November, 1984.

122

Kriss Kross Razors

by Kurt Moe

The Rhodes Manufacturing Co., Inc. of 1418 Pendleton Aven., St. Louis, Missouri, produced and marketed the Kriss Kross Stropper and Safety razor. The firm's president was Marcus H. Rhodes. A booklet dating from about 1925 describes an 18,000 square foot factory in St. Louis. In the last five years, the booklet says, the firm grew from a one room building into a large factory. It grew from an idea into a business with sales of nearly one half million stroppers. Tons of high grade steel, brass and nickel were needed for the stamping machines each day. Great bales of shell horsehide were shipped in by the car load.

National advertising was one reason for the Kriss Kross popularity. Collier's, Cosmopolitan, Liberty, Popular Mechanics, and Popular Science are a few of eighteen magazines listed and a few of the hundreds said to be used.

It's obvious that with 500,000 units produced in just five years, that the Kriss Kross stropper is not particularly rare. One of the stories repeated between razor collectors some years ago was of a response to a collector's ad. In a letter of response one of the stroppers was offered to the collector for a mere $200,000. Granted the device is interesting and satisfying to work. The blade holder regularly flips over to strop both sides of the blade as the device's handle is turned. Ten dollars should, however, be enough to pay for a good specimen with box and instructions. A patient

Illustration of the Rhodes Mfg. Co. plant shown in the company booklet from about 1925.

Early stropper with stamped instructions. Box shown is from a later period of manufacture and has a red & black plaid pattern.

collector might even get his stropper for less.

The "Mystery Razor" was given free for a time with the stropper. It is less common than the stropper itself and is usually priced a little higher. The head of this razor pivots from side to side in several different positions so that it can be used to shave with a

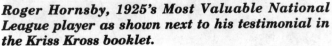
Roger Hornsby, 1925's Most Valuable National League player as shown next to his testimonial in the Kriss Kross booklet.

Illustration of Tom Mix from the booklet. "Next to Tony, the Wonder Horse, Tom hasn't a better pal in the world than his trusty Kriss Kross Kit."

diagonal stroke. Marcus Rhodes received patent No. 1,592, 540 on July 13, 1926, relating to this razor.

At one time a package of five Kriss Kross blades was included with the kit and guaranteed to be keen for life. At any time the blades could be returned for reconditioning or replacement if they no longer held an edge. Of course, nicked blades, rusted blades or blades used for purposes other than shaving were not included in the guarantee. The stropper itself was basically guaranteed for ten years.

The function of the stropper was to mechanically duplicate a master barber's stropping stroke but without human variation. The horsehide stropping disc smoothed a blade's microscopic teeth so they no longer pulled and chewed at a shaver's beard and face. The best time

to strop the blade was after each shave. This was said to remove invisible moisture and prolong the blade's shaving life.

Who were the best prospects for the Kriss Kross stropper? The man with a wiry beard who would get smoother shaves was a prospect as was the man with tender skin who would get a cool, velvety shave. The straight razor user who would like the three way adjustable razor was a prospect as was the barber's customer who would like to save the 25 cents a day that it cost to be shaved by the barber.

The booklet contained a final page which was to be completed by an "Authorized Sale Representative." The representative was to put his picture in the recommended space and have it and his signature marked with the seal of a Notary Public. By dealing with the person identified by the certificate a customer could be assured of a "square deal." Agents were said to be able to make from $175-$400 a month selling Kriss Kross Kits.

The company's product was said to be thoroughly inspected. A member of the staff actually looked over the product a second time to inspect the work of the inspectors. Even though the speed of one large press was 17,640 pieces per hour, tolerances were to be kept to one ten-thousandth of an inch.

Because the stropper was sold for so many years there are many variations in markings. The earlier stroppers are thought to have been packaged in a box with a brown pattern resembling burlap. The burlap pattern gave way to a red and black plaid pattern on the box. The marking of Rhodes Mfg. Co. gave way to the Kriss Kross Corp. marking. Rather than having a large number of instructions imprinted on the machine itself, later models had instructions printed on the box. There were also separate instruction sheets and if something was deemed very important, a tag with directions was attached to the stropper as well.

Instructions required that a little shaving cream be applied to the leather before ever using it the first time. The text suggested Colgate's shaving cream and recommended against beard softeners such as Molle and Barbasol.

One thing seems to remain the same throughout machine models. A small lever controlled pressure

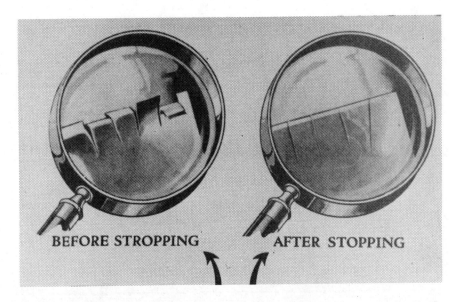

BEFORE STROPPING   AFTER STOPPING

Illustration showing how the stropper smoothed microscopic teeth on the blades edge for a smoother shave.

on the blade holder. This lever would rise slightly with every turn of the crank handle. When the lever reached the top of the slot, the blade required no more stropping. The lever was to be started half way up the slot for ordinary blades and at the bottom of the slot for very dull blades.

Several of the stropper machines have patent dates printed into them. These dates include: June 30, 1921; Sept. 25, 1923; and Jan. 18, 1927. Perhaps the 1921 date refers to a design patent. The Minneapolis, Minnesota library couldn't furnish me with an index of design patents for that year. A trademark, however, was registered No.141,423 to Rhodes on April 30, 1921.

The September 25, 1923 patent No.1,469,147 was issued to Peter E. Bird of Jenkintown, PA for his razor sharpener. Patent No.1,614,492 was issued to M.H. Rhodes on January 18, 1927.

As a part of its marketing policy, it appears that representatives of Kriss Kross generously supplied the stropper to well known and influential people for them to use and hopefully to like. The people from the business, sport and entertainment worlds in many cases responded with letters telling how pleased they were with the product.

A featured testimonial was by Rogers Hornsby, the National League's Most Valuable Player in 1925. The test goes on to say "Rogers Hornsby votes Kriss Kross the most valuable shaving outfit now and forever." A second testimonial was by Tom Mix, the cowboy motion picture star. The text says, "Next to Tony, the wonder horse, Tom hasn't a better pal in the world than his trusty Kriss Kross Kit."

This article appeared in Knife World September, 1988.

Razors and Accessories

by Kurt Moe

The "Star" safety razor with thick backed and hollow ground blades was one of the first to be packaged in tins. These packages were less expensive than the same razor put up in leather covered boxes. The leather cases were often lined with satin, chamois, or velvet.

Decades of time, mold, and even insects have a way of stripping the elegance from leather, satin, and velvet. Some cases have deteriorated to the point that they have literally fallen apart while others only have an offending odor. The tin containers are durable even though faded with age. The lithographed colors have given canned razors of honor in our collection.

Some of the finest examples of canned razors can be found in the hands of collectors who usually want lithographed containers that held coffee or tobacco. As a result, quality examples may be difficult for safety razor collectors to find.

In some cases, the firm making the containers put their name in small letters somewhere in the art work. Red, green, purple, and gold were some of those colors used along with black and tan. The detail on the cans was often comparable to that shown in photographs or the collectible lithographed prints. Illustrations of a man shaving which were used by the Kampfe Brothers show buttons, fingernails, eyebrows and even folds in the shirt.

There are at least two different styles of cans holding the Kampfe Brother's Star safety razor. A tan can with black printing on it has twelve U.S. patent dates shown. The earliest date is June 15, 1880, and the latest is August 7, 1888. Directions on the can suggest that the blade be stropped after use before returning it to the shaving frame. The stars on the blade were to remain up when the blade was in the razor. The large head of this razor was to catch lather scraped off while shaving. The nickel plate razor frame itself has patent dates embossed also. The embossing shows an award the razor won at the 1886 Mechanics Institute in San

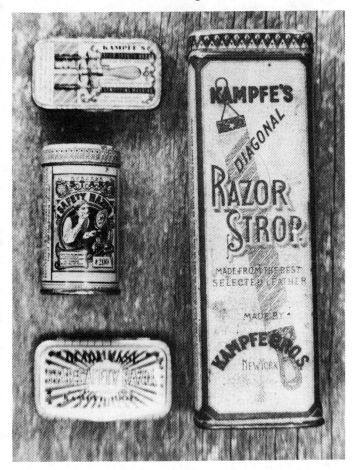

Right: Can holding Kampfe's Razor Strop. Left: Cylinder can holding Kampfe Safety Razor from about 1895. Notice detail on illustration of a man shaving. Small tins hold extra blades.

Dime Safety Razor and two views of Dime Razor containers.

Francisco, California. The can is marked "Somers Bros, Brooklyn, N.Y. Pat Apl 29, 1879."

Another Star razor can be found in a four sided metal can. The box has two hinged lids. The larger compartment holds the razor and stropper. The bottom lid covers a smaller compartment which holds extra blades.

This razor frame has embossing referring to the highest Paris Award of 1900 and the highest Pan American Award of 1901. It is called the "New Model" and appears to be silver plated. The tin box has much the same information printed on it with an illustration of a man looking into a mirror while shaving with a New Model razor. The razor's original price was two dollars.

Kampfe Brothers packaged blades in separate tins and their strop in a can too. The blade cases have brass holders that keep two of the thick, backed blades safe from harm. The holders are marked, "Patented June 4, 95." The bottoms of the cases show a Star safety razor stropping machine being used with a strop. One blade tin is marked, "American Can Co." the other is marked, "H.L. Hudson & Co."

The strop can carries the familiar picture of a man looking into a mirror while shaving. There are many printed instructions and patent dates on the back and sides of the can.

The "Gem Cutlery Co." has a round can holding a razor that is similar to the Star. The blade holding mechanism, however, is different from that used by Star razors.

The can contained instructions for shaving in English, German, French, and Spanish. The directions make no mention of shaving with the blade holder on a straight handle. This device is apparently only to hold the blade while it is stropped. The razor handle has threads that enable it to be screwed to the holder.

A 1915 Shapleigh Hardware Catalog shows a "Gem" safety razor packed in a four side tin box bearing the face of a man shaving. The description identifies the razor as having a hard rolled brass frame which is nickel plated. Its price was two dollars. This was the same price as the molded celluloid straight razors of the patterns we seek today. Patterns such as the crane holding a fish and the nude art design. Of course, some straight razors were more expensive but many were less expensive as well.

The "National Safety Razor" is packaged in a tin cylinder. The can is printed green with gold

Gem Cutlery Safety Razor, stropper, and tin container. Part of the handle can be screwed into razor or stropper.

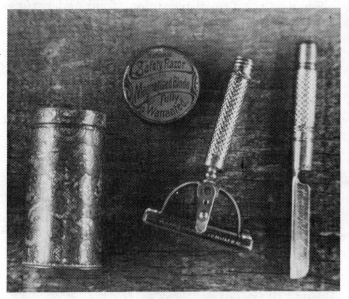

National Safety Razor stropper, and tin container; magnetized blade has thick back and is hollow ground.

designs on it. Its cover identified the blade as "magnetized." The razor has a large hollow ground blade but is more simply constructed than the Star or Gem razors. The razor itself is marked "National Warranted." Part of the handle is screwed into either the razor or the stropper.

"The Dime Safety Razor" is more simple in design and was cheaper than the earlier canned razors. The flat blades were available at 3 for 10 cents and the complete outfit in the can was only

10 cents at all dealers. The can shows a Patent date of "Dec. 31, 1907," and the company as "International Safety Razor Co., N.Y."

The razor blade has a safety guard that looks like wire. The handle is wood painted black. This particular razor had never been put together and used. The tissue thin paper of the instructions would not likely have survived being packed back into the can after the first shave. The container is marked "AmCan Co."

The "Laurel" Ladies Boudoir Safety Razor is both interesting and small. This one is packaged in a tin container instead of a cardboard box. The razor has a blade guard of Bakelite material with no teeth, comb, or serrations to irritate the skin. The purple, green, and gold hinged box is marked "Made in England" as is the guard.

The "Twenty Grand" Razor Blade Company of Spencer, Indiana had a tin blade holder with felt pads inside. The holder was to protect the blade from invisible rust on its cutting edges. The maker marked the tin, "Made and Lithographed in USA C.C.CO."

Don't forget that lithographed tin containers made nice "banks" to hold used safety razor blades. The "Gem" Record Book, the "EverReady" Treasure Chest, and the "Williams" Safe were some of the blade banks. We also expect to find talcum and shaving powder packaged in tins.

There were straight razors packaged in tin boxes also. A cigar shaped tin is printed on the inside and outside of the hinged lid, "Taylor's The 1000 Razor." A trademark of an "eye" and the word "witness" is also used by the maker, "Needham, Veall, and

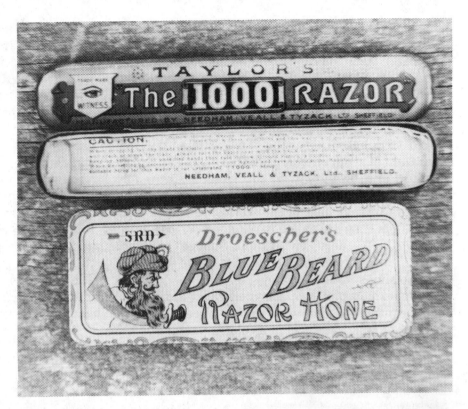

Top: Inside of the cigar shaped tin box which held "The 1000" razor. Taylor's eye witness trademark is also shown. Bottom: Lid of a box holding a Droescher's straight razor hone.

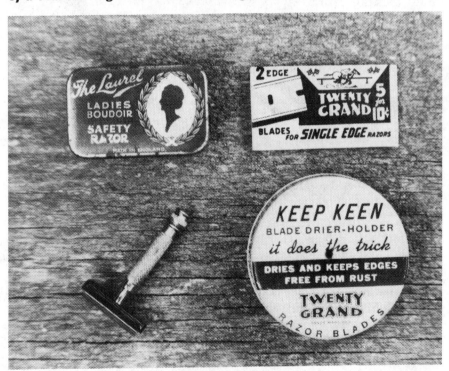

Left: Tin box which holds the Laurel ladies razor shown below it. Notice that the regular size Twenty Grand razor blade wrapped in paper is longer than the Laurel box. Twenty Grand blade holder is below the blade.

Tyzack LTD Sheffield." There is a cardboard liner to the tin box and paper instructions are enclosed. The razor itself has its blade etched "The 1000." The handle is plain black with a white spacer.

This particular razor has traveled thousand of miles. Many such razors were manufactured in Sheffield, England and shipped throughout the world to places including Australia and New Zealand. My parents found this razor in New Zealand and brought it to the United States for their razor collecting son.

Razors in that part of the world are called "cut throats" as they are called in England. Places with names like "Gallery" or "Antique Shoppe" sell the old razors for prices very similar to those found in antique shops in this country.

Several companies packaged razor hones in metal containers. The well known "Keen Kutter" razor hone was packaged in a colorful metal box as late as 1927. Since the hones were often used with oil or water, a metal box seemed to stand up better than cardboard packages.

Another colorful box is marked, "Droescher's Blue Beard Razor Hone" with an arrow through the letters "SRD." The bright yellow box has an illustration of a bearded pirate carrying a sword. The instructions suggest that full hollow ground razors need very little honing and that thicker razors need more honing in preparation. The hone itself is embossed with the SRD arrow trademark.

Carter liver pills for a time were packaged in a round container that looks like it might contain a safety razor. So if you see a person on his knees and holding his glasses so he can put his head to the floor, it might not be as serious as it looks. That person might be doing what I once did, trying to read the can on the bottom shelf of the display case. The can did not read "Carter" but "Gem Cutlery" instead.

This article appeared in Knife World June, 1984.

Safety Razors

by Kurt Moe

There were, of course, many stropping and honing machines designed to return dull safety razor blades to a usable condition. Several safety razor manufacturers recognized that not all self shavers wanted to use a blade a few times and then throw it away. Especially during the depression when times were not that good. In response to this need, some manufacturers designed the sharpening device to be a part of the safety razor. In fact, many razors did not even require that the blade be removed in order to strop or hone.

The folding models of the Durham Duplex razor have a special attachment to enable the razor holding a dull blade to be put to an ordinary straight razor strop. The attachment allowed the blade to be held at the correct angle to the strop.

The English Rolls razor case had a mechanism that allowed for a dull blade to be pushed across a hone surface or pulled over a strop surface depending on which side of the razor case was removed.

The AutoStrop Safety Razor Co. sold a razor set that included a strop. Again a blade could be stropped on both sides of an edge without even removing it from the razor.

These razors were popular and were sold in large numbers. While the devices are interesting to a collector, there are too many available for prices to go very high.

What the collector really wants is a complicated razor with a sharpening mechanism that did

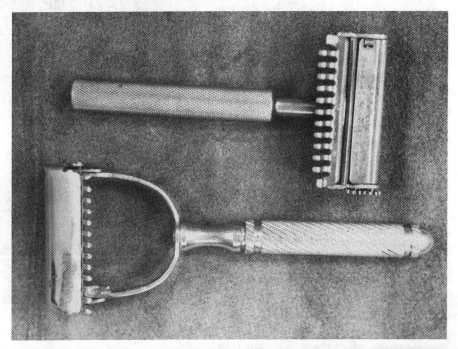

Top: Common and inexpensive Valet Autostrop razor. Bottom: Madden Safety Razor from 1920's was sold in a set with stropper.

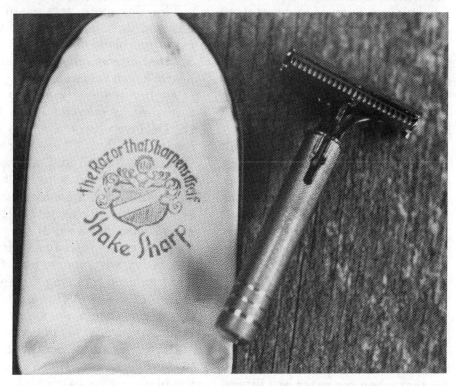

Shake Sharp razor. Mechanism showing in the handle allowed hone and guard to slip forward and back to hone blade in place.

not become popular. Perhaps the device had design imperfections so that even on its best day it didn't work well in the hands of an average shaver. Maybe the device was so complicated that an excessive selling price was asked. Whatever the reason, if the razor has an unusual shape or a complicated self sharpening design and was not produced in large numbers, the razor is now a sought after collectable.

The Madden Safety Razor Corp. of 1180 Broadway, New York, marketed an unusual stirrup shaped razor. The razor was the creation of Edwin C. Madden. The corporation dates from 1919, however, it took several years for the development of a blade and for the marketing to begin.

The blade was of Swiss steel 9/1000 in thickness with a high percentage of carbon. The double edged blades were hollow ground, hardened, and tempered to hold a sharp edge. They were guaranteed to give service for five years.

The Madden De Luxe set containing a razor and stropper retailed for $6.50. Also available was a miniature set without a stropper for ladies use which retailed at $5.00.

A second razor has its own built in hone. Sold by the Shavety First Corp. of 271 Fifth Avenue, New York 16, N.Y., it was called the G.E. Jones Shake Sharp razor. The razor that sharpens itself.

The razor's instructions indicate that this razor was plated in genuine 22 carat gold. The razor I have apparently escaped the gold plating process.

The Shake Sharp used a standard double edged blade. The head of the razor contained a hone so that when the razor was flipped or snapped with a wrist action the blade could be sharpened by

Ronson razor with special blade and box.

removing it from the razor. The guard and hone slid past the blade's edge sharpening with each wrist movement.

The DeHaven was a similar safety razor. Hugh DeHaven received three patents on May 24, 1932, relating to his combined razor and blade sharpener. These were patent numbers 1,859,554, 5, & 6. Surprisingly, the patents were applied for on July 24, 1925, nearly seven years earlier.

An invoice and instruction sheet for a DeHaven razor was furnished by collector Keith Danielson. This material shows that the DeHaven Razor Co. was a Division of the Pilliod Cabinet Co., Swanton, Ohio. There were two models, the Club model was Chromium plated and sold for $5.00 in 1933. There was also the Director's model which was gold plated. The DeHaven was sharpened with a shaking action. The key to the type of cutting edge produced was in the use of Syncrokeen Compound. The razor's case had a small compartment holding this compound that some collectors refer to as a jeweler's rouge.

A heavy, wiry, coarse beard required a course cutting edge. This was produced by using the sharpening compound as frequently as every other day. A fine beard required the compound to be used only about once a week. Syncrokeen was removed before shaving by shaking the razor in water.

Darwin's Ltd. of Sheffield, England, had a razor using a thick blade. British Pat. No.419,495 is marked on the blade. A screw in the blade seems to regulate the blade edge to guard distance for closeness of shave. The bottom of the razor's handle turns out and is a small screw driver.

The Darwin's case contains a strop and by sliding the end of the case in and out the blade could be stropped. The razor case is marked English Pat. No.397,334. The razor and the case look similar to the more common Rolls Razor.

Another type of razor had a cylinder shaped strop roller as a part of the razors head. Ronson Products, Inc. of Aronson Square, Newark, NJ marketed the Ronson Razors.

Several patent numbers are stamped into this razor. No.1,489,102 was granted to William G. Adams on April 1, 1924. Patent No.1,492,233 was granted to Adams on April 29, 1924. These patents bear little resemblance to the Ronson razor, however.

Patent No.1,565,704 was granted on December 15, 1925, to Raoul Boizard. The patent by Mr. Boizard of Paris, France included two cylinder shaped roller strops.

Louis V. Aronson's patent No.1,826,410 of October 6, 1931 was for a thoroughly thought out and drawn razor design. Mr. Aronson assigned his patent to Art Metal Works, Inc. of New Jersey. A second patent No.1,887,911 was granted to L. Aronson on November 15, 1932, for more details of the combined safety razor and sharpening device.

This is a very complicated razor. A brisk downward strike with the palm against the roller sharpened one side or bevel of a razor blade's edge. Part of the complicated design was to allow stropping of both sides of both edges of a razor

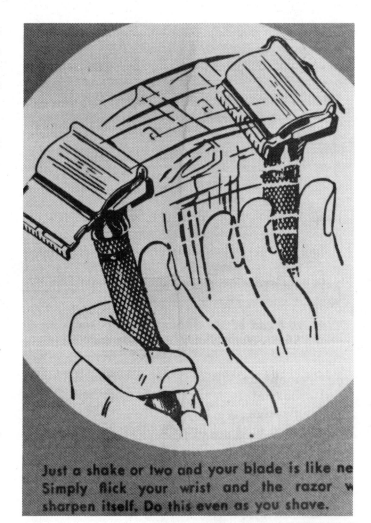

Just a shake or two and your blade is like ne
Simply flick your wrist and the razor w
sharpen itself. Do this even as you shave.

Illustration from Shake Sharp instructions. Shows hand movement necessary to operate hone.

blade. Thus four sides of the blade could be sharpened without removing the blade from the razor. The head was marked 1,2,3,4 so that it was easier to keep track of the edges already used for shaving or the sides needing stropping. The spring loaded handle could be telescoped together so that the blade holder projected from the head end of the razor. Once in that position the blade holder could be flipped over or turned end for end.

This razor was said to require a special Ronson Blade. The blades were of Stainless Steel made in Sheffield, England. The blade appears thicker than most other brands and has slots in the ends that fit projections on the razor head.

Still another reason for the obsolescence of some of these self sharpening razors may be that they required special blades. The original idea may have been to design a razor requiring special blades in order to create a captive and repeat blade market. In a few years the special blade

Close up of Ronson razor. Top shows stropper roller. Blade bevels #1 and #2 are showing. The blade holder can be flipped or rotated to put any of 4 bevels next to the roller strop.

Close up: Head of the Shake Sharp razor open to receive blade. Hone shows just above guard.

English Darwin razor (and case) is similar to the more common Rolls razor. Razor handle screws out to become screwdriver.

requirement backfired. Most retail outlets and mail order catalogs carried the common double and single edge style blades. When a Ronson razor user needed another Ronson blade I can imagine the store owner laughing and telling him at the same time, "Why don't you try looking where you bought the razor or else write to the manufacturer?"

This article appeared in Knife World October, 1988.

Windmill Pattern Razors

by Kurt Moe

All the windmill razors are being sought after for their handle pattern. Most are molded of ivory colored celluloid, sometimes with grain lines similar to real ivory. I have even encountered one handle completely stained a shocking pink. There may be more than three variations of the molded celluloid windmills but I haven't seen them yet.

The pattern must have been popular around the turn of the century. The 1902 Witte Hardware Company catalog shows an assortment of fancy celluloid styles. Two windmill patterns are included, both the rowboat style in ivory color and the sailboat style in black celluloid.

The first pattern variation has a smaller windmill than the other designs and was the most difficult for Cindy and me to obtain for our own collection. The blade in this razor has a shank marked "W.H. Morley & Sons," a four leaf clover trademark, and "Germany."

A more common version of the scene has a sailboat below the windmill and rocks around the block base of the windmill.

This particular razor is marked on the shank, "Oxford Razor," "Warranted Germany." The reverse side reads, "Germania Cutl. Works, Germany." This is the same "Germania" stamping that I've found on razors marked "Wadsworth Razor Co. XLNT."

Probably the most common of the variations is the style with a rowboat in the water. This razor's shank is difficult to read, but it marked "205 S...Eider & Chapman, Germany." Another

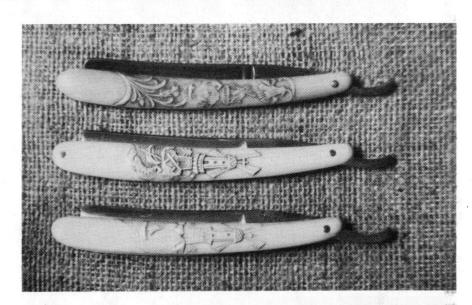

Windmill pattern molded razor handles. Top: A difficult to find windmill pattern handle with a W.H. Morley and Sons blade. Middle: More common windmill pattern with rowboat and S__eider and Chapman on blade. Bottom: Windmill pattern handle with sailboat and Oxford Razor on blade.

razor of this style is marked on the shank "55S Sheffield Steel E, Made in Germany." The reverse side reads, "The Admirals."

The Admiral razor is unusual because it is not common for fancy celluloid handles like the windmill pattern to be paired with fancy etched blades. This blade is etched with the busts of three Admirals. Though the etching is incomplete due to wear from honing and stropping, the Admirals appear to be Sampson, Dewey, and Schley. These men were naval heroes of the 1898 Spanish American War. Several books were written within a year of the war's end of the exploits of these American Admirals. One such book is "Pictorial History of Our War with Spain for Cuba's Freedom."

According to this book, the American public wanted action following the sinking of the USS Maine in the Havana harbor. The three Admirals furnished some of that action. Admiral Dewey accomplished the destruction of the Spanish fleet in Manila Bay. Admiral Sampson defeated a Spanish fleet attempting to escape his blockade of Cuba. Admiral Schley fought a very successful Battle of Santiago.

Spain, as a result of their losses, agreed to relinquish Cuba, and cede Puerto Rico, the Philippine Islands, and Guam. Most remarkable is that the Admirals achieved their victories with very little loss of American life. No wonder the Admirals were considered fitting subjects for a commemorative razor.

This article appeared in Knife World August, 1982.

Wedge Blades & Lather Catchers

By Phillip L. Krumholz

Once upon a time, the Brothers Kampfe invented a whole new razor, the "safety"...

The STAR, as it was known, was first patented in 1880, and featured a thick, wedge-shaped blade resembling a straight razor blade that had been cut off in a Radiac saw. This blade, which was about 1 1/2" wide, set the tone for a safety razor blade width that would last for many years.

And while the Kampfe Bros. were setting blade width, they were also establishing the "right" way for other manufacturers of razors to design razors. And that was:

- Use a thick wedge blade.
- Have a lather catcher.

And with only a few exceptions, this is the way all safety razors were produced for the next two decades!

Two exceptions are the Victor and the John Watts. These British safety razors deviated in that they did NOT have lather catchers; in fact, they did not have much of anything. They were basically bent pieces of metal formed into a "handle plate," with a platform on which to rest the blade. Usually, an adjusting screw was present for tightening the blade.

As for the wedge blade, a Star advertisement even showed an illustration of a portion of wedge

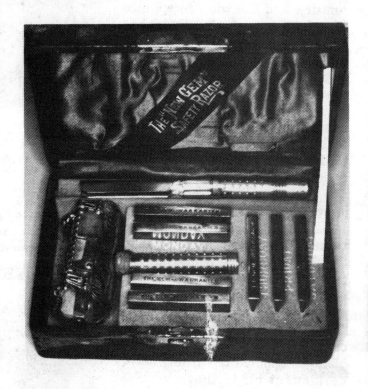

This new Gem featured seven day's worth of wedge blades and fullsized lather catcher.

blade (cut / broken?) from a straight razor, with the caption, "The same blade as used by your Grandfather."

But what is this lather catcher business? How did it get started? There were no lather catchers on the blades of straight razors, and men shaved with them for centuries. Patents clearly show the lather catcher in place with the first drawings of the Star, so the Kampfes must have felt that the invention was important, or perhaps they felt the invention needed a little extra boost to get it accepted by the Public. These full-sized lather catchers wrapped all the way around from the back of the blade, forming a tiny trough, to connect with the razor frame at the edge of the blade. The shaving lather and whisker bits (sounds like a cat food) were collected until the razor was rinsed.

Thus the lather catcher... and the nickname "Lathercatchers" for razors of this type. And a razor is a "Lathercatcher if it has this trough, no

Circa 1905 Gem has only a half-sized lather catcher and takes either flat or wedge blades.

matter how small the trough might be..."

Small the lather catchers became. With the turn of the century, and the wide acceptance of safety razors, the designers produced more economical, streamlined razor heads. Other improvements included different types of blade adjusting screws to allow a "customized" shave. Lather catchers went from the full-sized troughs to about halfsized. These vestigial lather catchers end not far from where the handle screw meets the shaving head.

Lather catchers saw the transition from the wedge blade to the flat single edge blade, but the true Lathercatcher would accept either. The advantage for the manufacturers to switch to the "improved" flat blade meant they could produce a more disposable blade as opposed to turning out a permanent blade that could be honed and stropped ad *infinitum*.

At least that was the mindset they were trying to instill in the shaver of the day.

So, by around 1910, the lather catcher was a vestigial part of the razor - it was there but its function was limited (if it **ever** had a real function) and razor designers continued to chip away at it. The 1912 Gem, for example, has no lather catcher at all, only a small strip of metal connecting the blade platform to the handle. This strip was not capable of "catching" anything!

The ads of the day began to tout the old fashioned lather catcher razors as being heavy and cumbersome. We think of them

A Griffon is shown next to an early 1900s Star. By that time, Star had designed a smaller lather catcher.

A Yankee has a fullsized lather catcher.

today as being quaint, like an old Model T Ford.

A growing number of collectors are taking a fancy to the heavy headed wedge blade razors, and especially so if equipped with the cute lather catcher. Prices are rising accordingly.

The nicest thing is, there are many brands and styles to keep them collecting for a long, long time!

This article appeared in Knife World February, 1993.

Are They Really Razors?

Kurt Moe

All cutlery devices that look like razors are not necessarily useful for the shaving of beards.

A piece of cutlery that looks like a huge straight razor has black handles 7-1/4 inches long. The handle halves are pinned together on each end just like a straight razor. The cutting edge of the razor sharp blade is a full 4 3/8 inches long. The shank is marked "Made in Germany" and "Spencer Lens Co., Buffalo, N. Y." The back of the shank has script initials "S", "L", and "Co."

The piece appears too big to be used as a razor. A lumberjack's axe might feel as good in the hand while shaving. Someone might conclude that this razor-like device was made for display purposes.

A firm like the Spencer Lens Co. doesn't sound like one of the cutlery firms importing razors. In fact it sounds more like a company specializing in the optic field.

The grind on the blade is not similar to the wedge or various concave grinds that are used on straight razors. The back side of the blade appears level with the shank. Only the front of the wedge blade has been ground to leave a shoulder. It has been suggested that the blade grinding was not completed so that the piece could be used as demonstration of a stage of the manufacturing process.

Another piece of cutlery is marked, "Central Scientific Co., Made in Germany." Again the back side of the blade is straight with the shank but this time the front is hollow ground.

A third device is marked with the block initials B & L in a circle. Sometimes "Made in Germany" & "Section Cutter" markings are found with the B & L stamping. This blade is also flat on the back

Three razors having back sides of their blades level or flat with their shanks. Top: Spencer Lens Co. razor. Center: Microscopic section cutter shank mark shown with blade having hollow grind on front only. Bottom: Shank has B & L inititals in oval marking.

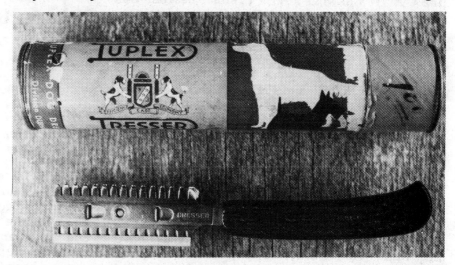

Duplex Dog Dresser for grooming dogs. Uses same blade as Durham Duplex razors.

and hollow ground on the front.

A fourth instrument again has the back of its blade nearly flat with the shank. It again has plain black handles. The shank stamp in this case reads, "Microscopic Section Cutter."

My choice of explanations for the use of these cutlery pieces is that they were razors used for shaving thin sections of tissue from a larger sample for examination under a microscope. Their larger size, unusual grind, and markings make their use for the shaving of beards seem very unlikely.

Another cutlery device is marked, "U'ROWN HAIR TRIMMER, PATENT PEND., MADE IN USA." The piece looks very much like an Arnold $ Razor patented in 1907. It has a flat metal handle with a finger hole. There is a single edged replaceable handle with a wrap around comb guard.

Directions which are supplied with the device are for trimming hair. The trimmer is held very much in the manner that a razor would be held. The middle finger goes through the loop with the little finger and ring finger resting on the end of the handle. The thumb and index finger grasp the handle near the comb. Illustrations show how two mirrors can be used to trim one's own hair and also show how to remove the comb for cleaning.

Another variation of the comb guard found on this device might enable it to be used for shaving. The comb guard on this example, however, extends past the blade on both sides.

It does not appear possible to get close enough to the skin with this U'ROWN device guarded as it is to be able to shave a beard.

Two razor reference books do list the U'ROWN as a razor. Some definitions of the word razor, however, include its use for the cutting of hair as well as the shaving of beards. Was a variation of the U'ROWN used as a razor to shave beards? Was a patent ever granted? Did the application mention shaving or hair trimming? I don't know.

A WECK cutlery device looks very much like their folding razor and appears to use the same blade but has a handle only 4 1/8 inches long. The bright metal handle and the blade guard are both marked "Hair Shaper." The fingers of the comb guard appear to be closer to the blade's edge on the hair shaper than they are to the blade of WECK's razors. The shaper probably would not shave well and further more why argue with the use that the manufacturer stamped on the device

A small folding piece has a real tortoise-shell handle 3-5/8 inches long. The blade is slightly curved. The seller suggested that the curved blade enabled the device to be used by a lady to shave her legs. The stamping is probably a poor "Tiemann & Co." There is a blade stop keeping the blade from opening past 180 degrees. Perhaps this device could be used to shave but that doesn't seem to be its originally intended use.

Levine's Guide to Knives and Their Values, 2nd Edition has a chapter titled "Folding Medical Instruments." In the chapter Mr. Levine illustrates some Tiemann & Co. instruments including one such example having what is described as a probe-pointed bistoury blade.

Finally we have a non-folding piece of cutlery

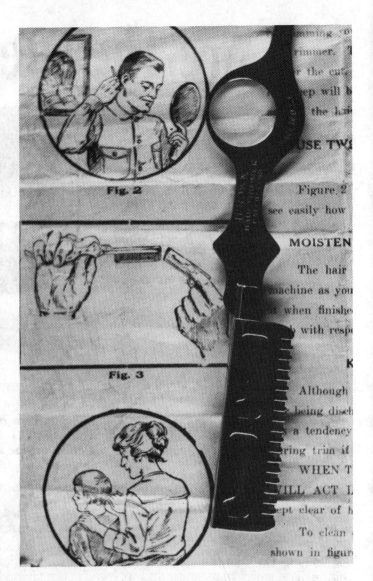

U'ROWN Hair Trimmer has guard extending past both sides of its blade. Directions show use as a hair trimmer.

using what appears to be the same blade and guard system used in Durham Duplex razors. The comb blade guard is marked "Duplex Dresser." The black handle resembles imitation stag. The blade and guard appear to be similar enough to that of Durham Duplex razor that it could be used to shave a beard.

Unless you chase cars for fun and your barking keeps neighbors up at night the Duplex Dresser wasn't intended for your use. The tube package the device was found in identifies it as the Duplex Dog Dresser. The instructions tell how the device can be used in grooming different breeds of dogs.

It just goes to show, not every cutlery piece that looks like a razor was meant to be used for the shaving of whiskers from the faces of men.

This article appeared in Knife World August, 1993.

Automatic Razor Strokes

by Kurt Moe

A person using the old fashioned straight razor could develop an easy cutting diagonal shaving stroke. Most safety razors were held in a manner that made this diagonal stroke difficult to duplicate.

Anyone would agree that a steak knife using a sawing stroke on a very tough piece of meat works better than simply cutting straight into the meat. A number of safety razors tried to imitate this sawing stroke automatically. One method used was to obtain a reciprocal or sawing motion of the blade itself.

One razor using this method was the King Oscillator Razor. This razor used a fluted roller that moved across the face. The roller contact ensured the correct shaving angle for a Royal shave. The turning motion of the roller was mechanically changed to a reciprocal motion of the razor blade. The razor required a special blade that was cut out to fit the razor's mechanism. The expectation was that a blade moving from side to side would cut easier, so that a less than sharp blade would still cut smoothly. The motion was compared to that of a farmer's mower cutting the hay field.

Patent #2,089,414 was granted Aug. 10, 1937 to Winfred Parkin and was assigned to Theodore W. Foster & Bro. Co. of Providence, Rhode Island. A second patent #2,116,280 was granted May 3, 1938, to the same inventor and assigned to the same company. Both patents were said to be improvements upon the razor

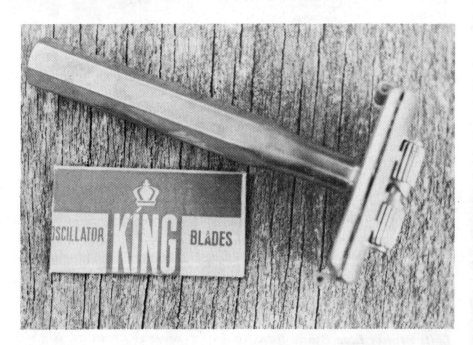

Gold plated King Oscillator Razor with special blade. Fluted roller turns when drawn across the face to move blade from side to side.

Vibro-Shave electric razor, box, and special double edge blade.

disclosed in patent #1,890,733 granted to John L. King for his razor using a reciprocating blade.

This razor was advertised as the razor that "clicks" while you

141

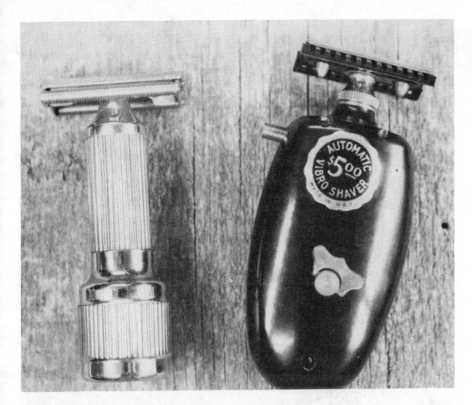

Left: Stahly Live Blade Razor sold for several decades. Right: Automatic Vibro Shaver which winds like a clock.

Collins silver plated razors using round blades. Left: Spring motor in the large handle slowly turned the round blade in this rare razor. Right: Fixed blade Collins razor using the same round blade and guard.

shave. The razor itself was marked "22 KT Gold Plate."

When considering the value of safety razors such as the King,

the box it was packaged in, instructions, and even an unused blade of the same brand enhance the razor's worth. A near mint razor with these additional items could easily be worth double the value of just the razor in average condition. This particular King razor came in a bronze colored metal box. The instructions gave the seller as the King Razor Corp., 342 Madison Avenue, New York 17, N.Y.

Another brand of razor obtained a reciprocal motion of its blade using a different principle. The TARK was a razor that plugged into a 60 cycle 110 volt electrical outlet. A two wire twisted cord carried currant to a vibrator in the handle. The device was rated 5 Watts.

The gold colored plating used on the head of some TARK razors is nearly always in poor condition. Other models of the TARK have heads with a nickel silver appearance and can be found in better condition.

The box and instructions of a TARK Aristocrat razor show the manufacturer to be Tark Electric Razor Co., Inc., Long Island City, N.Y. "Whisks The Beard Off Like Magic." The box and instructions also carry the National Recovery Administration symbol. Most packaging marked with the recovery eagle dates from 1933-1935. One source indicates The Tark Electric Razor Co. filed for incorporation on 10 October, 1932, and was dissolved on 15 December, 1938. The Tark Sales Corp., 261 Fifth Avenue, N.Y. was responsible for distribution of the razors and wasn't dissolved until 16 December, 1940.

Phillip Krumholz in his recent book "*A History of Shaving and Razors*" has a great deal of information about shaving and about safety razors in particular. There are a large number of photographs in the book as well. As might be expected in an undertaking of this size, a few errors may have crept into the work. One such error may be that the book's TARK listing indicates that the Tark razor "accepted a double edge razor blade." Those models of this razor that I've seen have all required a special single edge Tark blade. This blade has a small hole in the center for a vibrating post to fit. The photograph shown in his book also seems to be that of a single edge razor.

A very similar razor which does use a double edge blade is the Vibro-Shave Electric Razor marketed by the Electric Razor Corp. The box shows a 522 Fifth Avenue, New York, address. The instructions show the address as 40-09 21st St., Long Island City, New York.

The instructions also show two models of the Vibro-Shave. Model A is Chromium plated at $5.00. Model B is gold plated with a switch and sold for $7.50. Both models had a plug to screw in a light socket. I suppose the assumption was that every bathroom had a light bulb socket so that power would be available for the razor even though there were no plug outlets there. My question is, after the light bulb was screwed out so the razor could be plugged in, what did the shaver use for light to shave by?

If the shaver's community had only direct current instead of the usual alternating current, a Vibro interrupter device could be purchased for only $2.50. The razor was then adapted to use with direct power.

The razor box shows that a medal of award was received at the Sesquicentennial International Exposition in Philadelphia 1776-1926.

Patent #1,552,455 was granted to Saul Shaler on September 8, 1925, for his Vibratory razor. This patent was then assigned to the Electric Safety Razor Corp. of New York. The patent describes a solenoid magnet and a spring return to provide blade movement. This Vibro-Shave was a 6 Watt, 60 cycle, 110 volt razor.

Not much is known about another razor called the Automatic Vibro Shaver. The razor itself has no permanent markings. A sticker on the razor gives us the name and the information that it was priced at $5.00 and was "Made in U.S.A." The razor winds like a travel alarm clock and vibrates when a button is pressed in. There is little information on the razor's box except its name,

Vibro Shaver and the slogan: "It soothes as it shaves." The Phillip Krumholz book lists this razor and the previous razor under one listing, VIBRO-SHAVE, and gives credit for manufacture of both to the Electric Razor Corp.

I feel that the two razors do not belong under the same listing for several reasons. The first reason being that the names are only similar and not exactly alike as the book listing shows them to be. One is the Vibro-Shave and the other is the Vibro Shaver.

My second reason is that there seems to be no similarity in construction. The electric model uses a special double edge blade. The clip on closure to hold the blade is unique and is made of all metal parts. By contrast the wind up model uses a regular double edge blade. The method used to hold the blade to the head is common for Gillette style blades. The guard is not of metal but of a composite material.

Finally, right after the listing of the razors and their pictures, the Krumholz book shows an advertisement reproduction for the Vibro Shaver. The ad shows that the Vibro Shaver was sold by SeaJay Co., Cottage Grove Avenue, Chicago, Illinois. The ad does not mention the Electric Razor Corp. connected with the plug in vibrating razor.

The Stahly Live Blade razor is another vibrating type of razor. An anonymous history indicates the Stahly was invented by Emil Harshberger in about 1939. U.S. Patent records show, however, that Russell P. Harshberger applied for patent January 20, 1922, and was granted patent #1,760,496 over eight years later on May 27, 1930. This patent referred to a vibratory movement of the razor blade relative to the guard. Since the opening paragraph seems to be contradicted by official U.S. patent records, I won't quote the remaining two typewritten pages of anonymous Stahly history! R. Harshberger had earlier been granted patent #1,200,493 on October 10, 1916, for a vibrating razor design.

Patent #2,054,418 was granted to Ilse Hartmann Nee Bohm September 15, 1936. This patent referred to a design where the whole head of the razor including the blade vibrated. This appears to be the type of vibration that the Stahly uses. The blade was expected to make circular oscillations enabling it to cut whiskers easier. An off center fly wheel with either an electric or spring motor could be used.

The razor itself was named for P.G. Stahly of South Bend, Indiana. This razor was apparently sold over several decades with periodic engineering changes. It was a high priced razor. A catalog said to be from about 1960 shows the English Rolls Razor to be expensive at $13.95. The Stahly shown in the same catalog was even more expensive at $22.50.

Any double edged blade could be used in the razor. The mechanism moved the blade at 6,000 gentle strokes a minute. There are suggestions that the complicated mechanism suffered breakdowns yet there are indications that the device continued to be sold as late as 1970 by a firm called General Precision Corp.

My wife, Cindy, spotted this next razor in a store window during a community Centennial celebration some years ago. She recently tracked the device to its owner, Harold Renner, and secured his permission to photograph it. This razor is probably the most valuable and uncommon of those shown in this article. Surprisingly, its owner is not a razor collector but certainly has good taste in that he finds this device interesting. The razor itself is not marked with a brand name but is marked "Patented Feb. 9, 1915, Silver Plate." Cap. Bertrand Collins of Des Moines, Iowa received patent #1,127,409 on Feb. 9, 1915. The razor in the patent as well as Mr. Renner's device has a disk shaped blade that slowly rotates when the spring drive mechanism is switched on. Winding was done by twisting the bottom of the handle.

The wind up version of the Collins uses the same blade as at least two other fixed blade versions of Collins razors. The round blade with its gear shaped cut out is about the size of a silver dollar. The fixed blade razors and their boxes are marked Collins. They all seem to have a portion of the handle which when turned changes the clearance between the guard and blade.

One of the earliest patents granted for electric razors may have been #616,554 issued to John O'Rourke of New York on December 27, 1898. There have been many other patents over the years that I have been unable to connect with specific razors that were actually manufactured. This article is by no means intended to be a complete listing of vibrating razors. There are probably a dozen manufacturers of vibrating razors that I haven't mentioned simply because I have so little information about them.

Tark electric razor with special single edge blade.

A patent which is different enough from the rest to mention is #1,390,702 granted to Joseph Hammond on September 13, 1921. This patent describes an electric mechanism to give a swinging and cutting stroke to an ordinary straight razor type of concave blade. Although this patent was assigned to the Hammond-Howard Manufacturing Co. of Deming, New Mexico, I would be surprised if it was ever manufactured to the design shown in the patent drawings.

The electric and vibrating razors are not just a memory from the past. Remington currently manufactures the Lekto Blade model of razor in different colors for use by men and women. An AA battery powers on oscillating motor for a gentle shearing action of the blade. It uses a standard twin blade cartridge and is said to be submersible.

The Freedom Blade razor uses a twin blade disposable cartridge also. The handle holds a motor vibrating at 11,000 RPM. There is no drag on the skin and the blades sever hair with many tiny rapid movements. This modern razor has a battery which uses an adapter to recharge.

Panasonic and Windmere as well as lesser

known novelty brands of razors are currently marketed using the same vibrating concept started last century.

A final interesting design was patented July 22, 1913, by G.N. Moore. This patent involved an improvement in rotary safety razors. The device was meant to be driven by a flexible shaft such as used by electric massage machines some barber shops had in the early 1900's. Several rotary safety razors could be driven at once from one power source.

The Moore patent seems to be an improvement largely because of the speed at which it could be operated. The flexible shaft arrangement reminds me of the apparatus used for decades to shear sheep. Perhaps an Army Induction Center could have used the concept. Five barbers using machine driven clippers and the rotary razors would need a man full time just to sweep the floor of hair and whiskers.

This article appeared in Knife World May, 1989.

Blades and Banks

by Kurt Moe

There are many edged collectables with more status than safety razor blades. But the blades are more glamorous than they may seem at first thought.

While some countries still have the colorful blade wrappers, new technology in razor blade marketing virtually eliminated both blade wrappers and blade banks from the USA. Dispenser packages were developed that protected the blades until they were ejected for use one at a time. Individual paper wrappers were no longer needed. The same dispenser often had a section that accepted the used blades just removed from the razor.

Some of the more difficult old blades to obtain are those marked with names usually associated with other products. For example, there are "Coca Cola" brand blades. The box is marked with white letters and trim on a red background. How valuable are these blades? The proceeds from the sale of a box containing five Coca Cola double edge blades would certainly pay my air fare and hotel expenses to one of the upcoming knife shows! Don't throw away any cigar bands or gum wrappers marked Coca Cola either.

Winchester, the company well known for its rifles and pocketknives, also marketed a safety razor. And of course there are single edge razor blades marked "Winchester" to fit the razor "As Good As the Gun."

The Marlin Firearms Company marketed blades for several years. Some variations of this brand have outlines of lever action rifles on them. In 1951, magnetized "Marlin" blades were sold in packages of 12 for 25 cents.

Many of the major hardware distributors marketed blades also. A.F. Shapleigh, E.C. Simmons and Hibbard, Spencer, Bartlett & Co. are a few examples of firms that had their trademarks on razor blades.

Most of the private brands have blades and boxes marked similarly. Some brands, however, used stock paper wrapped blades marked "Quality Guaranteed" or similar phrases and had their own brand on the box only. "Pontiac" is one such brand. "Waltham" is another such brand and was

Display of Speedway blades containing 25 packages of 4 blades each. Red, black, and silver colors are eye catching.

packaged twenty boxes to a carton.

Some of my favorite blades are those with illustrations on their colorful wrappers. King Gillette's portrait is probably one of the most common. Other subjects include horses, dogs, airplanes, castles, swans, and ships to mention only a few.

The discriminating collector may want only blades in packages on their complete original counter display. Most such displays grouped a number of packages containing paper wrapped blades. Each package was removed from the display when sold.

The "Speedway" brand can be found on razors and in variations on paper wrapped blades. One

147

Top: Gem blade bank was free with purchase of a package of 10 Gem Double Life blades. Bottom: Blade box showing the ship "Hood." Ever Ready blade bank shaped like a treasure chest.

particular display sells them at "4 blades for 10 cents." While not as eye catching as some other blades with illustrations, the "Speedway" blades make use of red, black and silver colors.

Of course, not all brands of blades had different manufacturers. "Speedway" as well as "Bryford", and "Liberty" were brands of International Safety Razor Corp. Some companies were said to produce over one hundred private brands for sale through various distributors.

Recently there have been a number of "Honey" displays available featuring bee hives on the display, blade boxes, and each individually wrapped blade.

One unusual display contains only twenty-four individually wrapped blades. Each features one of six different color poses of the nude female figure. Judging by the subject shown, the distributor, "Gay Products Co." probably never heard of the more current definition of the word "Gay."

Blade and wrapper collecting is perhaps more advanced in other parts of the world. I've corresponded with collectors from Great Britain and Italy with over 7000 variations each. They have, of course, been collecting both blades made in the U.S. and other countries for many years.

One of the benefits of the blade collecting that I've enjoyed is corresponding and trading duplicate blades with other collectors across the country. It is not necessary to have a large amount of money invested in blades and the shipping costs are affordable too! I'd like to find a bargain Remington Bullet, or pearl handled razor at the next flea market that I visit, but if instead there are some more blades to add to our collection and trade, then I'll be happy.

Before blade slots became a part of every home's medicine cabinet there was a problem as to safe disposal of razor blades after they were used. There were many variations of banks to keep people from cutting themselves on rusty blades.

One tin bank is shaped to look like an old fashioned ledger book. The book's colors are black with red corners and back. The front cover reads, "Record Shaves," and the back cover reads, "Purchase Genuine Gem Blades, the Blade of Quality." The book top reads, "File old Blades Here" next to a slot. The book bottom reads, "Patented, Made in USA, Gem blades will give you more and better shaves than any other blades in the world."

A second Gem variation has less printing on the little tin book. However, the book spine is removable so that used blades can be disposed of and bank used again.

A third tin can with the same shape is mostly orange and gold. It looks like a treasure chest, however, instead of a book. The slot "For old Blades" is on the domed chest lid. The chest also reads, "Insist on Genuine Ever Ready Blades," and "Keenest edges in the World, Patented, Uniformly Perfect, Made in USA." The chest has detail such as hinges, lock and keyhole printed into the design.

The 1929 Sears & Roebuck catalog shows that these banks were included free when a package of ten "Ever Ready" or "Gem" blades was purchased for 55 cents. Both brands were part of the American Safety Razor Corp. which must account for the similarity of the bank design and of their promotion.

Listerine offered at least three variations of blade banks. Two of the designs were patterned after political party symbols. Usually the glaze has long since crazed or cracked on the white porcelain donkeys and elephants. There are slots on the tops of the banks and black stamping on the bottoms which reads, "Free with Listerine Shaving Cream offer made in USA., Pat Apd for." The bottoms also have an irregular 1/2 inch diameter hole that was part of the molding process.

According to the Warner-Lambert Co., the donkey and elephant banks were part of a special promotion for Listerine Shaving Cream in 1932 that took as its theme the Presidential election of that year. In case you're wondering, the 1932 Presidential candidates were Franklin Roosevelt and Herbert Hoover.

I suspect that many elephant and donkey blade bank pairs have found their homes in collections of political memorabilia. This probably makes them more difficult to obtain and more costly than the Listerine frog blade bank.

Since so many years had passed since the Presidential promotion, I had nearly given up hope of learning more about the banks until collector Herb Shearer furnished copies of promotional literature for all three Listerine banks. A "Merchandising Scoop" as it was called, was for the retailer to give a Republican elephant or a Democratic donkey with a purchase of a combination package for 35 cents. The combination package was a tube of Listerine Shaving Cream and a bottle of Listerine Antiseptic for use on the skin after shaving. There was a counter display to create interest as well.

According to Warner Lambert Co. information, the Listerine frog bank promotion came a few years later. The frog has an art deco style to it and a black base. Blades go into the frog's mouth. The bottom has raised porcelain letters reading, "Listerine Shaving Cream, for used Razor Blades, Made in USA." Promotional literature indicates that lithographed window displays were in full color. Advertising phrases were based on the frog shape and include, "What a ripple he'll make in shaving cream sales." No more would the wife or children be cutting their fingers on discarded blades because the frog would be eating them.

Herb Shearer has a number of interesting items in his blade bank collection. Some examples are a "Burma Shave" jar which when empty could be "For used blades or coin bank," by using the slot in the cover. Some of his other banks play on words. One example is labeled the "Whetstone," for dull ones, I also like the "Razor Back Hog." Mr. Shearer's extensive collection also includes many blade banks featuring barber poles and barbers with handle bar mustaches and their hair parted in the middle.

Many shaving talc cans became blade banks after their contents were used up. A blue and white "Williams" after shaving talc can has a long narrow slot on top to dispense talc. The direction for use include, "After powder is gone, use slot for old razor blades. Fit all makes, Patent No. 2234151."

The J.B. Williams Co. also had a tin can printed to look like a "Safe" for old razor blades. Its detail includes hinges as well as a combination dial. The bank is marked "Williams Shaving Cream and Aqua Velva for the perfect Shave."

An orange and black "Fitch's" powder can also have a slot in the top. Its directions read, "Notice, after the contents have been used, the empty container will serve either as a child's bank or as a depository for discarded razor blades."

After finding a blade bank and bringing it home, the fun still isn't over. Every old blade bank that I find with used blades in it is painstaking emptied with a knife blade and a technique that I perfected as a youngster on my piggy bank. At worst I could get a finger cut and need a tetanus shot. Then again I could be rewarded with a blade bearing the Coca Cola trademark.

This article appeared in Knife World October, 1982.

Collins Rotary Razor

by Kurt Moe

Cap B. Collins was inventor of the Collins rotary razor bearing the patent date of February 9, 1915. This razor uses a round blade that is slowly turned by a spring wound mechanism.

Patent #1,351,507 was applied for July 27, 1918, and granted in 1920. This patent describes several improvements made to the rotary razor. An improvement was made to the blade driving mechanism whereby the blade could more readily be disconnected for cleaning. Another improvement enabled the guard to be adjusted to vary the closeness of the cut. A third improvement was to the motor powering the razor.

The Chicago, Illinois, factory in about 1919 included a special Model Department. Six mechanics were said to be employed building models with tool makers equipment and testing new mechanisms and inventions. A prospectus showing illustrations of this factory makes no mention of a slim non-winding Collins razor handle with a fixed blade.

Razors are seldom design patented, however, the Collins razors and blade have been granted design patents. Keep in mind that these patents use a different series of numbers from that used for regular patents.

Patent #53,884 was granted for the ornamental design of the Collins rotary razor. Patent #53,885 was for the new original, ornamental design for the blade used in the razor. Both patents were applied for on June 20, 1919, and granted October 7, 1919, to

Illustration from prospectus showing the interior of the Chicago factory's Model Department in about 1919.

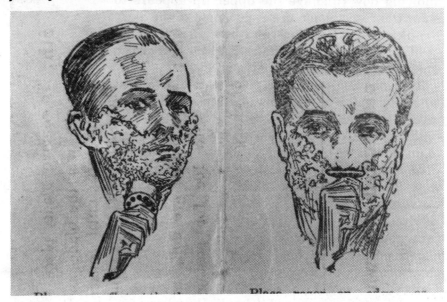

Illustrations from shaving instructions. Note technique advised for shaving the upper lip. Looks dangerous!

Cap B. Collins.

There has been some question whether the rotary windup version or the fixed blade version of the Collins razor was manufactured first. Application for a design patent wasn't made for the ornamentation of the fixed blade razor until later- March 24, 1920. This fact supports the theory that the rotary version was manufactured first. Design patent #56,283 was granted September 14, 1920, to Henry H. Johnson who assigned it to Collins Safety Razor of Chicago, Illinois. H.H. Johnson was Vice President of the firm.

One may speculate that the complicated rotary razor was difficult and costly to manufacture for the limited shaving benefit received from the slowly rotating blade. Even though the fixed blade razor appears more easily manufactured it still carried a price of $5.

A recently examined box fitted to a fixed blade Collins Safety Razor yielded a number of pieces of paper wadded under the razor itself. The first of these papers was the printed instructions telling how to shave with the Collins razor and its round blade.

The lathering described was, of course, important to a good shave with any razor. The next step was to raise the blade into position for shaving. This was done by turning the bottom of the razor handle clockwise until it stopped. Six illustrations show the hand grips and strokes to be used on different parts of the face. The illustration showing how to shave the upper lip appears to show the razor blade at a right angle to the skin. Frankly I don't understand how such a blade position could do more than scrap the lather off, unless, of course it were to cut skin!

After shaving the whole razor was to be rinsed with hot water and the handle screwed back to return the blade below the guard. The blade cap could be rotated counter clockwise with the fingers to unscrew it for blade removal.

At the bottom of the instructions in bold print were the words, "Agents wanted everywhere." The instructions were identified as by "Collins Safety Razors, Franklin, PA." Blades when dull could be returned there for resharpening free of charge except for 10¢ postage. Cap Collins has been shown to be a resident of Franklin during 1923. This could also be the approximate time of manufacture for the fixed blade, slim handle razor.

A second set of instructions found with the razor is on light onion skin paper also marked Collins Safety Razor. It appears to be the carbon from typed copy. In this case my deepest sympathy extends to the poor secretary with the boring job of typing the same copy over and over and over! The second set of instructions implies that some Collins razor buyers were not totally delighted with their purchase.

H. H. JOHNSON
Vice-President

H.H. Johnston, inventor of the Collins fixed blade, slim handle design razor. He was also Vice President of Collins Safety Razor Co.

Apparently the razors were shipped holding a blade that was not sharpened. The typed set of instructions advises that this round blade should be removed and replaced with a new sharp blade before shaving. Surely we all agree that this step is very necessary. The 'Joy Shave" was promised to those following the revised directions.

During the years from about 1914 to 1923 Cap Collins is said to have resided in Iowa, South Dakota, Illinois and Pennsylvania. Several of these moves seem to be an attempt to be close to manufacturing operations involving the versions of the Collins round blade razor.

What happened to Cap Collins when it appeared that his shaving inventions may not enjoy the popularity of competitive shaving tools? It appears that he made an effort to diversify the use of his inventions. Patent #1,480,668 was applied for in 1920 and was granted in 1924 for more improvements to a spring motor mechanism. Several possible uses for the uniform speed motor were mentioned in the specifications including its use as a telephone time-limit meter.

Patent #1,507,768 was granted in 1924 as well for a portable electric light. Rather than employ batteries requiring frequent replacement this device held a spring motor generator. Its appearance was shown to be like that of a flashlight. It twisted to wind the spring motor in a manner similar to the principle used in the rotary razor. When a switch released the spring, a dynamo turned, producing current to light a bulb.

The flashlight invention doesn't appear to be an illuminating success either. While his inventions would prove to be interesting collectables they probably never made Cap Collins financially independent.

Two yellowed columns from the Des Moines Tribune were also found in the razor box mentioned earlier. These were written by Elizabeth Clarkson Zwart and referred to the Rotary Safety Razor invented by Cap Bertrand Collins and patented February 9, 1915. There is an error in both columns in that they refer to the Rotary wind up version Collins razor while they illustrate a hand holding the slimmer handled, fixed blade razor.

Surprising information found in this Tribune column was that Collins was reported to have later been a carnival high diver. To make the act more daring and exciting, the shallow water tank was rimmed with spikes. Collins was said to have had an accident involving the spikes and as a result became more involved in management than as a carnival performer. Cap Collins' career made an often natural progression from inventor to manufacturer. I would have never suspected an individual to move from inventor and manufacturer to carnival high diver!

This article appeared in Knife World August, 1992.

Two different handle designs for fixed blade Collins Safety Razors. Handle on right is most similar to drawing for Design Patent #56,283. May be missing guard. Bottom shows round cap used to hold blade firm.

Collins Safety Razor

by Kurt Moe

THE PATENT: Cap Bertrand Collins made application on May 9, 1914 for patent on his rotary safety razor. Patent #1,127,409 was granted February 9, 1915. Collins' home was given as Des Moines, Iowa. Using the value of patents on other and said to be inferior razors as a basis, the company considered the Collins patent to be easily worth two million dollars. One should probably consider that Collins may have been looking for investors when the value statement was made. The principle basis of the patent was a round blade slowly turned by a spring wound mechanism in the handle. This resulted in a more efficient cutting method which was called the Circular Cutting Method.

THE COMPANY: Collins Safety Razor Co. was said to be organized in South Dakota. C.B. Collins was, of course, President. J.A. Stransky and H.H. Johnson were Vice-Presidents; W.T. Doyle was Secretary and H.N. Aikens was Treasurer. There were said to be some 6,000 stockholders through out the U.S. having invested about $600,000.

THE NEW INDUSTRY: A prospectus describing the Collins factory makes reference to the largest three companies in the safety razor industry having a combined capitalization of $41,000,000 and gross sales of $12,432,000 in the year 1918. The number of safety razors placed in the market by them in that year was said to be 7,000,000. This information was probably included in the booklet as an indication that

Collins Safety Razor Chicago factory on West Lake Street.

Illustration of the factory demonstrating room. Hundreds of shaves were done here weekly.

safety razors were in fact replacing the old fashioned straight razor as the preferred shaving device.

THE FACTORY: The prospectus tells us that one of the first factories was located at 4309-19 West Lake Street, Chicago. The land alone was said to be worth about $25,000, the factory building about $150,000 and the manufacturing equipment about

155

Cap Bertrand Collins, inventor and president of Collins Safety Razor Company.

The wind up version of the Collins Safety Razor in its box. Note the round blade.

$200,000. The company had high expectations of success and owned additional space for expansion. The capacity of the Lake Street factory was 1,000 razors per day. Plans were being made to increase production to 5,000 razors per day.

GENERAL OFFICES: The offices had plenty of space for an expanded work force of stenographers and bookkeepers. The Electric Surface Railway, the Elevated Electric Road, and the Northwestern System were modes of transportation located nearby. This was expected to attract the highest grade of help. W.A. Woodlief was General Sales Manager, Howard Temple was Assistant Sales Manager and H.S. Hasselquist was Superintendent and Works Manager.

ENGINEERING & EXPERIMENTAL DEPARTMENTS: Apparently the working design of the Collins razor was still being adjusted. Plans, figures and drawings were made with the thought of improving the razor itself or its manufacture.

THE MODEL DEPARTMENT: High grade tool maker's equipment enabled the making of plans into reality. Six expert mechanics were employed in the model work and experimentation. Any chance of irregularity in the Collins design or mechanism was to be ruled out before the full scale manufacturing process.

TOOL & MACHINE BUILDING DEPARTMENT: Twenty four tool makers and machinists each with his own set of tools worked on dies, jigs, fixtures, gauges, and in adapting equipment for the purpose of manufacturing the Collins Razor. Shafts rotating near the ceiling supplied power. Belts dropped to each individual machine. A twist in the belt reversed the direction of motion.

RAW MATERIAL STOCKROOM: Materials for the manufacture of the Collins Razor were received and held here until needed. In thirty days time, 54,234 pounds of brass and steel were taken

Automatic department as shown in Collins booklet. Belts bring power down from rotating shafts near the ceiling to individual machines.

Punch press and machining department as illustrated in Collins booklet.

in. This represented about $50,000 in value.

AUTOMATIC DEPARTMENT: This department consisted of automatic equipment for machining all parts of the Collins Razor made from brass and steel rod.

PUNCH PRESS & MACHINING DEPARTMENT: All operations performed on flat stock were done here by punch, sledging, and automatic stamping presses. Pillar plates, bridges, gears, and springs were some parts made here. The dies used in the punch presses were made in the factory and were pillar type compound dies.

CHEMICAL LABORATORIES: Steel used in the circular blades and the gold & silver used in plating the Collins Razor were thoroughly analyzed here.

GOLD & SILVER PLATING DEPARTMENT: Tanks for nickel, gold, and silver plating were here. This implies that gold plate Collins Razors exist.

POLISHING & BUFFING DEPARTMENT: This appears to be the only department having individual electric motors near the ceiling with belts dropping down to the polishing machines. A suction system removed lint, dust, and metals from the air. Metals were retained by the system and precious metals were extracted and refined for use again.

THE ASSEMBLING ROOM: Each person performed one particular operation in assembling the razors. This was to ensure the greatest efficiency and accuracy.

PACKAGING: The Collins wind up razor accompanying the prospectus was packaged in a black oilcloth covered box a little over four inches long and with a stop sign shaped cross section. One end and part of the top of the box unsnaps to reveal the razor itself. A purple ribbon has gold lettering which reads, "Collins Safety Razor, Self Shaving." The box interior is lined with a dark blue velvet like material. A small round black box holds more round blades separated by pieces of octagonal shaped cotton. One of the blades has no sharp edge. Perhaps the razor was originally packaged with a dummy blade to avoid cutting potential buyers. For shipping, the whole box slips into a cardboard tube which is a little larger than the ones found in the center of toilet paper rolls.

THE WINDUP RAZOR: The razor itself differs from the picture

shown on the booklet cover. The cover picture shows a higher dome on the guard than is on the razor itself. The picture shows four bands of marks to help give a good grip. The razor has only two bands. The picture also shows a screw in the handle while the razor has no screw. The picture shows lines on the switch to be vertical and the razor's switch has horizontal lines.

The razor is not marked with the brand name. It is marked only "Patented, Silver plated, Feb. 9, 1915" on the bottom.

FIXED BLADE RAZOR: Examples exist of Collins razors using the distinctive round blade but having no mechanism to turn the blade. There was no mention of these models in the prospectus.

FACTORY DEMONSTRATING ROOM: Every man who shaves was invited to come and try the Collins Razor in the demonstrating room maintained in the factory. Most of the factory's employees were said to shave here. Hundreds of shaves were done in the room weekly. A smile of satisfaction was said to be characteristic of those who shaved with the Collins Razor.

This article appeared in Knife World December, 1989.

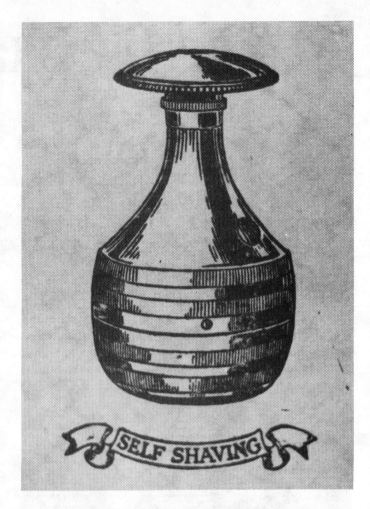

Collins Safety Razor as shown on booklet cover. Production razors had minor differences in appearance due to design changes.

158

The Eureka Patents?

by Robert K. Waits

The challenge of the search and the delight of discovery are what motivate many collectors. The recent uncovering of examples of an obscure Eureka safety razor sold by the George W. Gillette Razor Co. (the *other* Gillette) is an instance of such a discovery. Within the past two years, two Eureka razors have been found in Ohio by Mr. Don Perkins of Indianapolis, Indiana.

Phillip Krumholz has traced much of the brief history of the Eureka razor (*"That Other Gillette,"* Knife World, August and September, 1989), but as is often the case, the more information that is unearthed, the more questions arise.

To summarize Mr. Krumholz's chronology, the George W. Gillette Razor Co., was founded in late 1905 in Cleveland, Ohio, by a nephew of King C. Gillette (THE Gillette). The company moved from Cleveland to Oxford, Ohio about 1906-7 and was renamed the Eureka Safety Razor Co. in 1907. The company was dissolved in 1908. The total period of activity was little more than two years, from November, 1905, to February 1908.

Four years later, in 1912, the name "The Eureka" was registered as a trademark for safety razors by The Eureka Safety Razor Co. of Kansas City, Missouri, claiming use since February 1, 1912. There was probably no connection between the two Eureka razor companies. According to John Goins' "Encyclopedia of Cutlery Markings," the Kansas City company was owned by George F. Rich, Edward Smith and John Merkt.

"Eureka, Eureka!" (I have found it!), was the wild cry of Archimedes as he ran naked through the streets of Syracuse, Greece, upon discovering the first law of hydrostatics* while immersed in his bath. Archimedes had been searching for a way to determine whether a crown purchased by his relative, Hieron II, the tyrant (king) of Syracuse, was of pure or adulterated gold. So the story goes, the crown was proven fraudulent. As a result, the name Eureka, symbolizing a sudden brilliant insight or discovery, has been used for everything from cities to vacuum cleaners, and recently, even for a comic strip. There have been at least three Eureka safety razors. According to Goins, there was a short lived Eureka Cutlery Co.

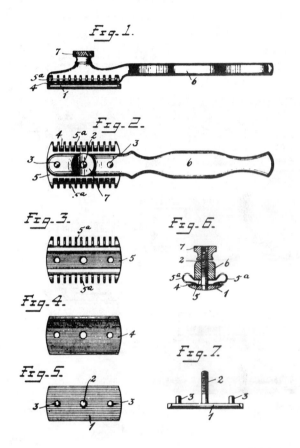

No. 842,927.   PATENTED FEB. 5, 1907.
A. A. WARNER.
SAFETY RAZOR.
APPLICATION FILED JAN. 23, 1906.

Fig-1.
Fig-2.
Fig-3.
Fig-6.
Fig-4.
Fig-5.
Fig-7.

Witnesses
G. J. Rasmussen
Geo. N. Mitchell

Inventor
ALONZO A. WARNER
By his Attorneys

Patent #842,927

in Nicholson, Pennsylvania circa 1911-1915, and EUREKA JB was a mark used by James Basil of Newark, New Jersey, about 1909. All in all, "Eureka" has not had a particularly distinguished history as a cutlery appellation.

Mr. Krumholz proposed that the name Eureka may have been chosen by George Gillette, because, in 1895, after conceiving the idea for his safety razor, King Gillette wrote his wife (who was in Ohio visiting relatives), "I have got it; our fortune is made."

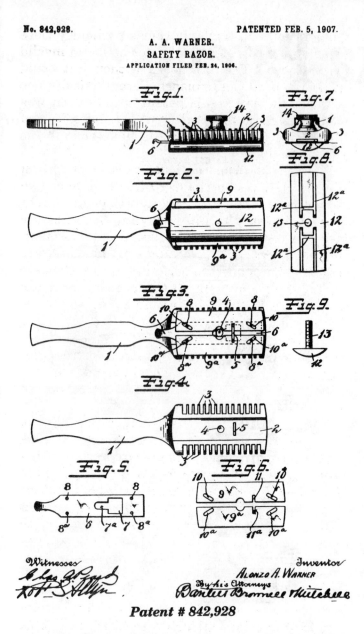

Patent # 842,928

In the matter of names, George was a favorite name of the Gillette clan. King C. Gillette's father was George Wolcott Gillette, his older brothers were Mott and George H. Gillette. All were inventors and tinkers. It was Mott's son, yet another George W., who is believed to have founded the company that sold the Eureka. This George had a son who, naturally was named George W. Gillette Jr.

Getting back to the George W. Gillette Razor Company, Mr. Krumholz speculated that the patent pending mark, (PAT. APL'D FOR), on the razor handle was a subterfuge and that nephew George was allowed to use King C. Gillette's patents because he (George) may have had a hand in inventing the original Gillette razor concept.

Although Mr. Krumholz stated that the Eureka "was clearly an infringement" of King C. Gillette's 1904 patents, that contention is debatable since the main claims of the Gillette patents refer to a flexible detachable blade having two opposite cutting edges. Indeed, the Eureka employs two single edge rigid blades, which seems to be an effort to avoid infringement.

According to the definitive history of THE Gillette and his razor ("King C. Gillette- The Man and His Wonderful Shaving Device" by Russell Adams, published by Little, Brown, 1978) all of the contemporaneous notes, drawings and models that King Gillette made while developing his idea were lost in 1904. According to Mr. Adams, in all of King Gillette's writings in the 1920's describing the events surrounding the razor invention or in sworn testimony and affidavits filed in connection with patent litigation prior to 1910, no mention is made of others contributing to the concept. Of course, if such a contribution had been mentioned, it may have put the patent in jeopardy. It is also curious that Mr. Adams does not mention the George W. Gillette Razor Co. or the Eureka; but then again, only major competitors are mentioned. King C. Gillette's nephew George was quoted in Mr. Adams's book and "the late George Gillette" was mentioned in the acknowledgments as providing photographs and family lore. Was this latter George the nephew or his son, George Jr.? And did either of them tell Mr. Adams about the Eureka enterprise?

Two U.S. safety razor patents exist that show many of the design features of the Gillette Eureka. The patent applications were filed in January and February, 1906, and the patents were issued on Feb. 7, 1907, during the brief life of George Gillette's razor company, and thus these dates are consistent with the patent applied for marking on the Eureka razor. The inventor was Alonzo Abner Warner of New Britain, Connecticut; the patents were assigned to the Landers, Frary & Clark Corp., also of New Britain.

First, a brief digression on patents. The full patent or patent specification has three sections. The first part states the objective of the invention- why it is new and better than what came before- and the second part describes the invention in great detail, usually with several drawings. But the most important part of the patent is the third section, the list of claims at the end, which usually follows wording such as: "What I (we) claim is—."

The claims *are* the meat of the patent as far as infringement is concerned. If it is not in a claim, it is not part of the invention. The claims are the invention. Summaries of patents called abstracts are published in the weekly Patent Office Official Gazette and usually consist of one drawing and a list of the most important claims.

One of the Warner patents, number 824,928, describes a razor having a straight handle "formed of any suitable material— such as hard wood, rubber, or ivory," a spoon-like head with a comb guard, and a split blade secured by a cap and thumb-nut. All are features of the Eureka except for the handle material and design. The objective of the invention was "to provide simple and effective means whereby the cutting edge of the blade or blades may be adjusted relative to the guard portion." This feature, which is the only claim of the patent, is missing on the Eureka, and was dependent upon having slanting slots in the blade that ride on pins on an adjustment plate between the guard and the clamping plate. A similar but much simpler approach to adjustable blade exposure that makes use of a split guard rather than a split blade was described in patent 919,910, issued April 27, 1909, to John J. Meehan, of Denver, Colorado.

The other Warner patent, No.824,927, shows a razor of similar shape that uses a Gillette-type, three hole, double edge blade. Adjustment of edge exposure is accomplished by a guard in the form of curved spring "teeth" that flex inward as the thumbnut is tightened, thus exposing more blade edge. The patent describes the relationship of the handle to the blade as "another feature of substantial advantage... that makes it possible for users of the ordinary razor to instantly adapt themselves to the use of...(an) improved safety-razor." In other words, it was not a "hoe" design like the Gillette from Boston. The patent claim, however, was for the means (or mechanism) to adjust the blade edge exposure. As illustrated in the patent drawings, the blade is thin enough to be flexible but is shown pressed against a flat cap. King Gillette's blade was flexed against a curved cap when in place in the razor. This Warner patent, if not an actual infringement of the Gillette patents, certainly comes perilously close (even an issued patent may later be found invalid by the courts). The razor looks as though it would be able to use Gillette blades. Parenthetically, one of the witnesses to this patent specification was G.M. Landers. If this is George M. Landers, one of L.F. & C.'s founders, he would have been in his 90's at the time.

The Eureka razor is similar in concept to first Warner patent described: 824,928. It has two blades (what a pain to replace!) that slip under four blade clips attached to the cap but lacks the mechanism for blade edge exposure adjustment. The only apparent advantages of the razor are that the blades have no perforations, are cheap to make and the design avoids infringing on Gillette's patents. Having no blade exposure adjustment, it also seems to also avoid infringing on the Warner patent! Two types of Eureka blades have been found, one type is perfectly rectangular and the other has a long notch on the side opposite the edge. It is easy to see why the Eureka was not a best seller.

One could theorize that George W. Gillette, having inherited the entrepreneurial spirit of his grandfather and uncles, and searching for a hot product, offered to market a non-adjustable version of the Warner design. Perhaps Landers, Frary & Clark manufactured them for him. At that time Landers, Frary & Clark was well on the way to becoming one of the largest cutlery manufacturers in the United States (See "New England Cutlery" by Philip R. Pankiewicz). Of course, at this point this is all speculation. We do know that, whatever it's genesis, the Eureka project was a failure. Later, in 1910, L.F. & C. brought out their own UNIVERSAL straight safety razor that had also been invented by Alonzo Warner (Patent 969,626, issued September 6, 1910).

Perhaps continued detective work by razor collectors will uncover more details and add more mysteries to "that other Gillette" story. It is a certainty that other "lost" safety razors are out there awaiting rediscovery by an astute collector.

A floating body loses weight in an amount equal to the weight of the liquid displaced.

This article appeared in Knife World June, 1990.

That's Korn Razor, Not "Corn" Razor!

by Phillip Krumholz

It's just a little place, with only 1,838 townsfolk at last census. It is located eight miles from Ellicottville, and 21 miles from Gowanda, "cutlery towns." Springville is nearby; so is Olean. This whole area has gone down in cutlery history.

Little Valley is known as the county seat of Cattaraugus (where have we heard THAT word before?) County, and rail stop of the New York & Lake Erie Railroad. It's mostly known as a cutlery town, too, and has seen the following companies in its time: J.B.F. Champlin & Son, Case Manufacturing Co., Cattaraugus Cutlery Co., Standard Knife Co., Little Valley Knife Association, J.D. Case, Kinfolks, Case Bros. Cutlery Co., W.R. Case & Son Cutlery Co., and ....G.W. Korn.

Korn had his own manufacturing plant in Little Valley at the turn of the century and had the opportunity to hob nob with the cutlery immortals...Jean Case, Andrew Case, John D. Case, J.R. Case, Elliot J. Case, and Dean J. Case. He knew the Champlins and probably Crandall and one or two Platts. Everyone knew everyone, and they all knew cutlery.

George William Korn was born in Breslau in 1846. When he came to the United States he settled first in Buffalo, New York, than later moved to New York City. Korn worked for August Weck as a cutler, and therein lies the seeds for his own cutlery business years later, plus the training ground for a mind filled with ideas. Korn was a man from the same mold as the Kampfe brothers or J.B. Rhodes or George Schrade - fertile minds that continually come up with unique ideas for patents. Korn's first trip to the Patent Office, about 1881, was for a pair of button hole scissors. Meanwhile, Korn worked with August Weck and Hermann Heinrich on cutlery inventions, most often relinquishing patent rights, it is thought. He got to know more and more people in the cutlery trade, and those people recognized in Korn a genius for invention.

In March of 1883, Korn received approval for a patent (#273,858) filed October 2, 1882. This early patent was for a "fly-opening" knife, one of the earliest designs known in this country for a

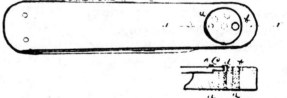

U. S. Patents #306,839 and 306,840 were assigned to Korn for improvements to his fly-open knives.

switchblade knife. On October 9, 1882, Korn took out a patent (#283,900) for a cork turner for removing corks from bottles. At least three patents follow for cutlery, one for a fly-open knife (#306,839), one for a handle for such a knife, and one for his REAL transitional straight/safety razor.

One day, Korn met E.E. Kelley (then sales agent

for Cattaraugus Cutlery Co.) and later entered into a quiet partnership with him. It was this partnership which formed the basis for Korn's relationship with Tint Champlin. Champlin, you may recall, was the son of J.B.F. Champlin, onetime sales agent of Friedmann & Lauterjung, and later founder of J.B.F. Champlin & Son Cutlery and Cattaraugus Cutlery Co. Tint was not only deeply involved in these firms, but also had an interest in Kinfolks. He would later become, along with Korn and his wife, Pauline Korn, E.E. Kelley, J.D. Horning, Cecil L. Horning and W.H. Merow, a Director of the G.W. Korn Manufacturing Co.

The date was May 19, 1900, and a very happy day in the life of a certain immigrant cutler. Korn had just signed the incorporation papers for his company, and the future looked bright, yes, very bright indeed. Newspapers of the day were publishing optimistic statements about the economy: "The expansion of our commerce and industry showed an unguessed national vitality. The subsequent recovery of business from its inflated condition without a serious crash showed an unguessed shrewdness. American enterprise can now be counted on for trade expansion when conditions are as favorable as today."

It is believed that Korn sold patent rights for some of his early inventions to raise capital for his company, and some help was forthcoming from Kelley, of course. The razor company he formed produced only shaving and corn razors, and not knives of any kind - at least none have been seen by me or anyone I've talked to on the subject. Straight razors were produced (some probably

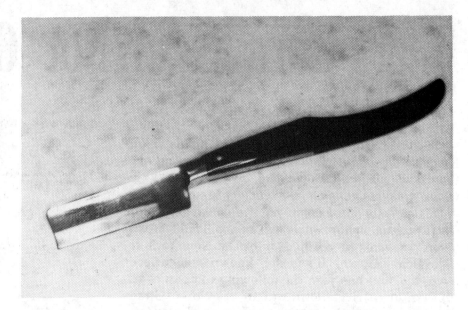

A REAL nonfolding straight razor with black compo handle.

1903 advertisement for a REAL transitional straight/safety razor offers the device for $2.00.

subcontracted, some possibly imported, some assembled from parts) for the following brands: FIT-U, SIGNATURE, BLACK PRINCE, OUR SIGNATURE, and BLACK TANG. Probably the most famous product that Korn is known for is THE REAL razor. REALs are seen both as a straight-handled non-folding shaving device, and also as a transitional straight/safety razor that came with a slotted safety guard. Product was invariably of high quality.

Sales were good for several years and the company prospered by the diversification of its shaving line. Ultimately, though, the tremendous competition from Gillette, American Safety Razor Corp., and others was causing THE REAL, the flagship product of the company, to lose ground. One example of this was the certificate filed on September 13, 1918, for an increase in capital stock to help shore up the firm. Things may have continued to roll along for some time, however, except for the death of the then 73 year old Korn on June 7th, 1919. The firm named E.E. Kelley President; his leadership involved a lifetime of cutlery commerce, and with people like Tint Champlin on the Board of Directors, it was thought that the company might struggle along.

The products just could not keep competing, and as new shaving technology came on the market, the Korn Mfg. Co. did worse. It was decided that the company should be dissolved while the available assets could still pay off the bills. The first step to put the dying firm out of its misery took place on August 10, 1925, when a petition was filed for "Voluntary Dissolution Of The G.W. Korn Razor Co." It stated, "Company is solvent and its property is sufficient to pay all its debts. Due to the growing popularity of safety razors, the business is gradually declining. It will soon be insolvent. It is in the best interests that a temporary receiver be appointed to continue in his discretion. He is empowered to borrow $1500."

Cecil Horning, one of the directors, was appointed Temporary Receiver. He wasted no time in filing, on August 28, 1925, the Petition For Temporary Receivership.

On January 20, 1926, a permanent receiver was appointed to oversee the final gasps of the company. Soon it was no more.

Yes, a few fine old razors may yet be seen, and some old European switchblades carry the

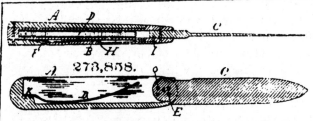

273,858. POCKET-KNIFE Geo. W. Korn. New York, N Y Filed Oct. 2. 1882 (No model.)

Claim.—The combination of the handle A, blade C, having holes O and E in butt-end, the lock-lever B, working on pivot-pin H, having pins I I in one end, actuated by the spring F at the other end, and the

GAZETTE.   March 13, 1883.

273,858.

fly-opening spring D, all constructed and operating substantially as and for the purpose shown.

March 1883 patent for a fly-opening knife.

unmistakable fingerprint of a Korn patent.

If you are in Little Valley, and care to see further evidence of a once-proud company, stop by the building that houses the paint shop of the Cattaraugus County Highway Department. It was the home of the G.W. Korn company.

This article appeared in Knife World March, 1989.

The NRA Eagle Emblem 1933-1935

by Kurt Moe

Soon after Franklin D. Roosevelt's 1933 inauguration as president of the United States various measures were taken to help deal with the Great Depression this country's economy was suffering. A National Recovery Administration (NRA) was created to carry out an industrial program intended to help in the nation's recovery. Some NRA goals were to increase commerce, production, and employment. Further goals were to eliminate unfair competition and improve labor standards. This National Recovery Administration was active for only about two years following mid 1933.

Many U.S. made products from that era show an eagle emblem on their packaging. As a general rule, that meant that an employer promised to pay workers a minimum of $12 a week for a 40 hour maximum work week. The eagle design has its wings outstretched and is holding what appears to be a gear and lightning bolts. The design is said to have been based on the American Indian Thunder Bird. The symbol was intended to show the public who deserved their support.

In a message to the people concerning the NRA eagle, President Roosevelt said in part, "...those who cooperate in this program must know each other at a glance. That is why we have provided a badge of honor for this purpose, a simple design with a legend, 'We do our part,' and I ask that all those who join with me shall display that badge prominently."

The Emblem was a badge of honor for those cooperating in the effort to abolish sweat shops and child labor. Every employer displaying the Blue Eagle Emblem was to have already raised wages and created new jobs. Consumers were expected to support those employer efforts and buy his goods.

Often a certain style of packaging could have been used by a manufacturer for many years. A package marked with the NRA eagle emblem, however, has a very great likelihood of having been printed during the period from July, 1933, to September, 1935. We could wish for the odds to be this good at one of our Minnesota Indian reservation casinos. Most collectors are delighted

Small boxes which held Gem, Smith, and Gillette razor blades. The boxes show NRA emblems to date from about 1933-1935.

when they are able to determine the manufacture date of an item this closely.

Those readers wishing to know even more about the eagle emblem may wish to read Hugh S. Johnson's book, *The Blue Eagle From Egg to Earth.* Mr. Johnson was the head of the National Recovery Administration and his book is the source of most of the Blue Eagle material shown here. You will note that in actual practice the so called Blue Eagles were sometimes white, brown, or black.

Another emblem was jokingly discussed by

those involved in the NRA. This symbol was thought to apply to those not supportive of the administration's efforts and was a design of a Black Buzzard.

While the administration goals seem patriotic enough, there were apparently many who opposed the NRA's methods. The Code System and the eagle symbol were said to have been abolished in September 1935.

The American Safety Razor Corporation marketed razors and blades under several different names after about 1919. These names include Gem, Ever-Ready and Star. The Gem Safety Razor Corporation of Brooklyn, New York, used the NRA eagle on several variations of its blade packages. The single edge blades for the Gem Micromatic razor had an NRA marking in white on the box end flap. U.S. Patents and dates shown were No. 1,739,280 Dec. 10, 1929, and 1,773,614 Aug. 19, 1930.

There is a larger version of this single edge blade box that measures 9-3/4" x 5-1/4" x 4". It shows much of the same information except that the eagle emblem on the large box is brown. This box is constructed of cardboard not much thicker than that used to make the small blade box. It would probably not be strong enough to handle the weight of enough blades required to fill it. My guess is that the large box was intended to be used only as a display.

The Gem Micromatic razor was a single edged razor, however, blades were also manufactured for it with two edges. While only one edge at a time was available for shaving, the blade could be reversed to double the number of shaves possible. This double edged blade is said to have been

GEM micromatic razor in its box. NRA emblem on box side not showing. Cardboard blade.

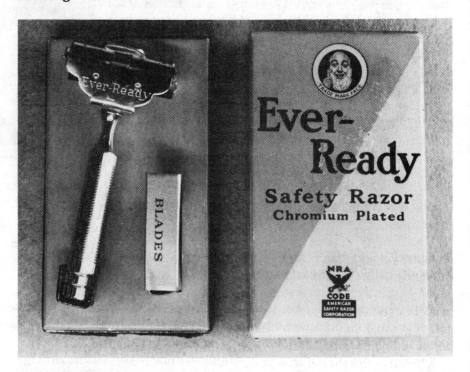

EVER READY razor in turquoise and yellow box showing NRA emblem. Cardboard blade box.

introduced in about 1932. The Gem Doubledge blades for the Micromatic razors were packaged in a yellow box with a red circle. One flap is marked with the same Patents #1,739,280 and 1,773,614. The box may have been already printed and

168

Two large Gem boxes about 9-3/4 inches long each were probably for display. Boxes show the NRA emblem.

warehoused when the NRA program began. In any case, the NRA eagle symbol was attached as a red, white and blue sticker on an already printed blade box.

The large version of this yellow and red box measures 9-3/4" x 2-3/4" x 6-1/8" and has the eagle emblem printed on the box. Its light construction also suggests that this box was intended for display only.

Another Gem box looks as if three small yellow blade boxes were laid side by side. A side panel reads, "This is a dummy carton. It is designed for display purposes and does not contain blades." There is a small black NRA eagle emblem on the box.

The packaging of a Gem Micromatic razor is silver, red, and black with its NRA symbol on the side. The razor was packed with a cardboard blade. Printed instructions suggest that the blade rest against two stop hooks and that the razor be held flat against the face while shaving. A separate tag makes the same shaving suggestion and tells how the handle should be twisted to open and close the razor.

So many of these Gem Micromatic razor boxes are seen that perhaps a great many were printed in 1933-1935 with the NRA emblem and warehoused until needed in later years.

An Ever-Ready razor has a turquoise and yellow box with black printing. The eagle emblem includes the words "NRA Code" and "American Safety Razor Corporation."

The packages of the Ever-Ready and Gem razors are of a similar size, about 4-7/16" x 2-7/16". They have wording inside both their lids including "Chromium plated" and "with two blades." Each has a silver cardboard box marked "Blades" that appear to be identical to each other. The Gem and Ever-Ready razors themselves were probably manufactured in far too great of numbers for them to ever have much value as collectables.

The Star Safety Razor Corporation of Brooklyn, New York, used both the simple version of the NRA emblem and a more complete version with its red and blue lettering. The Star Super Edge blade packages were marked "4 for 10¢" and with the same patent numbers on the Gem packages mentioned previously. These blades were intended to fit Ever-Ready and all Gem razors.

The Smith Safety Razor Blade

Co. Inc. of New York had a mostly red box for its Smith Double Edge Blades. The eagle emblem on this box was black.

A Gillette Blue Blade box is mostly blue with a King Gillette portrait. The printed eagle emblem is blue. The patents shown on the box range from 1,633,739 to 1,924,262.

While the blade boxes mentioned previously are all marked with the NRA eagle symbol, none of the individually wrapped blades contained in the boxes were marked with the eagle.

A genuine Keen Kutter Razor made by Christy is packaged in a light blue box. This box is marked with an NRA eagle that appears to have been stamped on with blue ink after the box was printed.

The box for the New Tark razor has an NRA eagle emblem. This 60 cycle, 110 volts, 5 watts razor was said to whisk the beard off like magic. The box is marked, "Tark Electric Razor Co., Inc., Long Island City, N.Y. USA." All Tark razors that I've seen used a special single edge blade.

The only actual product that I remember having seen marked with the NRA emblem was a

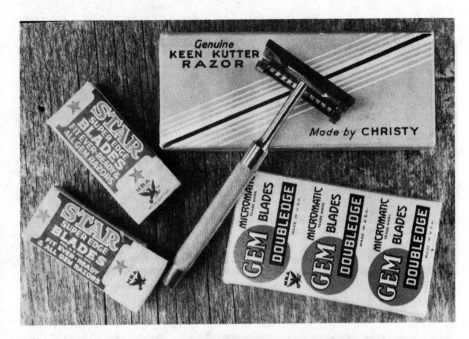

Gem box for display purposes. Two variations of Star blade boxes. Keen Kutter razor box. All marked with the NRA emblem.

magazine cover. Otherwise the symbol is usually found on the product packaging or instructions. There are indications in Mr. Johnson's book that the emblem could be used on letterheads, posters, and store window cards as well.

If sometime while reading about the NRA Blue Eagle symbol you thought of the National Rifle Association and its American eagle symbol you're probably not alone. The initials of the Administration and the Association are the same. I am not aware of any connection, however, between the two organizations or their eagle symbols.

This article appeared in Knife World June, 1992.

Safety Razors for Women

by Kurt Moe

With the popularity of the men's safety razors, ladies razors began to appear also. They generally fall into two categories. Those especially shaped for a day's use such as the "Curvfit" and the "Round Schermack" fall in one category. Those whose tiny size makes them convenient and feminine looking such as the "Kewtie," "Evans," "Elgin," "Vanity," and "Mayatt" fall into the second category.

Sometimes the tiny razors are mistakenly identified as salesman's samples or play razors. The large number of sharp surgical steel blades for these tiny razors would not be required for either of those uses. Some of the tiny razors still have traces of hair and soap in them. Also when one is fortunate enough to find an original box with shaving directions or see the advertising directed at the women users, one realizes that the razors were bought and used by women.

For the first time there was a social pressure on the ladies to remove their body hair. Swim suits no longer covered the legs and whole body. Advertisers suggested the razors as gifts and bridge favors or card prizes. They suggested that in order to be chic and dainty, a woman should be hair free.

An unusual looking razor that appears frequently is the "Curvfit," "The Womans Razor." The Sears catalog of 1927 shows a nickel plated "Curvfit" packaged in a cloth pocket inside a paper box. A 1938 Montgomery Ward Catalog shows a gold finished version of the same razor.

The razor's shape was designed to fit those hard to reach spots under the arm. The blades are about 1-1/2 inches long and were wrapped in wax paper. The blade boxes, however, are often colorful and show illustrations of ladies in swimwear or shaving under their arms.

Another curved razor is marked only "Pat. Pend" and gives no other clues as to its maker or use except the curved shape of the shaving head. The handle is relatively short and made of an olive colored plastic.

The unusual name "Schermack Round Razor," matches its unusual round blade shape. Its directions claim a scientifically correct shape for under arm shaving. This razor was marketed by National Production Co. Detroit, Mich. Its box and

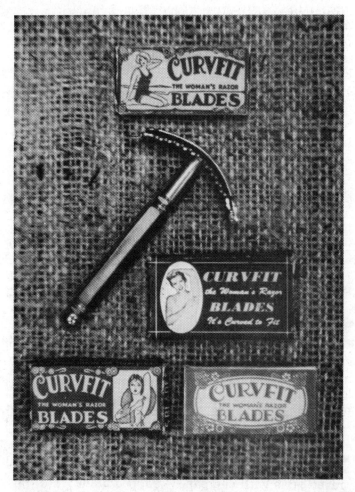

"Curvfit" woman's razor and various blade packages. Note the illustration of ladies.

directions illustrate a lady shaving under her arm.

The smallest razor that I've found has a hinged metal box about one inch square and 5/16 inch thick marked "Myatt Ladies Razor." Inside is a spring loaded letter "M" that may have been to hold extra blades in the lid. One part of the metal handle fits inside the other part for storage. The razor head is similar in shape to an old Gillette razor, but much smaller. It uses a blade about 7/8 inch long with three holes in it. The razor is stamped "W.J. Myatt Co. Ltd. Made in England."

A small leather pouch holds the metal box, perhaps to make it large enough to find in a purse?

The "Evans" razor isn't much larger. A gold colored example fits with its blades in a gold colored cylinder 1-1/2 x 5/8 inches. The razor is unmarked but the blades are marked "Evans Case Co." A second example is nickel plated and also unmarked.

Instructions found with the gold finished razor call it "The Miss Evans Little Shaver." The instructions are clear that this is considered a working razor for bathroom, dressing room, handbag, or travel.

The "Kewtie" razor is a common small razor. I've seen handles in pastel shades of blue, pink, and ivory as well as gold color. These little razors usually have plastic handles and hinged plastic boxes the same color. The razors are unmarked but the boxes are marked "Kewtie."

The cardboard box one set came in, indicates that the razor was "Scientifically Designed for Women" and was a Lapin product. A paper wrapped blade is marked, "This blade is designed to fit Kewtie Ladies boudoir safety razors made in USA."

The next razor takes a slightly larger, 1 inch long blade requiring only one hole in the center and notches on each end. Two styles of black paper boxes indicate that this is a "Vanity Razor," "A ladies razor that removes risk of cutting or after shaving burn."

The razor itself is unmarked and appears to be plated with real silver. Each razor came with one paper wrapped blade marked "Vanity Razor."

This next razor uses a regular blade but is small because it lacks a handle. It is packed in a red leather case. It probably is for a lady's use because it is marked, "daintee shave," and its shape seems suitable for shaving legs.

There are also ladies razors made by Gillette. In fact their "Milady Decollete" was probably one of the first. Later they marketed the "Bobby Gillette" to help ladies obtain smooth skin.

I once passed up an all wooden ladies razor with non-removable blade at a flea market. These collectors of advertising and old product packages sometimes cause prices of razors to be high.

A 1938 catalog illustrates and describes an "Elgin" razor for women in a fountain

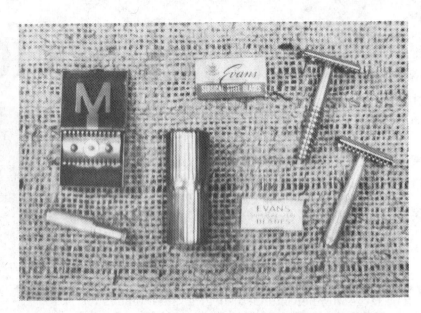

Left: Mynatt ladies razor in 1 inch box. "M" is probably to hold down spare blades. Handle comes apart to store. Right: Two Evans Case Co. Razors. Lipstick style tube held one "Miss Evans" razor and blades.

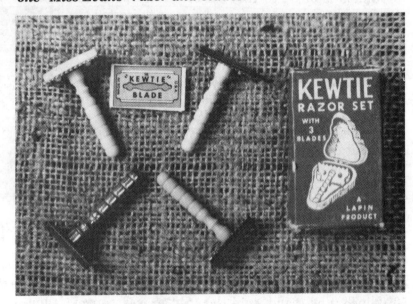

Four colors of "Kewtie" ladies boudoir razors. Gold and pastel blue, ivory and pink.

pen sized case. I'd like to bring that one home to my wife!

I've heard of a "Curvfit" model with mother of pearl sections on the handle that would also be a beauty to add to the collection.

Even with all the specialized razors for women, I'm sure there were ladies who would not or could not buy their own razor. I suspect that many times early morning peace was shattered by a man's loud voice asking, "Were you using my razor again?"

This article appeared in Knife World September, 1982.

Rolls Razor

by Phil Krumholz

There exists for razor collectors an unusual opportunity: the sometimes chance to purchase a shaving anachronism, a Rolls Razor shaving "system." An anachronism is something not in its proper place in time. How else could one describe the Rolls razor? In the late 1930s when the razor made its debut in this country, everyone had accepted the disposable blade single or double edge safety razor. Rolls designed its razor to have a permanent hollow ground wedge blade harking back to the days of the straight razor. When many manufacturers (in the late 1930s and 1940s) were spending big bucks to develop reliable electric razors, Rolls pushed its "semi" safety razor concept. When safety razor manufacturers competed heavily with one another to market the inexpensive blade (you may remember the "penny" blade prior to WWII), Rolls stuck to its "permanent" blade, expensive to replace when it went bad.

Author's Note: Apparently this phenomenon of "going bad" was not infrequent— particular care was needed to make sure the device was thoroughly dry after shaving since the high carbon steel blade rusted easily. Consumer's reports of the time also cast aspersions on the manufacturer's ability to properly inspect the blades after heat treatment.

The Rolls razor system was sturdily constructed, but its high price ($15) at a time when conventional safety razors were selling for a buck or two made it a luxury item. Perhaps the name gave this luxury connotation to sophisticated consumers. At any rate, the system certainly seemed impressive. It was produced at Rolls Razor, Ltd., Cricklewood, London, N.W. 2, England.

The razor arrived in a handsome nickel plated metal storage box or case which featured an embossed Art Deco design.

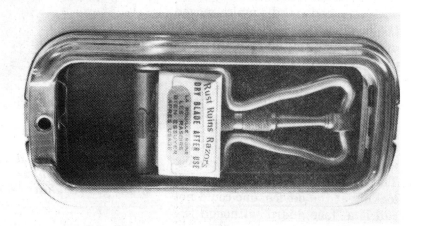

Rolls Razor in case showing stropping/honing mechanism.

Razor box, metal case and razor "ready to shave." System cost $15 when new.

Spring loaded buttons on the frame of the container opened lids exposing the razor and the mechanism for either honing or stropping.

Faced with the array of mechanical goodies inside the case, our shaver would immediately run to his directions lest he risk damaging one of the components just by removing them from the case. By religiously following the instructions, he could carefully remove the various parts of the razor, much like defusing a bomb in London during the Blitz.

The system consists of the frame and lids which form the storage case. The inside of one lid has a "Grey stone" hone and the inside of the other lid has a leather strop. The stropping/honing mechanism (it pushed the blade against the hone, and pulled it along the strop) featured a geared "rack and pinion" with attached spindle which moved the friction clip, friction clip wings, attachment pin– and all this was connected to the stropping/honing handle. (Yes, it DOES sound like a persnickety English two seater sports car, doesn't it?) The blade, with its integral blade guard, is detached from the friction clip and is screwed onto the shaving handle. The blade guard is aptly named– looking at the device, one could not call it a "face guard" although the razor was advertised as "the one blade safety." Yes, the guard functioned well to protect the blade from the face!

Results of users were mixed. Some reported excellent results while others felt the system was not any better than ordinary cheap safety razors. Most agreed that a month or more of practice was needed to get used to shaving with the necessary skill. Particularly vexing was coping with shaving with the blade nearly flat against the face, straight razor fashion, around the tender chin and upper lip areas. The buying public by this time was used to and liked the unfussy true safety razor, except of course for some old timers like my own grandpa who shaved with straight razors until the day he died.

Two faults were noted by users. If adjustment or repair was needed for the system, one had to package the whole device and send it to the distributor. The consumer, by necessity, had to procure another razor and supply of blades ANYWAY. The other fault was the tendency of the brass gear and clip device to lose its pressure because of wear, resulting in the blade not sharpening properly.

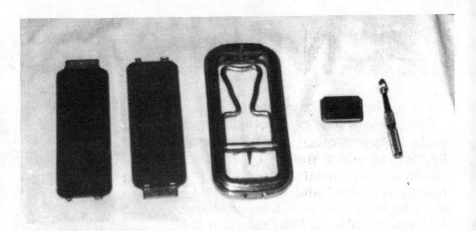

Parts of the Rolls Razor shaving system are from left: strop and lid, grey stone hone and lid, frame and mechanism, blade and blade guard, shaver handle.

My contact in England states "Rolls razors are very well known over here and are often found in junk shops. The firm was operating in the 1940s." The razor itself could be obtained in this country in the 1930s and 40's through Charles Levin & Company, 320 Fifth Avenue, New York, N.Y. As quality problems and general unpopularity grew, this distributorship was given up. As late as 1952, the razor could still be purchased or serviced, but only by dealing directly with the Rolls Razor Distributor at 338 Madison Avenue, New York City. Caution, by this time, was urged by a Consumer's Research Bulletin, which indicated that selection (of a razor) from dealer's stocks must be done carefully (and in person) to assure a proper fit between friction clip and brass roller.

Expense, inconvenience, and mechanical problems contributed to the ultimate demise of the company. The last straw was the inability on the consumer's part to obtain fast or reliable servicing of the product. Letters to distributor or factory were returned unanswered. The company was dead.

Other products seemed to have more of a following, but they couldn't keep the firm afloat. The Rolls Razor Company manufactured its badger shaving brushes, shaving bowl soap, two sided shaving mirror (plain and magnifying), Rolls Razor Strop Dressing, and Rolls Razor Imperial Shaving Soap Stick. The firm produced an early electric shaver, the Viceroy Dryshaver.

My contact states that Rolls also produced a mechanical version of the electric shaver. Several companies worked on this idea in the 40s and 50s for use primarily where no electricity was available, or where constant voltage was not available. These mechanical versions generally worked on the principle of the electric shaving head powered by sturdy windup springs. She states, "Rolls Razor produced a mechanical version of this (electric Viceroy Dryshaver). My dad had the mechanical version and used it for 30 years."

This article appeared in Knife World March, 1986

T. Noonan & Sons Co.

by Kurt Moe

T. Noonan & Sons Company of 38 Portland Street, Boston, Massachusetts sold several barber supply products. A Barber's Journal from May, 1925, has an illustration of a bottle of "Noonan's Hair Petrol." The advertisement describes the product as the best known remedy for dandruff and falling hair. It goes on to say that the product gives a beautiful luster to the hair and contains enough petroleum to stimulate the hair and scalp.

Hair was cut short and the wet slicked down look was in style. A second advertisement in the Journal suggested that barbers sell "SLIKUM" hair dressing for increased profit. If a barber's dealer couldn't supply him with this product, the barber was requested to write T. Noonan & Sons Co.

A third advertisement in the Journal was placed by the "Union Cutlery Co., Inc." of Olean, New York. The advertisement contains a complimentary statement by Mr. Noonan about Union Cutlery Co. razors. The ad copy refers to T. Noonan & Sons Co. as one of the largest, oldest, and most reliable establishments of the country.

T. Noonan & Sons also had razors marked with their own name. Their label is on a large cardboard sleeve that held "Copperdine" razors. The sleeve is similar in size to a box which held a half dozen "Case Red Imp" razors in their individual slide boxes. The "Copperdine" razors, however, may have had a different number of razors packed differently. There is a notation on the box of "Doz. No."

An ordinary looking razor has the mark "ZEPP" stamped into the shank. On the back of the shank "T. Noonan & Sons" is in an arc over "Boston, Mass", "Made in Germany." The celluloid handle does have a pretty butter and molasses color and has nickel silver ends.

A second razor has the word "Velvo" stamped on the shank and inlaid on the front of the razors black celluloid handle. The "T. Noonan & Sons Co." stamping is in three straight lines on the back of the shank.

The pin at the large end of the razor is protracted on both sides by a metal shield bearing the name "Velvo." The pin that holds the razor's

Advertisement for Noonan's Hair Petrol from a May, 1925, "Barbers Journal" and a T. Noonan & Sons razor marked "Velvo." The razor has metal inlays of wreaths and shields in black celluloid handles.

blade is surrounded by a wreath of metal leaves on both sides of the handle. Besides being unusual and more attractive than the ends of most razors, the metal wreaths also strengthen the handle at the pin.

The next razor's owner was absent the first time we saw it while on vacation. Several evenings were spent after the lights were out thinking about this beauty. We then back tracked many miles and found the razor to be for sale. The bad

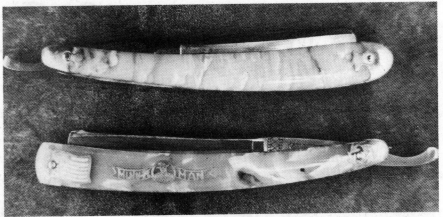

Two T. Noonan & Sons razors with celluloid handles. Top: Butter & Molasses handle with metal ends on a ZEPP razor. Bottom: Minute Man Razor with handles of mottled lime green color. There are also inlays of the bust of a man and the words, MINUTEMAN.

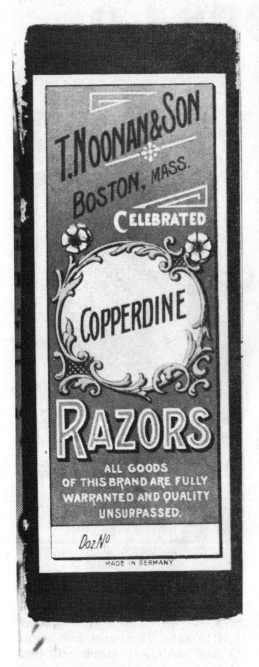

T. Noonan & Sons label on a box that held Copperdine razors. Blue, gold, red, and black colors were used on the white paper to make a bright, colorful label.

news was that it was a part of a collection that had been purchased as a whole.

A few years later another razor of this Minute Man pattern was displayed in a case at a national knife show. The razor was for display only and soon disappeared. The owner told me he removed the razor to avoid the frequent interruptions when people stopped to ask its price.

The razor has "Minute Man" marked on the shank. The usual straight line stamping was on the back of the shank. There is a nickel silver inlay of the bust of a man and the words "Minute Man" on the front center of the razor handle. The celluloid handle is a very colorful mottled lime green.

The blade's pivot pin has a wreath of leaves around it on both sides of the handle. The pin at the razor's large end has the same metal inlay of a wreath on the back side only. The front side has an inlay of a flag. There are seven metal strips with white celluloid between them. A second color of celluloid in an inlay is not often seen. The white celluloid has the remains of some red in every other stripe.

The flag inlay has only five stars, three red stripes and three white stripes. We could apply the faulty logic of some of the sharper "horse traders" doing business in the antique trade. This would be a pre Revolutionary War razor, in that case, because the flag doesn't have the usual thirteen stripes commemorating the original colonies. A more likely situation is that there just wasn't enough room in the flag inlay for thirteen stripes and the necessary stars for a United States of America flag.

While this is an exciting pattern of razor, it probably dates from close to the year 1900. Imitation ivory celluloid wasn't supposed to have been invented until about 1868 and this mottled lime green celluloid probably came years later.

The Minute Man inlay looks like he is wearing a coat and a tie. He doesn't look like a Revolutionary War Minute Man to me. Could the user of this razor have been expected to become a Minute Man by shaving in only 60 seconds?

This article appeared in Knife World February, 1985.

The Detroit Razormaker

by Phillip Krumholz

Frank Sherosky was a cutler. He was also a barber, a tool designer, a coal miner, an inventor, and a dreamer. He vigorously searched all his life for that elusive goal– Success. In the end, all he achieved were shattered dreams...

His story starts before his birth on March 30, 1910. Frank's father had claimed the name Sherosky on his citizenship papers, it has been said, in order to avoid a stint in the army back in Poznan, Prussia (now Poland). The original family name was thought to have been Petrosky.

The family lived in an area of mixed immigrants in Buffington, Pennsylvania known as "the Patch." Young Frank attended grade and high school, then went to work in the coal mines with his father. There are no illusions that life in those times in that part of the country was very hard, indeed. Frank married Josephine Tolistsky of Central City, Pennsylvania.

Frank was in his early twenties and the nation was in the throes of the Great Depression. Hard currency was scarce in Coal Country. On the eventful morning that Frank Sherosky left for the coal mines for the last time, his family had only $7 in the house. Perhaps you can imagine a young Frank Sherosky leaving for the mines, shirt sleeves rolled up, a kiss for Josephine, and a tin-lidded lunch pail tucked under one arm.

He went into the mines that day and nearly died.

A large boulder had shifted and

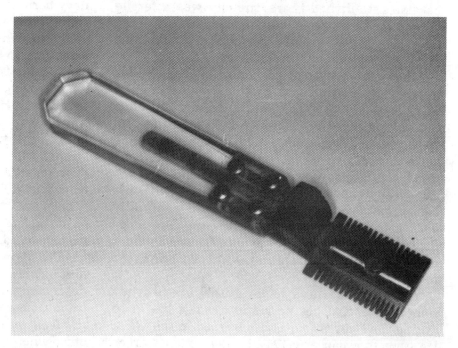

Frank Sherosky's first invention- a thumb actuated hair clipper.

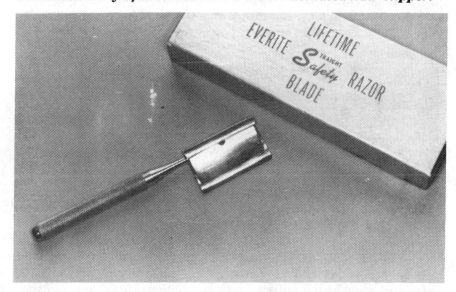

The Everite razor could be used straight or safety, hoe-type or transitional.

it nearly crushed him, so he left the job determined never to go back down into the big black hole. Convinced that his destiny lay to the West, Frank made plans to leave the next day for Detroit, where his brother Kelly was doing well. He took five of the seven dollars, kissed Josephine good-bye, and began walking and hitchhiking. Three days later he arrived.

Then, as now, the City of The Straits was a mecca for the inventor, the talented metal worker, the ingenious pattern maker, or experienced tool and die man. Even before the auto industry became established there, the city was a fertile ground for this type of man; indeed, that fact may have contributed greatly to why the city became an automotive center.

Frank Sherosky had an important goal on his mind: he had to find work that paid well enough to bring his family west. He went from machine shop to machine shop, and since work was hard to find in the early Depression period, I suspect that he represented himself as an "experienced" machinist. Errors were made and he lost his job...many times. He kept trying, and with his determination came the experience to eventually gain a toehold in Detroit City. Now Sherosky dreamed of becoming a setup man. That job paid a dollar an hour more than what an operator received.

"He had a helluva lot of guts!" his brother remarked about that period in Frank's life. Also during the Depression, Frank worked in the WPA. He went to a barber college and became a barber in a two-man shop. Later, he opened his own shop in Detroit. Always on his mind was the thought that maybe he could invent a better way to cut

hair or whiskers. He could also provide his Josephine with the money to buy some of the nice things she saw in the catalogs.

America entered World War II. Sherosky helped navy barbers cut hair on board the troop transport riding the Pacific. He participated in the invasion of Leyte and was wounded twice in the leg. He went back to barbering after his discharge.

In the postwar years, Sherosky suffered some heart trouble and he also developed severe cases of dermatitis. He left barbering because holding his hands and arms up for long periods of time bothered him, so he went back to the machine shops. The cutting oils in the machine shops aggravated his dermatitis. He had no choice but to continue working in them, and he made many friends and contacts that would help him later on.

In the late 1940s, Sherosky tried his hand at his first invention. The prototype featured a plexiglass handle attached to a "sickle-bar" hair clipping mechanism. The clipper was operated by depressing a large button on the top with your thumb. Sherosky was new to the patent game, and the feature he claimed was rejected by the patent office when a routine search revealed that German patent #631,433 contained a similar feature. Discouraged, Frank gave up on the project.

"I don't think he intended to invent," his son

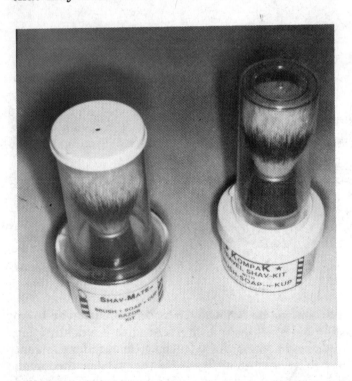

Sherosky's last products: the earlier KompaK Travel Shave-Kit and the Shav-Mate.

The Reddi-Brush and a similar Gillette product, the Brush Plus.

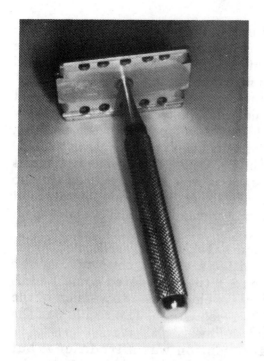

Sherosky made many other prototypes; this one was produced for a double edge wafer blade.

Prototype of a Marvex straight/safety razor. Only about a dozen were produced.

told me. "It was a natural occurrence from his machine shop days. Always trying to increase his efficiency so he could make more money on a piece/day basis brought out common sense, practical ideas. I remember that he developed a cutting tool for turning cork for fishing pole handles. He highly admired Charley Helin of Helin Tackle fame and spoke and dealt with him on a few occasions."

Sherosky continued to try to hit it big to bring prosperity to his family. His family by the time the Everite came on the market consisted of his wife, two daughters and an infant son.

The Everite. Sherosky filed his application for a "straight safety razor" on June 21, 1950, and patent #2,610,396 was granted in 1952. This unique razor featured a knurled, lathe-turned steel handle which could be screwed into the wedge type blade two different ways: the handle could be turned

into the middle top of the blade to form a hoe-type razor, or turned into the end of the blade to form a transitional-type safety razor. A sheet metal safety guard could easily be removed to create a straight edge razor.

The inventor didn't stop there. Sherosky came up with a unique storage container that held a hone/strop combination. The flat plastic box had a cut-out to help guide the user's hand when honing/stropping the razor. The instructions which came with each razor showed the address for the Everite Corporation as 14745 Manning in northeast Detroit. This address was the family home at the time. Sherosky embarked upon a campaign to promote his razor. He contracted with his old contacts at machine shops to produce the handles and he had boxes made up, instructions printed, and hone/strop units manufactured. Sherosky incorporated the business to protect family assets, and took as a business partner a man named Cy Lipcinski. Frank was akin to many inventors in that he was unsure of his business skills, and so his partner handled the business dealings.

Disaster struck in 1953. Sherosky suffered a heart attack which forced him to leave the machine shops. He took a drafting course and obtained a position at Chrysler. He worked in Tool Design for some twenty-five years until he retired.

Sherosky's son, Frank Jr., helped his father in their basement workshop. He did hand work such as packing, polishing parts, and running the drill press. He also accompanied his father to inventors' trade shows at various fairgrounds and exhibition halls. "I eased the fears of potential customers by showing them how easily the Everite could be honed," he said with a smile. "When one of Dad's customers would be reluctant to purchase a razor because of that reason, he would say, 'Come over here, son.' and I would go to work!" The Sherosky-Lipcinski partnership split up in the mid-1950s, and each man took a share of the Everite inventory.

Sherosky continued to experiment with different types of razors, including several prototypes which used double edge wafer blades, and in the late 1950s, he developed a razor he called the **Marvex**. This razor was similar in concept to the Everite, but featured a permanent thin stroppable blade. The patent feature was an adjustable blade angle, of benefit when the razor was used as a hoe-type. The Marvex was patented in 1960, #2,930,120, and Sherosky made up about a dozen prototypes. He gave a few to friends to shave with as a sort of market study, and formed the Marvex Razor Company. Meanwhile, Sherosky was still promoting his Everite razor inventory.

Disaster struck once more. Sherosky's wife Josephine began experiencing health problems, and in the next few years there were no private funds for developing his products. There were, however, trips to doctors' offices, cobalt treatments for the cancer that was found, and the inevitable death in early 1964. The crisis caused a suspension of Frank's razor company and an evaluation of his personal philosophy.

Sherosky was always a proponent of permanent shaving products, and he beat his head against the proverbial wall of a throwaway society. He felt there was a place for traditional, well-made products, and a commercial demand for them, as well. His ideology came through once more in his next enterprise.

Young Frank Jr. remembered his father tinkering at the kitchen table with a shaving brush, a liquid shoe polish kit, soaps and tools. This was in the mid-to late 1960s. Sherosky worked on this project for a number of years, perfecting it in his own mind. Perhaps the long time he spent was the result of his advancing years, perhaps he was more cautious because of earlier ventures, or perhaps the loss of his wife slowed his enthusiasm.

In the mid-1970s, Sherosky was actively promoting his patent #4,066,367. SherMark Corporation was formed of private investors who knew the inventor. Mark-Allen Company was given an exclusive license to produce and distribute the **Reddi-Brush**. The Reddi-Brush featured a squeezable base which delivered the proper portion of liquid shaving soap to the shaving brush top. The user could lather up quickly and easily. The applicator would furnish enough soap for a year, then a refill base could be installed. This invention appeared to be headed for great commercial success.

The product began appearing in army post exchanges and other limited distribution. Quality control problems developed with the product, however, when the soap chamber wasn't sealed per the inventor's design. Management problems plagued the firm as well, foreign patents took up much of the investment capital, and Sherosky felt the distributor overpriced the product and made it less competitive.

The Sher-Mark Corporation was doomed. About this time, Gillette caught the scent of the invention, and actually ordered some Reddi-Brushes, then developed its own version of the product in its research lab. The result was the successful Brush-Plus.

The final invention was a traditional but compact travel/home shaving kit which featured a shaving brush, razor and soap-container-in-the-base. Initially, Sherosky worked with a partner, Lawrence Craven, but again this partnership did not work out. Sherosky's patent #4,14,967 was granted and he began working with his son on the project. The first prototypes were called the **KompaK Travel Shave Kit**, then the product was developed further into the **Shav-Mate**. Frank Jr., a designer of automotive products by this time, helped financially and also with the design of kit components, vendor selection, prototypes and development. The father/son partnership provided the two with a business, Kompak Products, based on mutual trust and affection. This period was a special time in the lives of both father and son. The period would be all too short, however.

Frank Sherosky died on March 5, 1983, in Warren, Michigan. His final dream had ended.

Today, Frank Sherosky Jr. will tell you all about his dad, his invention, and his own dream of resurrecting the Shave-Mate product. Kompak Products Company exists at 40517 Michael, Mt. Clemens, MI 48044. You see, the father's dream has been transferred to his son. We wish the small company success. A dream is a terrible thing to waste, and it may just keep alive the memory of Frank Sherosky, the Razormaker of Detroit.

This article appeared in Knife World December, 1990.

Unsinger Patent Safety Razors

by Kurt Moe

Philip H. Unsinger made application for patent on October 17, 1908, and received patent # 932,518 on August 31, 1909. A group of safety razors that was simple, durable, and able to be cheaply manufactured is the result.

There are a number of razors showing the "PAT'D AUG. 31, 1909" marking on their blade clamps that are nearly identical in appearance to patent drawings. The razors use a simple unmarked single edge blade. Their bar safety guards and knurled metal handles are of similar design. Most of the razors themselves are not name marked.

Firms such as the Novelty Cutlery Company of Canton, Ohio, show a safety razor in their catalog with the August 31, 1909, patent date marking. The nickel-plated, razor frame and handle along with a blade holder for stropping and a dozen wafer blades were packaged to sell for $3.00. The same catalog shows the Novelty Cutlery's more well known picture handled knives and straight razors but shows no date.

Another razor example of an Unsinger patent is held in a dark green box with gold print. It reads "Price $1.00, Majestic Safety Razor Manufactured by Majestic Razor Co., Kansas City, Mo." A set of directions suggests that personal shaving is a more sanitary habit than visiting the barber shop.

The razor is suggested as an improvement over the old straight razor comparable to that of a lawn mower over the scythe for cutting

Left: Hodes-Hyman Spec. Co. "Adelene" razor marked with the 1909 patent #932,518. Right: Majestic Safety Razor marked with the patent date Aug. 31, 1909.

grass. The scythe is a single edged curved blade swung by hand to cut grass or grain. Sheep or goats would probably leave a lawn looking nicer.

The blades could be rehoned, however, the price of new blades at 50¢ per dozen post paid was said to be a price making it impractical to hone dull blades.

Another dark green box is printed, "The Globe Razor Co. Fremont, Ohio" with a Globe trade mark. The box holds a razor unmarked except for the 1909 patent date. There are indications that this firm could have been a sales agency for The Unsinger Razor Blade Co.

A third box is printed "Price $1.00, The Hayden Safety Razor made expressly for The Hayden Hardware, Dealers in Hardware and Implements. Sun Prairie, Wis." The razor inside has a slightly wider blade clamp. There is a card included with this razor giving directions for a perfect shave. It also described how to order a handle for 25¢ to hold blades while stropping them.

I would like to offer a personal observation here. The razors with boxes advertising individual stores were probably made up in small quantities. So few examples may have survived the decades that they may even be considered very rare. Because the razors in the boxes are not marked with a name, however, they aren't distinguishable from many other razors sold in boxes advertising different firms. This probably detracts from their potential value.

A "GLENN" razor with a wide blade clamp is marked, "G. C.

Mitchell Co., Aurora, Ill. in addition to the 1909 patent date. The dark green box has a hinged lid. Inside the lid is printed "Glenn Safety Razor sold by The Leather Store, Henry Lischefska, proprietor, Springfield, Minn., Price $1.00." This razor is special to me because it both advertises a store that was located in my home town and is a product of a trade with a collector who offered the razor because of that advertising.

Still another razor has a similar design and is found in the typical dark green box with printing on top. This razor is marked on its narrow blade clamp, "The Yankee." It is also marked with the Pat. No. 932,518 instead of the date.

The instructions for one of the previously mentioned razors indicated that finding the right shaving angle may take experimentation. The "Adelene" razor has its longer handle tilted at a small angle, perhaps to encourage its being held in a better shaving position. The razor's other markings include "Hodes-Hyman Spec. Co., Fremont O, Pat. No. 932,518."

Other dark green boxes have gold printed advertising for Hardware and Implement firms in Luverne, Minn., Burlington, Wis., Owatonna, Minn., Greene, Iowa, and Osmond, Nebr. All the boxes were marked "Price $1.00." Other products the firms dealt in were cutlery, automobiles, tinware, stoves, barbed wire, pumps, windmills, furniture, and harness. Patent #1,006,607 was issued to Phillip H. Unsinger of Fremont, Ohio on October 24, 1911. (Note that Phillip is spelled with an additional "L" in this document.)

Two sizes of razors are illustrated in the patent drawings.

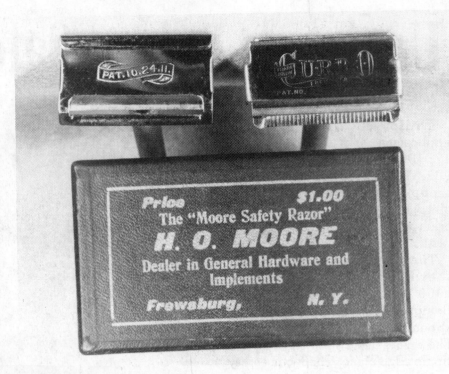

Left: Moore Safety Razor marked "PAT. 10.24.11" shown with its box. Right: CURBO razor marked with the patent #1,006,607 issued on the 10.24.11 date. Its features are those of the 1909 patent, however.

The smaller version was intended for either home or chiropodist use in paring of nails or corns.

The patent specifications describe that the razor's design is free of springs and corners enabling it to be cleaned easier in a basin of water. One change described is that the rear edges of the blade and guard now fit into a folded over area on the flat razor head. Another change is that the guard is now a part of the clamp holding the blade. In contrast, the 1909 patent design shows a lip against which the blade only rested. Its guard was instead a part of the flat plate attached to the razor handle.

A razor marked "The U.R.B. Co. Fremont, O. Pat. Apl'd for" uses the design changes detailed in the 1911 patent specifications. This razor was likely to have been manufactured from just before the December 27, 1910, application date to shortly after the October, 24, 1911, granting of the patent.

Two razors have "Pat. 10.24.11." in a ribbon marked on their wide blade clamp. The razors have a bulge in their handles near the blade holder. There is no name marking.

The razors are found in typical dark green boxes with gold print advertising. The razors are the Esser Bros., "Esser Safety" and the H. O. Moore "The Moore Safety Razor."

A quick check of references produced several other razor "brands" marked with Unsinger patent numbers or dates. There are likely many more such razors.

Finally we have a razor marked "C.U.R.B.O," trade mark,

Fremont, O., Pat #1,006,607." The Robert Waits <u>Safety</u> <u>Razor</u> <u>Reference</u> <u>Guide</u> indicates that the razor's marking is derived from the first letters of Unsinger. Razor. Blade. and the C. & O. of company. Peter and Philip Unsinger are said to have been in business in Fremont, Ohio.

The box is unusual to the extent that it advertises a pharmacy in Ithaca, N.Y. rather than a hardware store or an implement dealer.

While this razor is marked with patent #1,006,607 it does not use the blade holding or guard modifications shown in the patent's specifications. The razor instead uses the blade holding and guard system described by the 1909 patent.

The razors, blades, and their boxes as well as printed instruction cards found in the boxes are very similar in their appearance. In spite of the various "brand names" it is doubtful that they could be manufactured by many different firms. An Unsinger Razor Blade Co. letterhead indicates that the firm was a manufacturer of safety razors, safety razor blades & cutlery. I think it is likely that they made most if not all of the safety razors marked with the Unsinger patents.

Due to the excellent condition of the razors and even the boxes I suspect that some may never have been used. Collectors do not usually have the good fortune to find so many examples in such fine condition. The boxes all have the marking "Price $1.00." But would so many of these razors have been purchased and used so little? Could the advertisers have given them to customers? Could some customers have put their gift away and kept using their favorite shaving tool?

This article appeared in Knife World May, 1993.

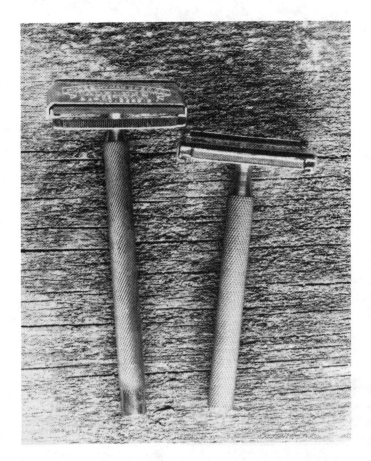

Longer "Adelene" razor on left and Majestic razor on right show difference in length and angle of handles.

Clark Blade & Razor Co.

by Kurt Moe

Osroe A. Clark applied for patent on January 9, 1909, for his safety razor using double edge blades. He was granted patent #933,020 on August 31, 1909. A safety razor based on this patent was manufactured and sold by Clark Blade & Razor Co. The blade used by this razor was said to fit the Gillette product sold at that time. The Gillette blade with its three holes would not, however, fit the Clark razor's projection which required a long slot. An obvious benefit of this to Clark was that

they could sell blades to users of both the Clark and Gillette razors.

The resultant patent infringement suit of Gillette Safety Razor Co. vs Clark Blade & Razor Co. et. al. was decided in Gillette's favor in May of 1911. *The Complete Gillette Collector's Handbook* by Phillip R. Krumholz contains several pages of information about this landmark case. Much of the argument before the court concerned the thinness and flexibility of blades and the requirement of external support necessary to ensure rigidity of

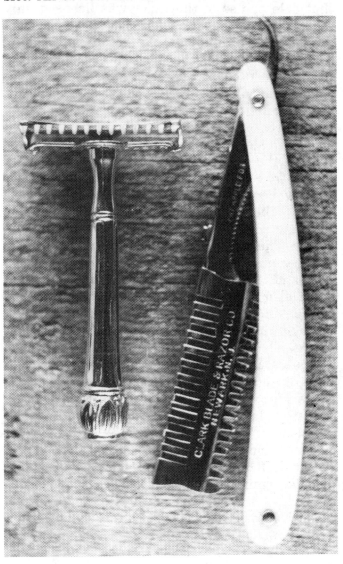

Left: Libby Gold Razor came equipped with Celebrated Clark Blade. Right: Clark's IUSA folding safety razor.

Libby Gold razor disassembled into its three pieces and label. Two metal blade boxes shown on right.

the cutting edge. *The Man and His Wonderful Shaving Device, King Gillette* by Russell Adams also gives an account of this and other patent infringement suits brought by Gillette in an attempt to protect their interests.

In fairness it should be emphasized that the defendant, Clark Blade & Razor Company, did manufacture their razor based on a patent which had been already granted to them by the U.S. Patent Office.

The court's decision did not appear to extend to thicker razor blades not requiring external support or to include single edge blades with thick reinforced backs. Clark Blade & Razor Co. continued to manufacture blades which did not come under the 1911 court decision.

Clark's secret temper hollow ground blades were made in at least fourteen styles. From the number sequence it appears that some numbers like 3, 6, & 7 were dropped as older razors came into disuse, and other numbers were added as newer razors became more popular. A blade from this large variety could be found to fit most of the single edge razors used at the time. While the following listings of razors that one of Clark's blades would fit could be boring to some, they show two things. One, the lists show which razors used similar blades. Two, the lists include both razors with familiar names and those whose names have long been forgotten except by the collectors.

Clark's No. 0 blades would fit Dandy, College, Young, Barnum, Nebulla and others.

Clark's No. 1 blades could be used in Burham, Dame Everybody's, Imperial, Roler, Vest Pocket, The Centaur, Shumate, A.D.S., and Grant Jr.

Clark's Silver King safety razor was sold for a time packaged with seven Clark's No. 2 blades. The set was in a plush lined box and had a price of $3.50.

A baby blue paper box with gold embossed lettering reads, "Clark's Trial King Razor, Newark, N.J. USA." The enclosed instructions tell us this is the same razor regularly sold at $3.50 but with only two blades included.

The user is warned not to condemn the razor as not satisfactory without testing the extra blade. Sometimes the one in the holder could be damaged by handling. To insert the blade, the handle is turned once to the left. The blade is placed under the side lugs but on top of the "flop" which is marked, "Clark's Silver King, Pat'd Oct. 10-11."

A December 7, 1910, application was made by Joseph Molkenthin Jr. for his improvements in safety razors. Patent #1,005,273 was granted October 10, 1911. This patent was assigned to Clark Blade & Razor Co. of Newark, New Jersey. The Silver King razor appears to have been made to this patent's drawings and specifications. Of primary importance is that it did not appear to infringe on previous patents.

On the same October 10, 1911, date J. Molkenthin Jr. also received patent #1,005,274. This patent was also assigned to Clark Blade. One feature seems to be that the handle could be pivoted at various angles to the blade holder. The Silver King did not have this feature.

The inside of the Silver King box lid advised that sale or use of the razor was licensed only when sold at $3.50. The lid further stated that this condition was annulled only for this advertising campaign. Whether this razor was given free or sold at a reduced price is not known.

Clark is also known to have conducted a Holiday offer that gave a Clark King Dollar Safety Razor free of charge to purchasers of 8 Clark blades. Dealers were required to purchase a gross (144) of the special blade packages to participate in the free razor offer. There were apparently window displays and other sales aids available for dealers. The stated result of these campaigns was to create a greater volume of blade sales for the dealer. The users of the free razors would need replacement blades on a regular basis.

In addition to Clark's King razors the No. 2 blade also fit Star, Ever Ready, Gem Jr., Sharp Shaver, Odell, Yankee, Very Sharp, The Eureka, Everyman's, Reliance, Columbia Junior, Shavewell, and Clemak.

Clark's No. 4 blade fit Auto Strop, Diamond Edge, Razac, Toledo, and Clauss.

Clark's No. 5 blade will fit the Imp, Clark's Jewell, Clark's Winner, Enders, and Wyths Simplicity.

Clark's No. 8 blade will fit Mark Cross, O.V.B., Federal, Klass, Penn, and Clark's Jewel is included again.

Clark's No. 9 will fit the Leslie.

Clark's No. 10 will fit Clark's Imp, Keen Kutter, Christy, Model, and Hoe.

Clark's No. 11 will fit Clark's Never Dull, Simplex, Weck, and Sexto.

Clark sold a razor very similar in appearance to the Weck. It was a folding razor with a long removable blade and guard. The razor is marked "Pat. Appld for, Clark's IUSA." The reversible guard is marked "Clark's Blade & Razor Co. Newark, N.J." The single edged blade had a thick back. It could be ejected from the holder by sliding a button toward the blade. The hollow ground blades could be stropped and were said to hold an edge as long as an ordinary straight razor. The razor, guard, and extra blade sets were priced at $2.50.

Clark's IUSA razor used the No. 12 blade which also fit the Shavrite, Graham and Simplex.

Clark Blade & Razor Company also manufactured blades to dealer specifications and would ship bulk or wrapped. Blades could be die stamped with a name. Paper blade wrapping could be custom printed with special advertising.

A black box holds a quality looking razor marked "Gold Razor" and two gold colored blade boxes. The razor is also marked "Libby" on the end of the handle. To remove or replace the blade the razor top is held and the spring loaded handle pushed into it until the cross bar is released. The handle can then be turned slightly

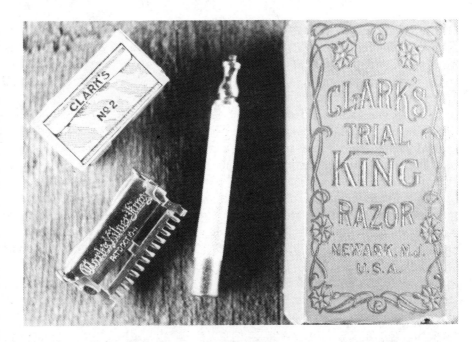

Clark's Trial King Razor box. Paper wrapped #2 blade. Clark's Silver King Razor marked "Pat'd Oct. 10-11".

and releases the blade.

The sticky label instruction is marked "Hotel Department, Libby, McNeill, & Libby, Chicago." The sticker advises that the razor is equipped with the Celebrated Clark Blade.

No. 13 was Clark's New Blade to fit the "Gillett" and similar type razors. What was the purpose of leaving the final "e" from the catalog spelling of Gillette? In any case the concerns of Gillette about their thin, double edged blades seems to have made a point. The catalog description of these No. 13 blades to fit the "Gillett" indicates that they were single edged and harder, thicker, hollow ground versions of the originals.

This article appeared in Knife World March, 1993.

Durham Duplex Razor

by Kurt Moe

The Durham Duplex barber type of safety razor combined the balance and principle of the old style straight razor with the modern ideas of an interchangeable blade and safety guard. Early Durham Duplex advertising suggested that the grip used on the razor ensured a smooth cutting diagonal stroke.

Many Durham razors are stamped with patent dates of May 28,07 or Nov. 7,11. Don't be misled by the patent dates on these razors to think that they are all old. While some of the razors could be from the early 1900's, catalogs such as Sears, Roebuck and Co. and Belknap Hardware and Mfg. continued to show folding Durham razors until the 1940's.

The Gillette hoe type of razor was actually patented before the Durham Duplex models were patented. The Durham designs, however, are sometimes called "transitional." Many shaving sets included a stropping attachment to hold the blade at a correct angle when using the traditional razor strop. For a person who could not bring himself to throw away a dull blade as suggested by Gillette, the Durham stropping attachment was desirable. By keeping the traditional straight razor grip and the concept of stropping the blade when necessary, the Durham design was an in-between step or transition to the modern concepts of an interchangeable blade and a safety guard.

Thomas Sheehan began as general manager of Durham Duplex Razor Co. in 1909. He was largely responsible for the

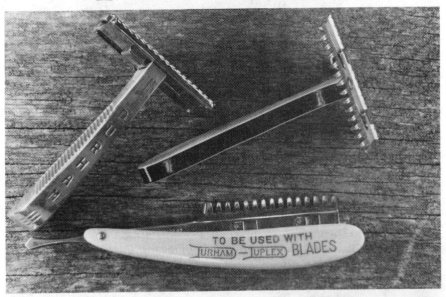

Two hoe style Durham razors in top of photo. Left: Razor using the unusual large Durham Duplex blade. Razor has aluminum handle. Right: Handle is imitation pearl on sides with a black edge. Bottom: Durham Demonstrator barber type or folding style of razor.

simplification of the razor design and the construction of the necessary equipment to produce Durham Duplex razors. The

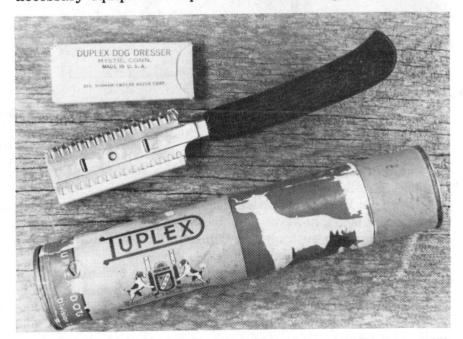

Duplex Dog Dresser shown with extra blades and cylinder package. This item was used to groom dogs.

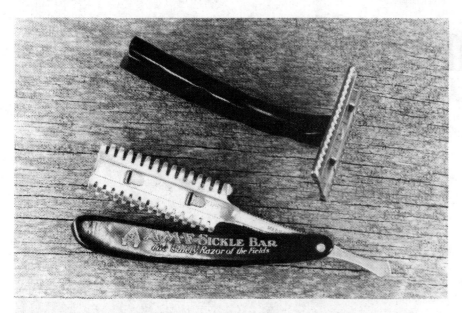

Two Durham Duplex styles of razors both using the same type of blade. Top: Durham Dorset hoe style of razor with faceted black handle. Bottom: AMF advertising razor in folding style.

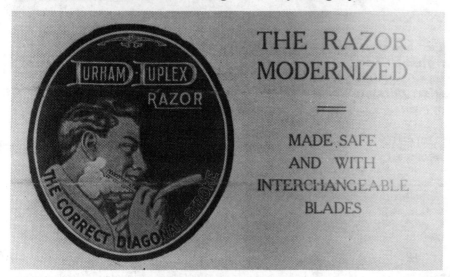

factory was said to be first located on Montgomery St. in Jersey City, N.J. In 1911 Sheehan became vice-president and director of the company and became involved in the selling end of the business as well.

A fire in 1916 crippled operations temporarily. New facilities were soon finished, however, and began to turn out 10,000 razor sets per month. By 1917 over five million Durham Duplex razors were said to be in use.

A marketing change had helped increase the number of customers using the Durham Duplex razor. The razor originally sold at $5.00 per set. The company decided to sell the razor for about $1.00 and intended to profit from increased sales of their unusually shaped blades. The Durham blades were longer than those used in most safety razors. The uniform excellence earned for the blades the slogan "The blade men swear by - not at."

Advertising copy indicated that each blade was stropped by the equivalent of 3000 inches of leather before being offered for sale.

The 1915-1916 Shapleigh Hardware Co. catalog showed a Durham Demonstrator razor with cheap looking black fiber handles. This demonstrator razor sometimes had lighter metal parts as well. The razor with a soap stick sold for 50 cents. The intention was that if a customer liked the blade and soap, he would probably purchase a better razor set and continue to purchase Durham Duplex soap and blades. It was this repeat business that was expected to be profitable. Most blades made by other manufacturers would not fit the Durham Duplex razor.

Not all demonstrator razors had black fiber handles. A variation of the demonstrator razor which found its way into our collection is marked on one side of the ivory grained handle, "Durham Demonstrator, Not to be sold," and on the other side "To be used with Durham Duplex blades."

Some demonstrator razors were accompanied by a coupon which was good for 50 cents on a better Durham Duplex outfit. A razor with silver plate instead of the usual nickel plate was one of those better outfits. Put up in a hinged leather presentation style case lined in chamois such a razor can also be considered collectable.

Still another Durham razor that I've been fond of is embossed in gold on its black handle, "AMF Sickle Bar Safety Razor of the Fields." This advertising razor was "Compliments of American Machine and Foundry, New York." It wouldn't surprise me if Durham Duplex had given AMF a very good price on these razors in order to have more of the Durham razors in the hands of shaving men and in turn have more demand for their blades.

Generally the handles of Durham Duplex razors are quite plain and the common models are very abundant. Nearly every antique shop has one Durham Duplex and flea markets have them by the dozens. The company was apparently very successful with their high volume production and marketing of their shaving device. Branch sales offices were located in Canada, France, and England. England became a manufacturing location for the holder part of the razor and later expanded manufacturing to include blades also. The large volume of razors produced over so many years by Durham Duplex and their simple but practical design makes the razor seem quite ordinary to many collectors.

Wade and Butcher is often one of the first names mentioned when someone is talking of razors. Over the years Wade & Butcher made a whole range of straight razors from the plain and massive razors to the ornate carved ivory and decorated models. It will probably be a surprise to many readers that in about 1920 Durham Duplex absorbed W. & S. Butcher Ltd and Wade & Butcher Ltd plants in England.

My special thanks to Dennis Ellingsen for providing copies of articles about Durham Duplex from the *American Cutler*. These articles from about 1920 were the source of much of the historical information on Durham Duplex written here.

A 1927 Winchester-Simmons catalog offered several Durham Duplex outfits to its dealers. A red handled folding model was packaged in a hinged white celluloid case. Other models were in black sheep skin or red leather folding cases. An all metal hoe type razor was offered with knurled handle and the same wide blade as the folding razor. Some of the hoe type razors were packaged in mottled blue imitation leather hinged cases. Others such as the Du Barry set were packaged in white celluloid boxes grained to look like ivory.

Other variations of the hoe type of razor can also be found. The Durham Dorset razor had a faceted black plastic handle. The Dorset was designed especially for trouble free shaving with brushless shaving cream. The blade package is marked "Durham-Enders Razor Corp. Mystic Conn." Even if a chin sprouted baling wire, this hollow ground blade was said to be able to conquer

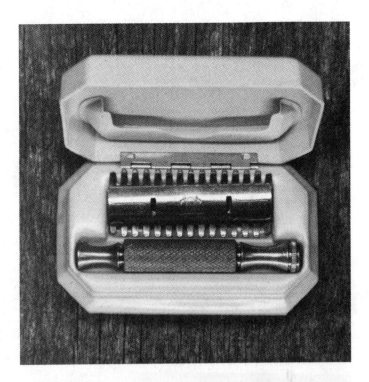

Du Barry set packaged in imitation ivory celluloid box. Same Durham Duplex style as shown in 1927 catalog.

it. Another variation of the hoe type razor had what appears to be an aluminum handle and was marked "Durham." Still another variation has a handle that looks like imitation pearl and has a black plastic handle edge.

An interesting Durham item is not for shaving at all but is for grooming dogs. The Dog Dresser could be easily mistaken for a man's shaving device unless one also had the orange and blue cardboard cylinder this item was packaged in. The razor and blade package makes it very clear that this item was intended for use on dogs. Individual trimming charts for dog breeds from Airdales to Welsh Terriers were offered as was a trimming instruction book.

Someday I expect that a flea market dealer will proudly show me a Durham Dog Dresser. Then he will either proceed to tell me the story of how his grandfather used to shave with one like it or perhaps offer a more imaginative tale of how it was the personal grooming tool of one of the Punk Rock singing stars! When I tell the seller that the Dresser was more likely used by movie and TV star "Lassie," the price will probably double. That's part of what makes trekking through a flea market so interesting.

This article appeared in Knife World November, 1986.

192

E.C. Simmons

by Phillip Krumholz

Resting on a gentle curve of the great Mississippi River is St. Louis, Missouri - home of the Arch, Gateway to the West. If you were a 19th century farmer, rancher or miner heading west, chances are that it was here that you crossed over and headed away from civilization. You could outfit yourself at Hawken's Gun Shop and also pick up any miscellaneous "necessaries" at one of the numerous hardware companies.

And were there hardware companies! A turn-of-the-century book on St. Louis explains it this way:

One of the few business branches, which even in earlier years, made St. Louis the center of an extensive trade, was the hardware branch. This was chiefly due to two specific causes: the immense river traffic between St. Louis, St. Paul and New Orleans made our city the distributing point for the North, West, South and Southwest and the boats running on the Missouri River secured the trade of another vast territory: hardware of all sorts, but especially for building purposes, formed one of the principal necessary commodities and therefore a very large part of freight. The other cause by which St. Louis became the great distribution point, was not less natural: the hardware manufacturers of Pennsylvania, particularly of Pittsburgh, sold a large part of their output to St. Louis jobbers and wholesalers and this gave our city a prestige in this line, which it still possesses.

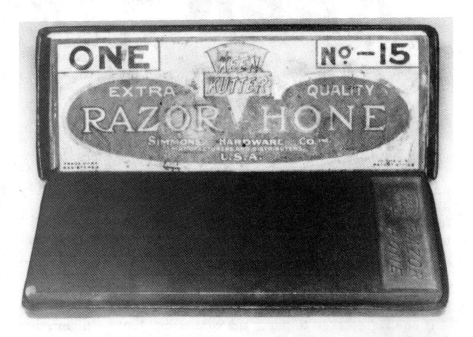

An early Simmons Keen Kutter razor hone in its original box appears to have been produced for export. The directions are in both German and English. (Photo courtesy Lon Furness)

Below: A new-in-the box Simmons Keen Kutter safety razor is shown between Simmons and Shapleigh boxes of razor blades.

Certainly, August F. Shapleigh's hardware firm was the oldest, being established in 1843. But E.C. Simmons is the most famous; the two companies became commercially and personally intertwined, as you will read later on...

Edward Campbell Simmons established his hardware company in 1870. At this time a "hardware" store sold much more than hardware, and usually a full line of home furnishings could be

193

KEEN KASTER

Ser. No. 386,745. SIMMONS HARDWARE Louis, Mo. Filed Dec. 14, 1936.

KEEN KLIPPER

For Safety Razor Blades.
Claims use since Dec. 2, 1936.

1930s trademark for fishing equipment.

1936 trademark for razor blades.

purchased from stock or ordered. Any cutlery items could be obtained, as well as a full line of tools. Appliances such as cookstoves, iceboxes, and heaters came from here, and sporting goods were also obtained in this manner. "Store bought" toys were purchased there for Christmas. E.C. Simmons was no exception. The retail store on Broadway also sold silverware and cut glass.

If one were asked to name the commodity the E.C. Simmons was most famous for, the answer would certainly be KEEN KUTTER. While this trademark appeared on axes, picks, hoes, hammers and hundreds of other items, it is best remembered on knives and razors.

At this point, it may be well to mention other E.C. Simmons trademarks. The company produced Senator, Royal Keen Kutter, Hornet and Barber's Pet straight razors. Another brand of straight razor was ChipAway, which is believed to have been inherited from Herman M. Meier, a St. Louis cutler of the 1850s who originally made the Indian-derived trademark popular.

Another brand used by Simmons was KEEN KASTER; this one was for fishing equipment. The fishing line under this trademark was produced by the Cortland Line Company, Inc., of Cortland, New York, who also used this trademark in the late 1930s.

KEEN KLIPPER was a trademark for safety razor blades, a brand less expensive and nominally of lesser quality than the famous KEEN KUTTER blades. Most cutlery items sold under the E.C. Simmons label were produced on contract by the Walden Knife Company of Walden, New York. Simmons gained operating control of this company in 1902. In the early 1920s, the Simmons firm merged (after the death of founder E.C. in 1920) with the Winchester Arms Company,

creating Winchester-Simmons. Cutlery products were produced under the KEEN KUTTER and Winchester brands at Walden for about a year, and then the small plant was closed down and the operations moved to the Winchester plant at New Haven, Connecticut.

The Winchester-Simmons merger lasted just a few years, until 1929 or 1930, at which time the companies became separate and unique once more. The association with Winchester, however, enhanced the public's perception of the firm, and old E.C. Simmons products today command recognition as high quality items.

With the advent of the safety razor, E.C. Simmons marketed the KEEN KUTTER and KEEN KUTTER, JR. razors using the Christy patent safety razor design. Christy, a longtime company of Fremont, Ohio (known today for its slide-blade knives) produced the KEEN KUTTER razor under contract, as well as blades, and some cutlery boxes seen today bear the legend that the KEEN KUTTER safety razor was "made for E.C. Simmons by the Christy Company."

Large inventories and reduced sales during the Depression put many companies out of business, and E.C. Simmons hung on until 1940, when the firm was sold lock, stock and trademark to the A.F. Shapleigh Hardware Company.

This company was no stranger to E.C. Simmons. Back in the late 1800s Saunders Norvell, a bright but apparently fickle young man, was working for Simmons as a clerk. Through a series of rapid fire promotions, he became Vice-President of the firm. Won over by promises of greater opportunities at Shapleigh Hardware Company, he made a switch to that firm within a short period of time, taking some of the brighter executives from Simmons in the bargain. As Shapleigh like to brag, at the turn of the century:

"...Mr. Norvell had for many years been a vice-

194

president of the Simmons Hardware Company. Mr. Kelley, a department manager in the same house, in which Messrs. Yantis and Gordon had likewise held responsible positions. The valuable experience thus acquired by them added to that of the Messrs. Shapleigh, who had grown up in the same branch from early manhood, gives this formidable association of active, energetic business men a particular prestige, and placed the rejuvenated old firm at once side by side with its most prominent competitors in the country."

Within five years, Saunders Norvell had become President of the newly named Norvell-Shapleigh Hardware Company. Seeing the value of the traditional name, the firm was changed back to A.F. Shapleigh Hardware Company a few years later, but Saunders Norvell had by this time left an indelible impression on the company, and HE had done well by IT, too.

But what of E.C. Simmons? It was certainly a struggle staying afloat in the 1930s, and there were some rumors that the company lessened quality to cut costs. Perhaps the public misinterpreted some moves the company took, such as substituting plastic-type materials for metal in some products. At any rate, an offer was made by Shapleigh in 1940 that the Simmons Company could not refuse.

Now, Shapleigh broadened its product line with the trademarks made famous by E.C. Simmons-Shapleigh had its OWN set of house trademarks for many years. In some cases, the products were labeled A.F. Shapleigh Hdwe. Co. KEEN KUTTER (and other trademarks), but in many cases they were simply labeled with the trademark itself. Quality did, truly, suffer during this period of time.

The E.C. Simmons trademarks did remain viable for another twenty years until the Shapleigh Company was discontinued in 1960. The myth of Simmons and KEEN KUTTER had built up in the public's mind, and the public stubbornly clung to that quality symbol while the rest of Shapleigh was slowly winding down.

It is believed that Shapleigh will be remembered more for KEEN KUTTER than for DIAMOND EDGE, the leading house brand. It is the lasting legacy of Edward Campbell Simmons.

This article appeared in Knife World July, 1989.

That Other Gillette Part I

By Phillip Krumholz

If we were given a word-response test, and the examiner tossed out the word "razor," most of us would probably reply "Gillette." Then, if the examiner prompted "Gillette," most of us would probably say "King." For, wasn't King C. Gillette the man of legend who singlehandedly invented the "disposable wafer-thin razor blade" and razor that came to dominate an industry which annually grosses over 600 million dollars? If this is so, what about poor George Gillette?

As the legend goes, King Gillette was the visionary who thought up the idea for a disposable wafer blade at a time when razor blades were wedges, permanent or semipermanent, for all safety or straight razors. Folks back in 1895 did not subscribe to the idea of disposable items as we do today. Yes, we use an entire razor today and after a few shaves toss it away, but at the turn of the century, King C. Gillette was asking that people throw away only the blade, and THAT was preposterous! Gillette's idea was to make the blades so well, and so inexpensively, that the owner could afford to throw them away and purchase more instead of trying to sharpen (or have sharpened) the blade in its conventional razor. Gillette wanted to peddle convenience, but the technology was not there yet to support his idea. He struggled in a titanic effort of "function follows form" to make people believe in his idea. Legend has it that family and friends scorned his belief that the idea was sound, thinking him

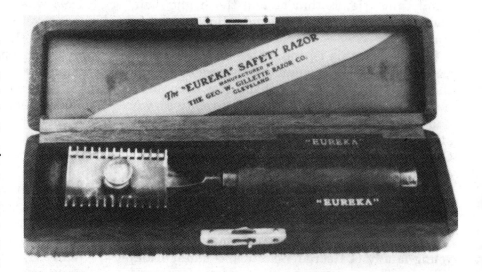

A George Gillette Eureka razor in its original wooden case.

a bit daft. They gave him little support, but he would show them someday! Gillette was also the butt of sarcasm among his small group of business and inventor associates. Metallurgists at universities laughed at his idea. Gillette persevered. Finally, engineer extraordinaire Bill Nickerson came up with a practical process for making blades of thin sheet steel. It was as though, since King Gillette dreamed up the idea, it was only a matter of time until technology caught up with his thoughts, that history caught up to his vision.

It was September of 1901, then, that the American Safety Razor

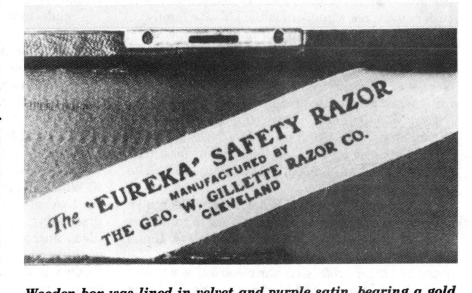

Wooden box was lined in velvet and purple satin, bearing a gold label proclaiming the "Eureka" Safety Razor.

Company (soon to be succeeded by the Gillette Safety Razor Company) was launched, and King Gillette was vindicated from his detractors' comments. Against all odds, he had proved to family and friends that he had the "right stuff," and this was the stuff of legends. How much of it was true?

Nowhere in this legend do we find the support and enthusiasm of his family. Nowhere do we find the sharing of ideas with them. Nowhere do we hear of the competition of one of his relatives, who had a product much like King's. So, let us do some stripping away of legend, to find the human Gillette and put everything in perspective. This account will intertwine with King Gillette often, but is really written to honor another razor maker who has remained unknown for over eighty years - George W., the OTHER Gillette.

The story starts out in Wisconsin, with the young family of George Wolcott and Fanny Camp Gillette. There were three sons: Mott, George H. and King Camp. The family moved to Chicago, but was wiped out by the great fire of 1871. From there, they went to New York City.

In 1879, twenty four year old King Gillette went into business with his older brother George H., and formed the Gillette Tap Valve & Faucet Company. The brothers were also associated with their father in the family business, the Gillette Clipping Machine Company, which produced clippers intended for animal hair. The Gillettes were all quite close, and all of them appear to be prolific inventors; not Edisons, mind you, but frequent visitors to the Patent Office. Cutting and cutlery were not strangers to the Gillette family.

King C. took out patents for bottle seals, a bottle capping machine, and (with his brother George) two 1889 patents for electrical conduit. Father George and brother Mott took out patents in 1893 for power applying mechanisms and flexible shafts. Mott patented a hair clipper in 1894, and the elder Gillette came up with a locking nut in 1895. Mott also took out an 1895 patent for a hair clipping mechanism, which he assigned to the family business.

It was 1892 when Mott Gillette's son George W. showed up in Cleveland, Ohio, all set to make his own fortune. George stayed with a relative, Linus Gillette, until he could get started in the city. His bread 'n' butter profession was electrical work, and in those early days, the electrical trade for home and commercial use was something of a boom

industry. In 1893, George moved to New Lisbon, Ohio, where he also worked as an electrician. He blew back into Cleveland in 1895 and lived at the corner of Webster and Brownell Streets.

1895 was a pivotal year. George's Uncle King was seeking a "disposable" item to invent, something that was used frequently and thrown away after some little use. Gillette had seen the tremendous profits realized by his friend who invented crown bottle caps, and he wanted a similar setup. As the legend goes, it was in 1895 that Gillette hit upon the idea (while shaving with a semi-dull STAR wedge blade razor) to produce wafer-thin blades. One account gives a Newton's Apple version where Gillette allegedly cried "Eureka! I have found it!" Also interesting is the fact that, at the time of his revelation, King's wife, Atlanta, was sweeping Ohio, visiting relatives on an extended tour.

While King Gillette was prospering in other projects and developing his razor scheme, George W. was involved in the short lived Gillette Construction Company. He moved to 1496 Central Avenue in 1896, and to 55 Bond Street in 1897. In 1899 he was listed as a foreman, living at 68 Auburndale Avenue. In 1901, he owned a sign business and lived at 221 Champlain.

This continuous movement with varied career patterns is typical of the man, who was described as "a restless spirit," and we will see more of the same as the years pass. In 1902, Gillette listed his occupation once more as an electrician. He also moved to 1309 Central Avenue. In 1903, he moved to 460 Willson Avenue and to 785 Willson in 1904. He made more moves than a person who never pays his rent!

Now, history is often a small part fact and a large part conjecture, and it is appropriate to play some "what if" games at this point in the narrative. According to Russell Adams' book *King C. Gillette - The Man And His Wonderful Shaving Device*, King told everyone who would listen about his idea for a wafer-thin blade. He was described by Adams as "enthusiastic" about the idea. What if: What if during a family get-together or holiday in the mid-1890s, the Gillette men were discussing, as usual, their current inventions, ideas and projects. What if King stated he was seeking an idea for something which could be thrown out but was used frequently. (In Adam's book, King was obsessed with the idea.) What if one of King's brothers, or his nephew, said, "Why

198

not make throwaway razor blades?" What if King liked that suggestion so much that he developed it?

Or what if: What if King Gillette was unsatisfied with his current shaving device. He wanted to make razor blades but was uncertain as to how he could go about it in an inexpensive way. What if one of his brothers, or his nephew replied, "Why not make them out of thin sheet steel? What if? We do see a collaboration among the family members for many other projects, despite the legend; even for safety razors, we see family help and encouragement. It is true that King's brother George H. took out a 1911 safety razor which he assigned to King's company. His brother Mott took out two patents in 1923 which he assigned to King's company.

One well known razor collector feels a difference of opinion developed within the Gillette family over the wafer thin blades. I also feel that nephew George held a longtime belief that wafer blades should be single edged, sheared from sheet steel strip, be rectangular in shape, have no markings, and feature no punched holes or other shapes which would require specialized tooling to produce. King Gillette, on the other hand, apparently felt the wafer blades should be punched from sheet steel and feature curved end shapes and three mounting holes, and be sharpened with two edges. This product would have been more difficult to produce and also cost more. This difference of opinion may have resulted in a degree of friendly family competition. While King Gillette's company was just beginning to do well in 1904, George Gillette was undoubtedly planning his own razor company, which would become a reality in 1905.

That year was a benchmark year for George Gillette. He was living at 6823 Cedar Avenue and working as an electrician. He and one of his close associates, Tom Thomas, filed two patents for electrical signs which changed letters, the type of

sign that was used for store displays and athletic events years ago. The pair assigned one-half of the patent rights to Sheridan Risley, another associate who appears to have been a financial backer. Gillette had been planning his razor company for some time as well, and that year he achieved the financial backing to incorporate his George W. Gillette Razor Company. As seen in the Articles For Incorporation, the company was formed on November 2, 1905, with the Directors being Sheridan Risley, B.E. Brodhead, D.C. Emmons, J.F. Castle and W.J. Monaghan. George Gillette was President, and Karl Zwick was Secretary. The firm was located at 709 New England Building, Cleveland.

The razor came in a paperboard box. Inside, the razor was housed in an attractive case made of thin wood and covered with a cloth material. Purple silk and velvet lined the case, and a stunning yellow gold label contrasted nicely with the furnishings. The razor itself was of transitional type, and the knurled handle ended in a head which was somewhat spoonlike. A threaded stud protruded from this head. The blade retaining plate fit over the stud and held the two single edge blades in place, while the screw nut held the plate tightly down against the blades. It is interesting to note the similarities to a King Gillette razor: The blade-retaining plate and the threaded stud have nearly identical dimensions to a Gillette hoe. The handle shows the "Pat. Pending" markings found on early King Gillettes. The workmanship of the razor is distinctive of King Gillette's workmanship. The cases were probably purchased on contract from the same company which made King Gillette's razors. Two packages of blades came with each new razor. It looked like a "class act."

The George W. Gillette Razor Company and its untimely fate will be discussed in Part II of that OTHER Gillette. Stay tuned.

This article appeared in Knife World August, 1989.

That Other Gillette Part II

by Phillip Krumholz

In Part I, we traced the beginnings of the George W. Gillette Razor Company. George Gillette, nephew of King C. Gillette, had started his razor company in 1905. His product had many similarities with that of the King Gillette hoe variety; dimensions of the threaded stud and blade-retaining plate are nearly identical. The workmanship of the entire razor is reminiscent of the workmanship displayed on a King Gillette hoe. The case is of the same construction. The "Pat. Pending" markings on the handle are done the same as the early King Gillette hoes. George Gillette was never issued a patent in his own name for either blades (single edge strip blades, two to a razor) or the ultra-rare razor, and his product was clearly an infringement of his uncle's patents. I believe that George Gillette was allowed to use his uncle's patents, and the Pat. Pending marking was a subterfuge.

But why would King Gillette allow the use of his patents to a competitor, even if the competitor was "family"? True, some competitive but friendly rivalry may have existed between the inventors of two different blade designs, but this is not enough. It could very well be that George Gillette aided in the development (or had the original idea) for the wafer-thin blade!

George Gillette incorporated his razor company in 1905, with himself as President and his friend Karl Zwick as Secretary.

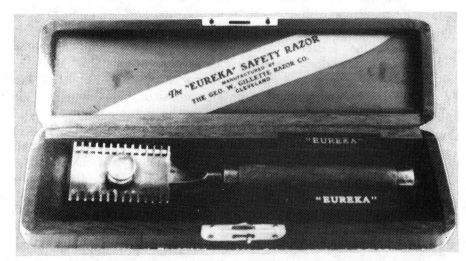

A George Gillette Eureka razor in its original wooden case.

Comparison of a Eureka blade with two early King Gillette blades. Note the Eureka would be much cheaper to mass produce.

Gillette probably met Zwick in New York or enroute from New York, when Gillette was traveling on business or visiting his family. Zwick owned a dry goods store in Oxford, Ohio and apparently was "cut from the same bolt of cloth" as Gillette. Zwick was described as being "sociable, a wanderer, who had a lot of restless ambition." He had grown up in Hamilton, Ohio and married an Oxford woman. Zwick left her to mind the store while he chased his dreams— buying dry goods stock in New York City, raising cattle in Colorado, trying to commercially produce and market chickens and gladiolus flowers, and managing a rice plantation in Louisiana. (Author's note: It is interesting that there were never any records of a Mrs. Gillette in Cleveland, unless they had separated years before or she had died. Yet, a George Gillette, Jr. showed up in town in 1910, working as a clerk, and living with Dad. Perhaps Mrs. Gillette was minding a store somewhere, as well.) It is thought that Zwick met George Gillette in the early 1900s, and they shared dreams. Gillette talked of safety razors and inspired Zwick to such an extent that the latter had to become a part of the enterprise.

As stated previously, the simple processing of the George Gillette blade as opposed to the King Gillette version should have made it cheaper to produce and to buy. Indeed, George Gillette sold his blades for fifty cents for a package of twelve, while King sold his during the same period for twice that amount. Of course, a shaver needed two George Gillette blades to make a double edge shaving tool - the customer was still nothing ahead.

The city records for 1906 show Gillette only as a "president"- that year he lived at 101 Elberon. On August 27th of that same year, he also formed the George W. Gillette Sales Co., located in Cleveland and formed for the purpose of "manufacturing and selling hardware specialties and supplies." The firm was capitalized at $10,000 and listed as Directors M.D. and A.H. Kilmer, E.L. Streiburger, J.C. Mansfield and A.W. Hill. M.D. Kilmer was named President and Albert A. Templin was named Secretary. Obviously, Gillette was positioning himself in a huge gamble to market not only safety razors but any other products that he felt were lucrative.

What about Uncle King? At this time, he was driving patent infringers out of business with a vengeance, but didn't bother George. In fact, more similarities existed as time went on. King Gillette offered, until 1906, the option to exchange six "fresh" blades for a customer's twelve used blades. George Gillette also did this. Both companies cleaned and resharpened their used blades, then sold them as new. To keep this good thing going, King marked on each blade, "NO STROPPING. NO HONING. NOT TO BE RESHARPENED." George Gillette stated in his ads, "NO HONING OR STROPPING." Both companies recognized the futility of this move as a plethora of blade conditioners, hones, and strops, mostly interesting mechanical devices, came on the market. To the customer's perception, these blade sharpeners were a good thing, for he saved even more money by doing what Gillette did and charged him for, and it was a fun way to pass some time as well. (Believe it or not, in pre-TV times people did things like this for fun.)

Several interesting things happened in 1907. Gillette, now living at 35 Carlyon Road, was calling himself a "commercial traveler." On April 7 of that year, he and Secretary Zwick filed an Amendment to the Articles of Incorporation of the George W. Gillette Razor Co. that stated, "The name of said corporation shall be The Eureka Razor Company, and the Article II of said articles be amended to read, 'said corporation is to be located at Oxford, in Butler County, Ohio, and its principal business there transacted.'" The document went on to state that the amendment was adopted by the votes of the owners at a meeting thereof, held on March 7th, 1907, at Oxford, Ohio.

This was a curious turn of events, certainly, and especially so if King Gillette really did say "Eureka!" at the moment of his revelation. The fact is, King Gillette's company was doing business at such an accelerated rate that he was unable to meet the demand for his products. King was still vigorously taking patent infringers to court, and was in the process of opening branches overseas. The belief the King "persuaded" George to change the name of his company is a logical one, brought about by concern that the Gillette names, and consequently the products, would be confused in the mind of the buying public. If you were purchasing Gillette blades at your neighborhood drug store, WHICH Gillette blades did you ask for? Also, while George Gillette's blades were of the same thickness and material as King's, they were inferior in grind, and the latter probably did not want the public's perception of his quality to be diminished. So, on the 7th of April, 1907, the name was changed to the Eureka Razor Company. On May 3, the George W. Gillette Sales Company was dissolved, perhaps so there would not be confusion with THAT company. (There was a Gillette Sales Company marketing King Gillette's razors, just purchased by the parent firm in 1906.) George W. Gillette left Cleveland once more, and did not return until the demise of the Eureka Razor Company.

The May 10, 1907, edition of the *Oxford News* listed the 58 new subscribers to the fledgling Oxford Telephone Co. The Eureka Razor Co. had phone #338. A small factory was located in the building which today houses the Capital Dry Cleaning Co., at 225 W. Spring Street.

An ad placed in 1907 was headed, "DON'T 'SCRAPE' YOUR FACE - SHAVE IT!" It went on to state, "so-called 'safety' razors either SCRAPE your whiskers off, or partly CHOP and partly PULL them out....And it is all on account of such razors being built *like hoes*." A direct slap at Uncle King's product!

The firm could not survive, however, even with that last-ditch campaign. Albert A. Templin (Secretary of the former George W. Gillette Sales Co.) filed a Certificate of Dissolution "the 27th day February, 1908, an amended petition... filed by plaintiffs praying that the Eureka Razor Company may be dissolved. This is to further certify that said cause is still pending in court." On December 4, 1908, the Dissolution was finalized and the razor company was no more.

George Gillette was back in Cleveland again. By 1912 he was an Assistant Superintendent living at 1384 Beach in Lakewood, certainly an exclusive sounding place. His son, a clerk, lived at the same address. The following year Gillette was listed as an electrical engineer living at 10621 Detroit Avenue. Gillette kept moving as always, and he was last listed in Cleveland in 1925. That year he ran an electrical contracting firm and his son worked at the same place. From there, the trail goes dead.

For collectors of cutlery, however, there is no need to go further, for the George W. Gillette Razor Co. had ceased to exist, and so too had the Eureka Razor Co. The firms collectively lasted only three years and one month - nothing more than an insignificant flyspeck in history.

NO
Honing
OR
Stropping

PLEASE READ

To enjoy the Luxury of a Velvet Shave, rub your face thoroughly with hot water and a cloth, then lather and rub your face with your hand; wash off lather with a cloth and hot water. Lather and shave with the EUREKA. To remove the lather while shaving, dip razor in water. When through shaving take razor apart; remove the blades. Dry it thoroughly and it is ready for the next shave.

Price of Blades ~~THE EUREKA RAZOR CO,~~ 50 cents a dozen
~~We will exchange for...~~
~~SUCCESSORS TO~~

The Geo. W. Gillette Razor Co.
OXFORD, OHIO

Advertisement follows the same line as King Gillette- no honing or stropping. Note that The Eureka Razor Co. is the successor to George Gillette, placing the ad in 1907 or 1908.

Maybe. But what if the idea for a "wafer" razor blade came, not from the fertile mind of King Gillette, but from an idea inspired by young

DON'T "SCRAPE" YOUR FACE—SHAVE IT!

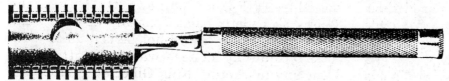

To prove this—
The Eureka Safety Razor is Sold on 30 Days FREE Proof Test

So-called "safety" razors either scrape your whiskers off, or partly chop and partly pull them out. This leaves your face sore and irritated. And it is all on account of such razors being built like hoes. Their handles are set so that you have to pull the blades over your face with edges set at an angle slanting toward your face. That scrapes, chops, and pulls your whiskers, makes your face sore, and not even the safety device can keep a blade set with the edge toward you from gashing your face occasionally. The Eureka Safety Razor is different. It is not built like a hoe. It is worked with the same old-fashioned downward gliding stroke of the clasp razor. It gives you a smooth, clean shave and leaves your skin smooth and your face unirritated, because the handle is set so that the blades cut your whiskers off squarely with the blade edges turned up and a little away from your face. This, with the safety device, protects you absolutely from cuts and gashes. Look at the cut. It shows the only Safety Razor that works with a razor stroke—that really shaves you.

Your dealer will make good this offer, or, if he has no stock of Eureka Safety Razors, we will make it good direct from our factory.

You can use one of these razors a month, and if that don't prove all we claim—don't satisfy you absolutely—don't convince you that the Eureka is the best and the only real Safety Razor made—the month's use you have made of it won't cost you a cent. A post-card to us to-day will bring you particulars, post-paid, by return mail. And the Eureka costs actually less than so-called "safety" razors of the hoe variety. Write us at once.

Address—

THE EUREKA RAZOR CO.   **EUREKA RAZOR WORKS, OXFORD, OHIO**

George? What if King picked up on that idea and developed it into a company worth millions today? What if King intentionally or unintentionally slowed the parallel company's success by a name change that ultimately drove it out of business? What if the Eureka Razor Company smeared the hoe-type razor out of revenge or jealousy? What if? What if? Intriguing, isn't it?

This article appeared in Knife World September, 1989.

Metal Gillette Razors Part I

by Phillip Krumholz

One of the comments I received as I was researching my book, *The Complete Gillette Collectors Handbook* (available through *Knife World Publications*) went something like this:

"There are all these styles - I don't know which is which or how old they are!"

Indeed.

So, perhaps you have some old Gillette razors in the drawer that you want to get. Perhaps we can match them up in this Part I of this article, find out when they were made and what the model was called. Go ahead, get them. I'll wait right here....

Ok, now we're ready. Let me start out by going over a bit of the "Legend." According to the writings of King C. Gillette, he was turning hundreds of ideas over in his mind, trying to find something to invent that could be used once, then thrown away. This "disposable" product idea was the result of the influence he received at Crown Cork, the firm that produced the pop bottle cap, and the advice of William Painter, founder of that company.

Also, according to the legend, was the morning in 1895 when Gillette was receiving an unsatisfactory shave from a semi-dull Kampfe Bros. STAR wedge-blade safety razor. He reportedly took a hard look at that massive, heavy, semi-dull blade and decided that, "I have done it!"

Variation old type from 1917 in a "Vest pocket" case.

Early single ring old type Gillette with leather covered case.

What he did was question why there had to be a heavy, usually forged, wedge blade supporting a razor's thin edge. He reasoned that all you really needed to support a razor's edge was a thin - he called it a wafer thin - strip of steel that could be better supported by the razor rather than the blade itself.

Further, he reasoned that if you could take enough material out of the blade, and process it cheaply enough, you could make a product so cheap that the customer could "use it once, then throw it away," thus insuring a never-ending demand for product (blades) as long as the customer lived.

So, you see that even in the earliest stages of the Gillette company, the real aim was not to sell razors, but rather to sell blades. But that is another story....

After Gillette had his idea, he had to make it happen. This proved to be very difficult, but it happened on the strength of his drive and determination alone, for there were no metallurgical processes at that time that could heat treat such a thin blade to make a hard edge, but with the resilience necessary to allow it to

American Button Company pocket set made for Gillette has decorative solid handle and rounded blade positioning studs.

New improved razor set is recognizable by the flat-milled guard and diamond pattern handle.

bend, or flex, in the razor. Metallurgists scoffed at Gillette. Finally, Nickerson at MIT helped him. Even then, it was not until 1903 that the first successful product rolled off the assembly line. Sales that year were a measly fifty razors.

Of course, these were the "double ring" type of handle. Look for the double ring (see illustration), since later "single ring" handled razors are identical except for this difference.

How rare are they? Gillette records (which admittedly were not kept very well at first)

suggest no more than 500,000 double rings were produced. Recent information that I have received indicates that the actual number may have been far less, perhaps only a quarter million. But they are rare - try to find one!

The Gillette Company produced the double ring razor until about June of 1906. Then, an improvement (probably to the machining operation) was put into place to switch to single rings, and that type was produced until the New Improved model was introduced.

Both double rings and single rings carry serial numbers, with one or two exceptions. From those serial numbers you can approximately date (using my book) the razor that you have. The serial numbers appear either on the screw-out inner "barrel" or on the top of the toothed guard. Exceptions: very early double rings had no serial numbers because the numbering system had not started yet. These will be stamped Pat. Pend. Also, very late single rings had no serial numbers, being inexpensive sets made up from parts after the introduction of the New Improved.

A new introduction was made in 1908, the Pocket Edition. The early Pockets were all produced by the American Button Company for Gillette, and are distinctly different. They feature solid handles with floral or other fancy embossed designs, and are quite attractive. The blade-positioning studs are rounded rather than bullet-shaped. They came in flat "pocket cases." While not rare, they are hard to find, and command premium prices because of their beauty and scarcity.

In the 'teens, Gillette brought out the short-handled Milady women's razors, the "barber pole" knurled-handle Bulldog, the heavy Big Fellow, tiny "vest pocket" sets, and the Gillette-produced Pocket Edition. All these can be tracked via their serial numbers.

Beware: It is a common practice for unscrupulous or unknowing dealers to sell "put together" sets that have mismatched parts. In my own observations, I would estimate that about one out of every four razor sets has some mismatched parts, case incorrect, etc. Only your knowledge can protect you from getting burnt.

A word about the Gillette-produced Pocket Editions: These serially-numbered razors featured knurled hollow tube handle construction as opposed to the solid American Button Company version. Studs were bullet-shaped. They were put up in similar (though usually thicker) metal cases. From this pocket razor concept evolved the Khaki-covered World War I Khaki Sets.

If your Pocket Edition does NOT have the serial number on the guard, but it DOES have the thinner cap-and-guard, then it is a transition piece made of leftover parts after New Improved razors were introduced. After August of 1921, pocket sets were produced by the millions and sold inexpensively throughout the 1920s. They are fairly common, and feature thicker caps-and-guards to avoid "corner bending," no serial numbers, and oftentimes cheaper cases or cardboard boxes.

The 1921 New Improved introduction signaled demise of the double ring and single ring era. This type razor would be called the Old Type by the Gillette Company - even the cheap pocket editions produced under the old patents in the 1920s.

The "new type" that the company was pushing as a premium razor was the New Improved. Starting at five dollars, a good chunk of change in the 1920s, the device was designed to bring the customer improved shaving comfort.

A dead giveaway to the New Improved is the flat-milled toothed guard with stamped serial number. Also, most handles were knurled in a diamond pattern. We'll discuss the New Improved in more detail in the final installment of Identification Guide To Metal Gillette Razors. So, if you haven't seen your metal Gillette in this issue, don't despair.

You'll see it next time.

This article appeared in Knife World June, 1993.

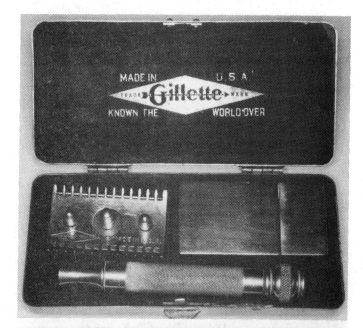

Two different 1920s pocket editions. Note the cap and guard are thicker than the pre-1921 version.

Metal Gillette Razors Part II

By Phillip Krumholz

Identification Guide To History was in the makin'.

The Gillette Salesman's Convention was held with much fanfare on April 14, 1921. Several tiny stages were set up, complete with little curtains. At the proper moment of anticipation, the little curtains were raised and on each little stage was a different model of New Improved razor. The salesmen were told how much better the new product was. They were pumped up. They were probably told, "and now get out there and SELL!!"

This razor was a "premium" product, starting at $5. It is characterized by a flat-milled guard with a serial number, tooth redesign, and several other minute improvements engineered to produce a more comfortable shave. These various models made up the premium end of the 1920s product line. As mentioned in Part I, Gillette also sold millions of inexpensive Old Type pocket sets in this time period.

The New Improved was a sturdy, dependable razor. It accepted the three-hole type of No Stropping - No Honing blade that had been around since the beginning of Gillette. But trouble was lurking on the horizon....

Keep in mind that King Gillette's original plan

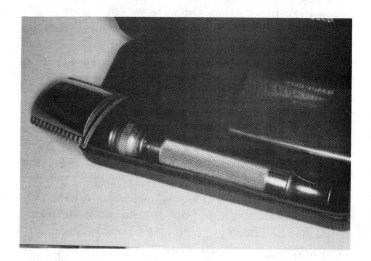

Two versions of Goodwill that were produced from old type parts.

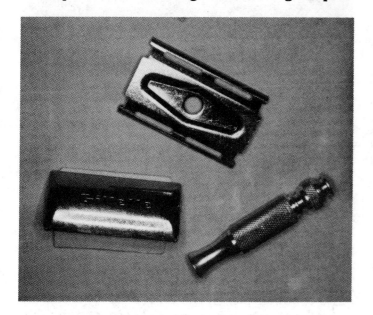

New razor set had ridge and matching slot in the cap and guard.

was to make his fortune by selling replacement blades, not razors. Of course, the basic patents had run out on the wafer-thin double edge blade, and many razor firms began emulating both the Gillette Old Type razor AND the double edge blade. We term these Gillette "clones." The blade makers were troublesome throughout the 1920s and stole tremendous market share from Gillette. The business of making blades was so lucrative that more and more firms entered the picture, and some high-production shops were set up in small buildings and garages. Blade cost was reduced by these competitors to as low as 1¢ per blade.

Coupled with these competitors, the Gillette–AutoStrop merger, and the Great Depression, Gillette was losing money at a rapid rate. Drastic measures had to be taken.

In 1930, Gillette brought out its NEW model safety razor. NEWs were characterized by a similar flat-milled style of guard that the New Improved sported, but the NEW had a groove milled in the flat center of the guard, and the cap had a matching ridge that mated with the slot. SURPRISE! There were no blade-positioning studs or mating holes in the guard. FURTHER SURPRISE! This change made impossible the use of the old Gillette three-hole type blade or any similar competitive blade! Owners of NEW Gillettes had to buy NEW, specially slotted blades, which were sold under the KROMAN or NEW brands.

Great quantities of razor parts existed for now-obsolete Old Type razor sets. Gillette used up these parts by producing various GOODWILL razors that were variously configured to use the slotted type of blade. These styles are pictured

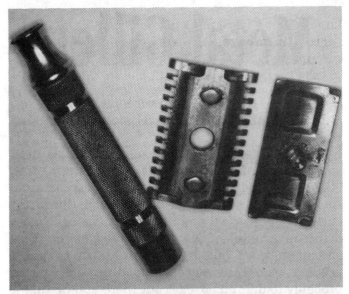

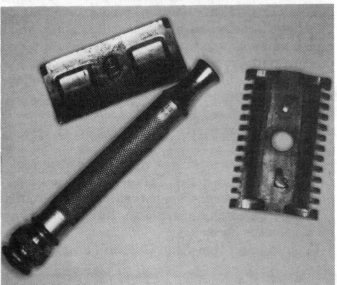

Two versions of Goodwill that were produced from NEW parts.

here. The special Goodwill Offer was a razor given free if you purchased a ten-pack of blades. (However, some fancier Goodwill sets are known to exist.) When Old Type parts ran out, a Goodwill was configured using unmilled NEW guards. According to Gillette records, about three million Goodwills were produced. The "Standard" Goodwill, made from NEW guards, is the most common, comprising perhaps half of the total Goodwill population.

NEWs were a different story. They were produced in tremendous quantities and are still quite common today. The trick is to find one all correct with matching parts and case, and in mint unused condition. Some NEW razors in the De

1934 Aristocrat TTO was the first product introduced after the Gillette/AutoStrop merger.

Luxe offering were put up in elaborate cases with serial numbers. These are infrequently encountered.

1934 marked the year that the first totally new product was introduced after the merger of Gillette and AutoStrop; the mechanics reflect the "gadgetry" of the AutoStrop influence. This razor - dust off the Aristocrat™ once again - featured a "barber pole" knurled handle design and a cap-and-guard that were hinged with little pins. Also, the knob at the bottom of the handle didn't take the razor apart when turned, but rather opened the hinges on the cap and guard! The innards of the razor were exposed, so you could simply shake the old blade out into the trash, and slide a new one from the pack. The emphasis was on safety since, if you were careful, you didn't have to handle the blade whilst loading or unloading it from the razor. The little knob was termed a TTO (Twist To Open), and this became the nickname for all mechanical Gillettes of this type.

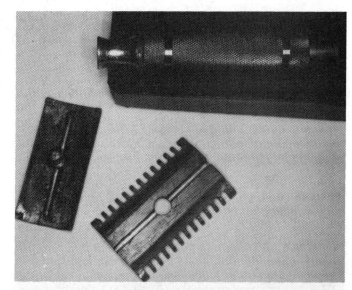

And there were more. The Sheraton. The Regent. The President. The TV. The Super-Speed. The Adjustable. Minor differences of style appear in razor and packaging. For instance, after World War II, the little rivet pins in the cap/guard hinges disappeared. Postwar improvements changed the style of hinge and the blade positioning bar had little cutouts to grab the blade from the new dispensers that were appearing.

Meanwhile, the TECH appeared. This was the 1938 introduction of the super-inexpensive razor set. Along with the TECH came the equally inexpensive THIN razor blade. This was the bargain shave that you could get for 49¢ complete. Millions of TECHs survive, and it is fairly easy to find one in the original box in unused condition for only a few dollars. The TECH lasted until the cartridge razor became popular.

TECHs were put up for sale in many variations. It was given out by our army in three wars, so you might find one in matte finish. Travel sets with TECHs abound. They are all characterized by a simple, cheap stamped sheet-steel guard, with a standard cap and a one or two-piece handle. Some are even made mostly of plastic.

The last major development in all-metal Gillettes came in 1958. This heavy razor, called the Adjustable, featured a dial indicator just under the head (later Adjustables featured the dial at the base of the handle). The dial made possible a setting change which positioned the

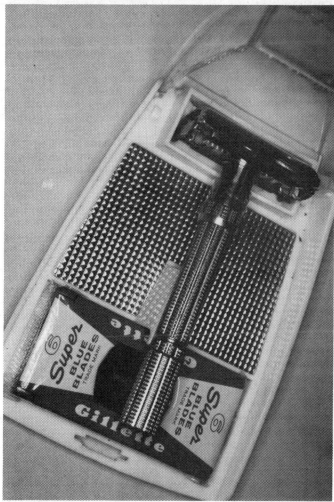

TECH razors were introduced in 1938. Gillette adjustable in case with blade dispenser.

blade closer to the guard, for a "custom" shave. Variations exist for the Adjustable, of course, one being the famous but shortlived Toggle Adjustable of 1960, which had a toggle lever instead of a TTO knob, which allowed faster opening and closing of the hinges. The complicated mechanism did not go over well enough to warrant the added manufacturing cost, so it was dropped in a short time.

Then came the cartridge razor, with razors made more of plastic than of metal. An era had ended....

This new period, beginning in the mid-1960s, reflected a changing world and a changing shaving world. You might have seen longhaired hippies running around, protesting against this and that, the Old Order, using NOT the metal or plastic razors!!

The world it was a'changing. And so, too, did Gillette.

This article appeared in Knife World July, 1993.

Gillette's Office Knife

by Kurt Moe

The courtesy shown to collectors by antique dealers often amazes me. This story begins with me talking to a dealer about razors at an antique show. Her face lights up and she begins to tell me about a sterling silver handle with a Gillette blade. As my face in turn lights up, she says the piece is packed away at home. Her home is half way across the country.

I wanted that piece so badly that I offered to pay for it in advance if she would send it to me. Instead, she would rather send a card the next time they visited Minnesota. Provided, of course, if she could locate the piece.

Time passes by and we get the card. Unfortunately, we had guests that weekend and could not make the six hour round trip to the show.

Now a year has passed. I am taking a thorough look at the antique show when I recognize some items but not the man behind the table. As I start to ask about razors, my antique angel arrives and pulls the sterling handle from under the table.

This was certainly royal treatment, actually better than I deserve. I was beginning to fear what the cost would be. That fear turned out to be groundless, however, as the price was modest for sterling.

But what was it? The piece fit in a blue hinged box which looked like it should hold a fine fountain pen. The box and the replaceable blades were marked with the diamond "Gillette" trademark. The inside lid of the box was marked, "Gorham Sterling Silver Handle."

The piece looked like a scalpel

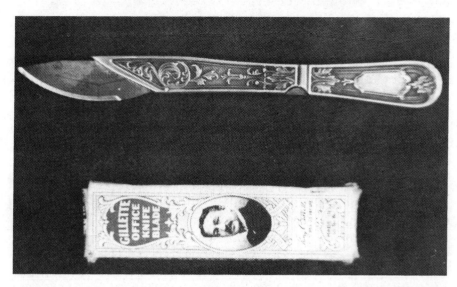

Gorham Sterling Silver handle with Gillette replacement office knife blade. Handle has a space for monogram box with King Gillette's likeness. Contains replacement blades.

but the Sterling handle with a place for a monogram made that use unlikely. The handle was marked with a lion, an anchor, a capital G, and the word "Sterling." This mark proved to be the trademark of the Gorham Mfg. Co. USA.

Finally my thoughts turned to a small box of Gillette blades a friend had sent me. For people with filing systems like mine, it means that you try to remember how long ago you saw something. Then you dig like an archaeologist through the pile until you reach that time period. I soon found the blades in the box were identical to the blades with the Sterling handle. The box was marked in three places, "Gillette Office Knife Blade" and held five replacement blades. Depressing a catch in the handle allows the old blade to be pulled out and a new one slid in.

A short time later another Gillette handle turned up. It was shaped the same as the sterling piece but made of aluminum. The handle, the blade, and the leather slip cover all had Gillette's diamond trademark. This piece was also no doubt an office knife but for someone with less money to spend.

These office knives are probably an attempt by Gillette to diversify in the 1920's. The green, black, and white blade package is similar to Gillette's razor blade packages of the time.

Thanks to a helpful dealer, I was able to add a nice related piece to my razor collection. Thanks to a helpful friend, I was able to identify the sterling piece and its aluminum counterpart. This whole adventure left me with a warm glow of happiness and general satisfaction.

This article appeared in Knife World March, 1982

Jacob Schick's Safety Razors

by Kurt Moe

Colonel Jacob Schick's dream was to conceive, perfect, and manufacture a practical dray shaving machine. We know that he did accomplish this feat. Along the way, however, the Colonel made several inventions used in the design of safety razors. He was also involved in the manufacture of safety razors.

Colonel Schick's military background and knowledge of the repeating rifle was said to be a large influence on his safety razor design. Several patents contained references to a case or a magazine containing thin blades in a stacked position. The blades could be stripped from this clip one at a time. This patent idea could easily have been adapted from the concept of a firearm's magazine allowing one cartridge at a time to be fed into a rifle.

In the early 1920's a firm named the Magazine Repeating Razor Company was organized. This New Jersey firm became active a short time later and placed their razor on the market in about 1926.

A long slender box holding one of the firm's razors is marked, "Schick Repeating Razor made by Magazine Repeating Razor Co. 285 Madison Avenue New York." Inside the box is a tube not much longer and about the same diameter as a lipstick tube. This razor is not much larger than the Elgin or Arnold pen style razors. The tube is of an aluminum like alloy. The vented cap pulls off to reveal the brass shaving part of the razor. The blade guard is a smooth bar.

The handle holds a magazine of extra blades. The handle is marked on the end, "Schick," and has a trademark that looks like a razor blade with wings. The end of the handle can be pulled out, and when it is pushed in again to the normal position, a new blade is injected into the shaving part of the razor. It is not necessary to touch the new blade during this process. The old blade is simply pushed out when the new blade is injected so it is not necessary to touch it either. The brass portion of the razor can then be turned a quarter turn to be ready for shaving.

Compare the simplicity and safety of this procedure to that necessary to change the blades in other razors of the time. The handle on an old style three piece razor was turned off to disassemble the razor. Possibly the old blade could be shaken loose without the use of fingers. The new blade, however, must have its protective paper covering removed. It must then be correctly placed and adjusted between the razor head parts and the handle screwed back on. There was great risk of drawing blood before the shaving even started. This risk was removed by the Schick system.

The round tube aluminum alloy razor is marked on the brass head portion with a patent date of 5-18-26. The drawings of patent #1,584,811 are not very similar to the round tube razor bearing the patent's date. The patent does describe a razor with a magazine of narrow blades. Individual blades need not be handled by anyone after packing at the factory.

The Literary Digest for June 9, 1928, shows an advertisement for a Schick Repeating Razor. This razor was approximately of the same length as the previous razor but was the squared version. The maker was shown to be the Magazine Repeating Razor Co. at the same New York address. It was not necessary to handle dangerous blades with this razor either. There were twenty blades stored in the handle waiting to be dispensed when needed. A silver plate razor was offered at $5 and a gold plate razor could be ordered for $7.50. An extra clip of 20 blades was 75¢.

A razor is packaged in a slim box marked "Magazine Razor, The Simplified Schick Automatic." This razor appears to be of the same construction as that advertised in 1928. The whole razor is of a brass color but has a more complicated geometric design on the squared body holding extra blades. The body is marked on opposite sides "Schick." The grip to inject new blades is marked "Blade." Razors of this design are known to have two different types of blade guards. One type has open fingers in a sort of beard comb. The other type has a closed bar with finger like bumps on it.

On its brass shaving head the razor is marked with the patent number 1,452,935. This patent refers to a magazine of wafer blades held in a razor's handle to be fed into shaving position when desired. The used blade could be ejected as well. The patent on this razor was granted on April 24, 1923.

This 1923 date of course, precedes the patent date of 5-18-26 found on the round tube type razor. Most sources consider the round tube style to be older than the square style. The round tube's design is more simple and the handle has less decoration. Generally, devices with a patent date on them are thought to precede those devices showing a patent number. The dates of the patents shown on these razors do, however, create confusion and some doubt as to which was actually manufactured first.

All three styles of these razors were able to have their shaving heads turned 90 degrees to a loading and storage position. The resulting small 4-1/4 inch and streamlined package could easily be carried in the pocket.

In about 1928, the manufacturing equipment was moved to Connecticut by the new

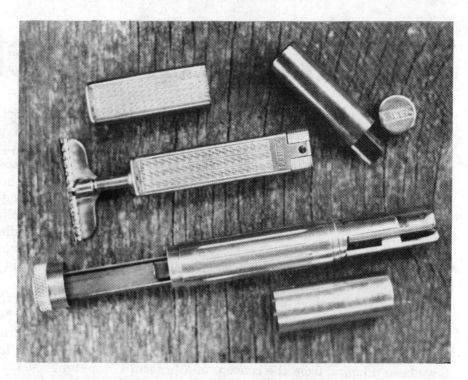

Top: Razor marked with patent #1,452,935 issued in 1923. Cylinder holds extra blades. Brass head is shown in shaving position. Bottom: Round tube razor marked 5-18-26 shown with handle end extended. Brass head is in loading position. Pushing in on handle loads new blade.

owner, American Chain & Cable Company. At some point the blade magazine was separated from the razor itself. The concept of the more common Schick Injector razor was born.

This article appeared in Knife World July, 1991.

Wade & Butcher

by Kurt Moe

Once in awhile something happens that bruises my collector's ego. In this case it was a Gun & Knife show advertisement that specified "No Razors." Wade & Butcher is one of those firms that I feel helps legitimize razors at least to knife collectors if not also to gun collectors.

Like many other blade collectors, I enjoy guns and have had a "National Rifle Association" membership for some years. I feel that those who collect guns, knives, or razors have common interests and should pull together. But for some reason that I don't understand, razors and even knives are not always welcome at weapon shows.

A possible objection to razors might be that they aren't very old. John Goins in his "Pocketknives" book shows the Butcher family began making razors in about 1730. That should be long enough ago to qualify a lot of razors as real antiques. Many other razors were manufactured during the same era that highly collectible Colt and Winchester firearms were made.

Another objection to razors might be that they are ugly. A person saying that probably has never held a Wade & Butcher razor with delicately carved mother of pearl handles. This carved razor has a pattern seen on several other Wade & Butcher pearl razors. There are two pieces of pearl pinned to each nickel silver liner. The tang end pearl is fully carved on both sides and the liner follows the contour of the

Wade & Butcher razors. Top: Carved mother of pearl handle. Center: Sterling razor that has traces of gold wash on the handle. Bottom: Ivory handle with monogram.

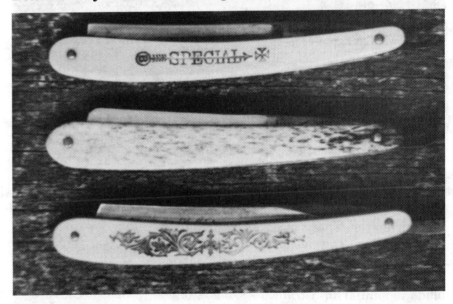

Top: Celluloid handle with Wade & Butcher trademark embossed as shown in 1927 catalog. Center: Coarse bone handle. Shank has illustration of bow. Bottom: Celluloid handle with gold embossed scroll.

pearl. The blade is marked "Wade & Butcher" in a ribbon.

Some people might feel that razors are too common and made of cheap plastic. They certainly haven't tried to acquire a matched pair of Wade & Butcher razors with carved ivory handles

217

Two Wade & Butcher razors. Top: Black celluloid handle with "Sterling" inlay. Bottom: Razor with dark horn handle and pewter like inlays.

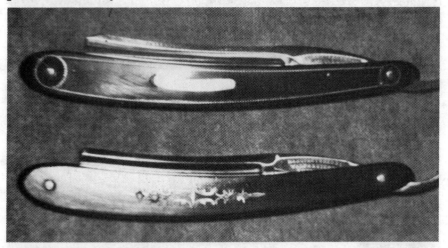

Two dark horn Wade & Butcher razors with mother of pearl inlays. Top handle also has twisted silver wire around pins and perimeter of razor.

decorated with over a hundred silver pins.

The ivory handles of this pair are carved at the ends and around the perimeter. There is an escutcheon surrounded with over a hundred pins. The design using different sized silver pins must have been the result of many hours of labor.

The blade in these razors is something special as well. The blade is similar to a frameback blade but is in one piece. At the middle of the blade the wide wedge suddenly narrows to a thin wafer blade for the last 1/3 inch. The blade is deeply stamped, "Superior Feather/ Edge concave Razor/ Manufactured by/ Wade & Butcher." The razor shank is stamped "Set ready for use/ Universally/ Approved."

In fact, most Wade & Butcher razors have natural handles of pearl, ivory, bone, or horn. The same materials that are used in the highly thought of pistol grips as well as knife handles.

Still another objection to razors could be that they were too

functional to be a source of pride to their users. There are examples of monograms artfully carved into ivory or engraved on sterling handles and examples of sets suitable for presentation. The quality Wade & Butcher razors were obviously thought good enough to serve as gifts or as deserving of a monogram as would the family glassware or sterling flatware.

One of the most ornate Wade & Butcher razors is marked sterling inside the handles and is marked sterling again in the deep relief pattern. Other hallmarks are difficult to read because they are also stamped into the pattern. Even the hinge pin is the center of one of the flowers.

Seven day sets are a desirable item for any razor collection. One set has ivory handles and appears to be marked with a monogram more artfully designed than legible.

Another seven day set of Wade & Butcher razors having similarly shaped ivory handles has some unusual markings. The back of the shank reads, "Curley N.Y. Aristos." The long tang extends beyond the pin nearly 1-1/2 inches and is marked "improved tang."

There are several shank stampings that are common. One variation is "Manufactured/ by/ Wade & Butcher/ Sheffield" followed by the firm's "B" in a circle, arrow, cross trademark. The word "England" is sometimes included, while sometimes the phrase "Manufactured by" is omitted. Older razors may have a crown "R" Wade & Butcher mark. It's a fault of several razors examined that the letter before the crown was not struck well or was worn off later. If a "G", "W", or "V" preceded the crown it would aid in dating the razor. The "GR" stamping was used during the reign of King George IV. The stamping became "WR" with William IV in 1830, and "VR" with the beginning of Queen Victoria's reign in 1837.

One interesting shank stamping is "Wade & Butcher/ Blank for concaving, Sheffield, England" and the firm's trademark.

Another shank has only an illustration of a bow. Wade & Butcher had what they called "The Original & Only Genuine Bow Razor." They used that etching on blades and the illustration of a bow.

There are certainly large variations in sizes of Wade & Butcher razors. A huge razor with heavy horn handle and a heavy wedge blade often turns out to be a Wade & Butcher. Some blades are as wide as 1-1/8 inch. There are other razors bearing the firm's name with long, narrow 7/16 inch blades as well as smaller moustache razors.

Various materials can be found as washers, caps or pin covers that surround the pin. Large brass or iron covers are common on the large old razors and probably helped strengthen the handle. Horn and ivory both tend to crack with their grain and need all the help they can get.

One razor does not have a clear stamping yet enough of it remains to convince me that it reads "Wade & Butcher." The blades and black horn handle are ordinary enough. However the pin covers are small mother of pearl buttons that appear to be slightly inlaid.

Some razors have pins that are similar to rivets used in knife handles. They do not have the covers. The pearl and sterling razors, the two seven day sets, and the carved ivory pair of razors described here have that type of

Pair of Wade & Butcher razors with carved ivory handles, inlaid silver pins and "Feather edge" blades. Front and back sides of the razor handle shown.

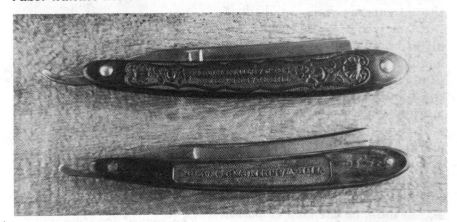

Wade & Butcher razors with pressed horn handles. Top: "The Washington Razor." Bottom: "The Real Kentuck Self Acting Shaver."

pin.

Some blades are marked deeply with decorations. One such blade has a number of masonic symbols. Another blade is deeply marked "Moustache Razor" in a ribbon. An illustration of a man sporting a very long handle bar moustache is at the top center.

Many razors leave no doubt that they were especially manufactured for the U.S. market. The deeply marked blade with an eagle and the words, "American Razor" is one.

The 1915 Shapleigh Hardware catalog shows a black rubber handled razor called the Wade & Butcher Special. Its blade is etched "Exclusively sold by Shapleigh Hdwe Co. St. Louis USA."

Some light etchings found on Wade & Butcher razors cover the whole blade with scroll and include "Fine India Steel." A more long winded variation is "Wade & Butcher's Celebrated Fine India Steel Razor." Another slogan is "You Lather Well- I'll Shave Well."

More desirable etchings are scenes. One such etching reads,

"Washington Razor" around a bust of our country's first president. A winged angel on one side of the bust and an eagle on the other side hold ends of a long ribbon. The ribbon reads, "America the land of the brave- the home of the free." The clear horn handle is embossed in gold, "The Washington Razor." Other desirable blades include etchings of a battleship, side paddle wheel and steamship.

Other collectors are fortunate if they have only one razor with its blade etched with a train scene. Charles F. Ochs II was able to display three variations of trains at the Tampa Knife Show. Two of the variations were on Wade & Butcher wedge blades. Each has different engines and cars. The handles have brass pins with iron caps and have no spacer between the handle halves. One razor is marked with a crown and "R" in addition to "Wade & Butcher" markings.

There are many slogans pressed into the horn handles of Wade & Butcher razors. The record length slogan must be the gold embossed statement, "Wade & Butcher's Celebrated Patent Frame Back Razor which for superiority of temper stands preeminent to any other manufactured." This frame back blade in dark horn handles is also part of Charles F. Och's collection.

There are several variations of the phrase "Wade & Butcher's Celebrated Razor" pressed into both flat and rounded horn handles.

One razor has its horn handle pressed "Original Arrow Razor." The blade and shank both have an etched arrow. The back of the shank identifies the razor as "Wade & Butcher."

Other razors have designs embossed in gold on the clear horn handles. A flat handle has groups of diamonds embossed near the pins. "Diamond Edge Razor" is pressed in the center. A rounded handle has a design full of curves and scroll embossed in gold.

Another razor has "Eyre Lane and Philadelphia Works," pressed into one side of the dark horn handle. "The Washington Razor" is pressed into the other side. Strangely enough, the lettering can be read with the blade over it on one side and the lettering can be read with the blade under it on the other side.

One of the nicest pressed horn razors is pressed "The Real Kentuck Self Acting Shaver" on both sides. There are shell and rose patterns pressed as decorations covering nearly the whole handle.

Wade & Butcher razors were sold through many outlets, a 1895 Montgomery Ward catalog and a 1897 Sears Roebuck catalog have several Wade & Butcher razors. Other catalogs from different years have Wade & Butcher razors as well.

The 1927 Sears Roebuck catalog shows a Wade & Butcher razor

The record length slogan must be the gold embossed statement, "Wade & Butcher's celebrated Patent Frame Back Razor which for superiority of temper stands preeminent to any other manufactured."

More desirable etchings are scenes. One such etching reads, "Washington Razor" around a bust of our country's first president.

with ivory colored celluloid handle. It is embossed with the firm's trademark in gold. There are also celluloid handles with a scroll decoration embossed in gold. One particular razor has its blade etched "Elite."

A 1927 Winchester Simmons catalog indicates that Wade & Butcher safety razors were free gratis, when the firm's safety razor blades were purchased. The blades were described as "cleverly curved" and the razor was similar to earlier Gillette safety razors.

There are several variations of Wade & Butcher razors with odd shaped escutcheons and eight pointed stars made of a pewter like metal. The metal was inlaid into dark horn handles with brass pins and no spacer between the handle halves.

Some knife shows have included razor categories in their competition. The 1982 American Blade Show and the Louisville NKCA Knife Show in March, 1983, are two examples. Other shows such as the Oregon Knife Show have included razors in their advertising.

I was able to attend the Louisville show and discovered that it had attracted some nice razor displays and more collectors with their razor rolls than I've ever seen in one place. Some of the Louisville visitors had trade razors and favorite pieces to show too. I was privileged to examine many razors including two dark horn Wade & Butcher razors. One of these razors had a twisted silver wire inlaid around each pin and around the perimeter of the razor handle. The center had a pearl escutcheon. The second Wade & Butcher razor had a very complex pearl inlay.

You will have to agree that Wade & Butcher used a variety of handle materials. They also made use of various decorations on handles and etchings on blades. Blades were made in a variety of shapes and types from wedge to modern hollow ground. Certainly collecting Wade & Butcher razors can not be considered boring.

A final objection to razors might be that they are dirty, rusty, broken, junk. I'll agree that razors fitting that description should not be displayed. However, we've all seen knives and guns that can be described in the same manner. It's hardly fair to exclude only razors on this basis.

Perhaps the razor did not perform as glamorous a job as did guns and knives. Simply shaving a

Some blades are marked deeply with decorations. Top: Marked with eagle and words "American Razor." Center: Masonic symbols and Bottom: Blade marked "Moustache Razor" in a ribbon.

face doesn't compare with winning the Civil War, downing rustlers and Indians, or surviving bar room brawls. But wait a minute, how many "Parker" shotguns were involved in those activities? In fact, how many of the weapons that are in top condition and sought by collectors today actually shed human blood? I would expect very few.

While our country was growing, while battles were fought and the West was won, razors were there. Before major events in a man's life and before usual Saturday night festivities, a lot of men used their own razor or kept a date with the barber's razor.

If you're still convinced that razors are worthless, there is no need to move that box of carved pearl razors from drawer to drawer anymore. Before someone cuts themselves, pack the razors carefully before sending and I'll pay the postage when they arrive here.

This article appeared in Knife World June, 1983

Star Safety Razor Part I

by Robert K. Waits

Recommended by Dr. Oliver Wendell Holmes

"In 1880 a hoe-shaped safety razor was manufactured in the United States. Oliver Wendell Holmes endorsed it enthusiastically." So states the opening entry in Volume 19 (Razor to Schurz) of the *Encyclopedia Brittanica*. This intriguing bit of information led me to track down the rest of the story and to discover that one hundred years ago this past April, Oliver Wendell Holmes was given a bon voyage gift...but I am getting ahead of my story.

First of all, which Oliver Wendell Holmes did the *Brittanica* refer to, the famous physician and author or his son and namesake, the associate justice of the U.S. Supreme Court? And where and when did he endorse the razor? The key to these puzzles was accidentally discovered in a 1913 article in *The Independent* magazine where an anonymous editor commented: "...it was, if we remember right, in 1887 that Oliver Wendell Holmes shocked Boston and the outside world by using the pages of the *Atlantic* to praise the new invention, the magic utensil...which a friend had given him as he embarked for his *Hundred Days in Europe*."

A search of the card files of a local university library turned up a book entitled "One Hundred Days in Europe" by O.W. Holmes. Since the razor was a bon voyage gift I presumed that it would be mentioned early on in the book. That was correct, but the relevant pages had been carefully razored out! (Who knows when or for what purpose or motive.) On to another library that had a set of 1880's *Atlantics*. There the quest ended with the March 1887 issue containing the first of a series of articles entitled "One Hundred Days in Europe."

Oliver Wendell Holmes, born the same year as Abraham Lincoln, had gained international fame as a physician, teacher, lecturer and author who commented in the pages of the *Atlantic* magazine on the manners and people of his day. He was best known for his series of *Atlantic* essays later published in an 1858 book, "The Autocrat of the Breakfast Table." Dr. Holmes was also the father of Judge Oliver Wendell Holmes, an eminent associate justice of the U.S. Supreme Court, and

"With the other gifts came a small tin box, about as big as a common round wooden match box... It proved to be a most valued daily companion..." An 1888 vintage Star safety razor tin sold by the Boston firm of Dame, Stoddard & Kendall.

whose life was the subject of Kathleen Drinker Bowen's 1944 biographical novel "Yankee from Olympus." It was the senior Dr. Holmes who had endorsed the new invention.

What did Dr. Holmes say that "shocked Boston and the outside world?" I will let him speak for himself:

The Cephalonia was to sail at half past six in the morning, and at that early hour a company of well wishers was gathered on the wharf at East Boston to bid us goodbye. We took with us many tokens of their thoughtful kindness... With the other gifts came a small tin box, abut as big as a common round wooden match box... It proved to be a most valued daily companion, useful at all times, never so much as when the winds were blowing hard and the ship was struggling in the waves. There must have been some magic secret in it, for I am sure that I looked five years younger after closing that little box than when I opened it. Time

"The tin box contained a reaping machine, which gathered the capillary harvest of the past twenty-four hours..." A 1888 vintage Star safety razor, blade holder and tin.

will explain its mysterious power...

Dr. Holmes continued the story a few pages later:

The first morning at sea revealed the mystery of the little round tin box. The process of shaving, never a delightful one, is a very unpleasant and awkward piece of business when the floor on which one stands, the glass in which he looks, and he himself are all describing those complex curves which make cycles and epicycles seem like simplicity itself. The little box contained a reaping machine, which gathered the capillary harvest of the past twenty four hours with a thoroughness, a rapidity, a security, and a facility which were a surprise, almost a revelation. The idea of a guarded cutting edge is an old one; I remember the "Plantagenet" razor, so called, with the comb-like row of blunt teeth, leaving just enough of the edge free to do its work. But this little affair had a blade only an inch and a half long by three quarters of an inch wide. It had a long slender handle, which took apart for packing, and was put together with the greatest ease. It was, in short, a lawn mower for the masculine growth of which the proprietor wishes to rid his countenance. The mowing operation required no glass, could be performed with almost reckless boldness, as one cannot cut himself, and in fact had become a pleasant amusement instead of an irksome task. I have never used any other means of shaving from that day to this. I was so pleased with it that I exhibited it to the distinguished tonsors of Burlington Arcade, half afraid that they would assassinate me for bringing in an innovation which bid fair to destroy their business.

...I determined to let other persons know what a convenience I

had found the "Star Razor" of Messrs. Kampfe of Brooklyn, New York, without fear of reproach for so doing. ...It is pure good will to my raze which leads me to commend the Star Razor to all who travel by land or by sea, as well as to all who stay at home.

Parenthetically, it was the judgement in 1913 of the Independent editor that these words about the Star in the 1887 *Atlantic* may represent the first appearance of the safety razor in literature.

Dr. Holmes, at age 77, had apparently changed a life long habit of shaving with a cut throat straight razor. It is doubtful whether he actually abandoned the use of a mirror, however. Photographs of Dr. Holmes show him to have been clean shaven save for luxuriant "mutton chop" sideburns. By the way, his trip to Europe, accompanied by his daughter, was to accept three honorary degrees: from universities at Cambridge, Edinburgh, and Oxford. He embarked (and was presented with the Star Razor) near the end of April 1886, returning on his 77th birthday on August 29.

The illustrations show a Star safety razor and round tin that was probably sold in Boston in late 1888 or soon after. Who knows, possibly as a direct result of Dr. Holmes' testimonial. The container is yellow with black printing. The lid is marked DAME, STODDARD/ & KENDALL/ FINE/ CUTLERY/ BOSTON,/ MASS. The tin bears no less than thirteen patent dates, the earliest is June 15, 1880, and the latest July 3, 1888. The tin is labeled in fine print at the bottom front MERSEREAU M'F'G CO. BROOKLYN N.Y., which was the manufacturer of the container. (A very similar, but not identical, round Kampfe safety razor tin marked "Somers Bros., Brooklyn, NY Pat Apl 29, 1879" was illustrated and described in an article by Kurt Moe in *Knife World*, June 1984. Somers Brothers was also a manufacturer of metal containers and the patent was for a type of lapped seam.)

The Star razor packed within this tin has an ornate Victorian style floral pattern that is embossed through the entire thickness of the head. The razor has only two patent dates, the original June 15, '80, date and Engl. Pat March 8, '87. The razor blade is held in place by a brass spring clip at the rear and two side channels each having a set screw adjustment that determines the blade edge exposure with respect to the comb guard. The handle is in two pieces that screw together. The outer piece is closed at one end and has a small rectangular opening that fits the head of the blade adjustment set screws. The open end of this piece fits into a simple blade holder that can be used as a handle for stropping. Dr. Holmes didn't mention it, but the ceremony of blade stropping was still required. The blade holder has no markings. The blade itself is a wedge type with concave sides, in essence, an inch and a half long section of a hollow ground straight razor.

The Plantagenet guard razor that Holmes recalled was made by Stewart & Co. in England. An example is shown in the illustration. Both the razor and guard are marked V (crown) R/ ROYAL LETTERS PATENT/ PLANTAGENET RAZOR. The guard will fit on only one side of the blade and is held in place by a set screw in a keyhole slot on the top of the comb guard and threaded into the back of the blade. The V (crown) R mark indicates that this razor was manufactured during the reign of Queen Victoria (1837-1900). The vintage is probably circa 1850. A U.S. patent for a similar, but reversible, guard design was issued in 1864.

Another question remains. Did Kampfe Bros. take advantage of Holmes' presumably unsolicited testimonial? Yes, they did. At least one time, anyway, 18 years later (and nearly 11 years after Dr. Holmes' death), in an advertisement appearing on page 40 of the April, 1905, issue of The Strand Magazine. (Which periodical, incidentally, brought fame to another Holmes, who solved many cases on their pages starting in July of 1891.) The Razor Dept. of Markt & Co. of London promoted the original Kampfe Star Safety Razors.... Recommended by Dr. Oliver Wendell Holmes in his book "Our One Hundred Days in Europe."

A subsequent article will continue the story of the early wedge blade Star Safety Razor.

This article appeared in Knife World December, 1986.

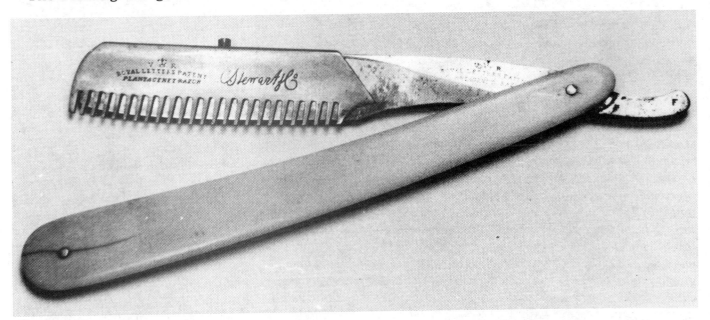

"I remember the 'Plantagenet' razor...with the comb-like row of blunt teeth, leaving just enough of the edge free to do its work." Example of a victorian-era Plantagenet razor manufactured by Stewart & Co., marked ROYAL LETTERS PATENT/ PLANTAGENET RAZOR.

Star Safety Razor Part II

by Robert K. Waits
All Others Are Spurious

Kampfe Brothers was founded by Frederic, Richard and Otto Kampfe. There is some inconsistency in the various dates that have been given (or implied) for the start of Kampfe Bros. and the advent of the Star safety razor. According to a booklet published in 1975 by their successor, the American Safety Razor Co., Kampfe Brothers began manufacturing the Star safety razor in 1875 "in a one room shop in New York City." Advertisements for Kampfe Bros. from 1901 to 1911 show addresses from 6 to 15 Reade Street, New York City. An April, 1905, Kampfe advertisement stated that "every blade bears a reputation of 29 years standing." This implies that Kampfe Bros. had been making some type of cutlery since 1876. A full page advertisement in the December, 1911, *The American Magazine* claimed that "over half a century of blade making experience is behind the Star Safety Razor. The Star itself has been made and used for thirty six years. We were expert cutlery manufacturers before we invented the safety razor."

From this one would conclude that Kampfe Bros. (or their predecessor) started making cutlery in 1860 or 1861 and that the Star was introduced in 1875. Over the years Kampfe Bros. and the American Safety Razor Co. have claimed that the Star was the "original safety razor" and "the first safety razor made in the United States."

According to the Official Gazette of the U.S. Patent and Trademark Office, the Star trademark name was first issued June 1, 1880. The first Kampfe safety razor patent application was filed on May 8, 1880, and was issued only 5 weeks later on June 15. The illustration for this patent is reproduced here. The removable handle, probably wooden, was short and stubby to enable it to fit within the blade holder for storage. The razor later became considerably more complex than this original design. The patent specification stated that the object of the invention was "to provide a safety razor which shall be simple and durable in construction, of small first cost, compact in form, and adapted to be used without soiling the fingers... (The)... refuse matter...will be retained

within the hollow holder...permitting the use of the device without danger of soiling the fingers of the user."

A patent model was submitted with the application, and if it has survived, would surely be a prize for any razor collector.

The STAR name and the trademark symbols, a single five pointed star and a row of three stars, were first used by Kampfe for safety shaving devices, razors and razor blades on June 1, 1880. A detailed illustration of a man shaving himself with a safety razor in front of a shaving mirror was first used as a trademark on January 14, 1885.

In 1897 the basic patent expired but in the interim design patents valid for seven years had been issued in 1894 and 1895 that protected the ornamental embossed star design of a tubular metal handle and the shape of the razor blade holder used for stropping. Also, in 1897, a 14 year design patent was granted for the safety razor casing (the razor head).

In spite of this, in 1898 Mr. Jeremiah Reichard, a former Kampfe employee, became one of the founders of the Gem Cutlery Co., which then introduced a similar razor. According to a 1901 Gem Cutlery Co. ad, they were at 41 Reade Street in New York, just down the block from Kampfe Bros.

By the end of 1899 at least 22 U.S. patents had been assigned to Kampfe Brothers. These included patents for various blade holding features of the razor, stropping honing devices, and a double ended container for razors and blades.

After the handle design patent expired in 1901 this feature was also widely copied. A Lakeside Cutlery safety razor sold by Montgomery Ward & Co. was described and illustrated by Kurt Moe in the December, 1985, issue of *Knife World*. It has a two piece tubular handle and blade holder for stropping that is identical in construction to that of the Star. It even has the socket opening in the closed end of the handle for use in adjusting the set screws that determine blade exposure. The only differences between the handles of the Star and the Lakeside are differing thread pitch where the two sections screw together and in the decorative design on the handle; the Lakeside has a spiral motif rather than rows of stars. The razor has the patent dates Dec. 31, 1901, and April 29, 1902, (both assigned to Joseph Turner). A Torrey safety razor having the same patent dates appears identical to the Lakeside razor. It is probable that the J.R. Torrey Razor Co. of Worcester, Mass. manufactured the Lakeside safety razor for Montgomery Ward.

The 1908 Sears Roebuck and Co. catalog featured "The New 1908 Model Wilbert Safety Razor/ Improved Model" for 94 cents (the Star was $1.50). The illustration shows a razor and stropping handle that appear identical to the Lakeside, even to the spiral handle design. Where the Lakeside was marked LAKESIDE/ M.W. & CO., the Wilbert is labeled WILBERT/SAFETY. One could conclude that Torrey made safety razors that were sold under their own name as well as manufacturing private label brands for both Montgomery Ward and Sears.

The competition was heating up. Star blade cases bore the proclamation: ALL OTHERS ARE SPURIOUS. The razor tins carried the legend, THE STAR LEADS THEM ALL. A 1905 ad in the *Saturday Evening Post* boasted five million or more users and warned "Beware of imitations and infringements." This ad also featured a frame back non safety razor having a replaceable blade and "modeled after an old style razor" for the die hard conservative who didn't want a guard between his beard and the blade.

King Camp Gillette introduced his flexible blade double edge razor in 1903 and had sold nearly one million razors by the end of

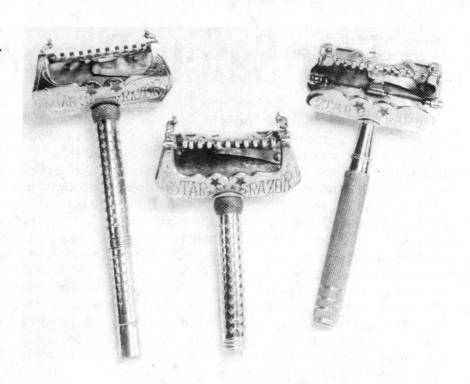

Three Star safety razor models. Left to Right: Last patent 1887, The Improved (1900, hinged guard, lower part of handle not shown), New Model (1902 hinged head, one piece handle).

1907. Kampfe Bros. fought back. A testimonial dated May 25, 1907 in a Kampfe advertisement stated "...from twenty years experience in using the Star Safety Razor, I have found it to be the only satisfactory safety razor that I have ever tried. My only object in trying other makes was the hope that I would be able to avoid the necessity of honing and stropping."

The writer was undoubtedly referring to (and refuting) the Gillette claim of "No Honing No Stropping."

A 1911 Kampfe Bros. advertisement still claimed five million daily users and that "Its many imitators prove its success." There were indeed many Star safety razor imitators. In addition to the Gem and those made by Torrey, there were others such as the Fox, Terry's Safety Razor and Dr. Scott's Electric ("electric" in name only) that came and went. From outside the U.S. there was Wilkinson, made in England, C.V. Heljestrand in Eskilstuna, Sweden, and J.A. Henckels of Germany. And these were only the wedge blade imitators. Becoming far more serious was the competition from disposable blade razors such as the Gillette with its flexible double edge blade as well as others having thin but rigid single edged blades exemplified by those manufactured by the Christy Co. of Fremont, Ohio.

Kampfe had also been guilty of imitation. An ad in the November,1909, American Magazine featured the Star Convex Flexible Razor. The illustration shows a single edge razor with a curved head. The ad claimed superiority over all the other thin or wafer blade razors due to an improved guard and because the

228

"convex curve which holds the blade firm produces the diagonal movement which cuts clean and will not scrape or irritate the skin." The Convex trademark, applied for in January 1910, depicted a five pointed star trailing the word CONVEX in a comet like tail. Yet another commercial tie-in to Halley's comet, which reached its peak in May of that year.

Some of the later competitors of the Star razor may have been made by Kampfe Bros. themselves. A razor similar to the Stoll safety razor illustrated in the 1916 Sears Catalog has SCS (for Stoll Chrome Steel) as part of a pierced guard design, but is marked "Kampfe Bros. Pat. Pend." on the back. A similar razor in the 1915 catalog is marked WILBERT CUTLERY CO./ CHICAGO. The Stoll blade for this razor was not a thick wedge type but was a single edge thin rigid blade having a folded reinforcing rib clamped to the blade opposite the cutting edge, that would "fit the Stoll, Superior, Ever Ready, Gem, Gem Junior, Star and other safety razors." This implies that this thin blade may have been interchangeable with the thick wedge blade. A similar Ever-Ready blade "to fit 'Yankee', 'Star' and 'Gem' safety frames" was offered as early as 1906 by the American Safety Razor Co. at seven for 50 cents (the thick Kampfe blades cost $1 each). This new style single edge blade together with the Gillette blade marked the beginning of the end for the wedge blade style safety razor.

It is interesting to trace the design evolution of the Star safety razor. Examples of the Star razors with their tins gives an indication of the changes in design over the years that were necessary to keep ahead of the imitators. Patent dates were displayed prominently on both the tins and razor parts, undoubtedly as a marketing ploy (even expired patent dates were sometimes listed), but of considerable value today in sorting out the design chronology. Based on the last patent dates found on the various styles on illustrations in advertisements the following can be inferred:

Around 1896 the word STAR was incorporated as a pierced design in a hinged guard plate. The name was obscured when the blade was in place.

The IMPROVED STAR was introduced about 1900. Its most distinguishing feature was a new spring loaded blade clamping arrangement. Screws still held the edge blade clamps in place.

Around 1901-1902 the NEW MODEL was available that had the hinge moved to the rear of the head or casing and a modified comb guard with Y shaped fingers. The adjusting screws had disappeared. By 1904 the price printed on the NEW MODEL tin had been reduced from $2 to $1.50 for the razor with one blade (the Gillette sold for $5.00).

In 1904 the stropping blade holder design was changed from one having eight round holes in the back (1895 and 1899 patents) to one with eight diagonal slots (patented 1904). Also around 1904 a one piece knurled metal razor handle was introduced. Previously the handle had been either a one piece wood or two piece metal.

Various Kampfe Bros. trademarks were registered with the U.S. Patent and Trademark Office. These included three stars arranged in a triangle pattern used on cases and razor parts starting June 15, 1900, an outline of a heart with three S's inside first used February 1, 1903, and three K's in a triangle outline filed in 1905.

Early Star razors along with blade and stropping handle were packaged in round tins. Around 1899 a double ended rectangular tin was introduced that had two compartments, one held the razor and stropping handle and the other, shallower section, held two wedge blades. A round tin pictured in a 1907 English catalog was marked A. JORDAN Sheffield Eng & St. Louis Mo USA/ EUROPEAN AGENT. The razor illustrated on the tin appears to be the NEW MODEL described above, and the blade bears the three K's within a triangle trademark. The price shown on the tin was $2.00.

Several Star razor sets in fitted cases were shown in the 1895 Montgomery Ward catalog and in the 1902 Sears Roebuck catalog. Included were The Gem case containing a razor and two blades ($3.30), the Favorite case with a razor and seven blades ($9.00), and the Traveling case set containing razor, two blades, stropping machine, shaving brush and soap and comb ($5.40). The prices given are for 1902 which differed little from those of 1895. The sets were put up in fitted morocco imitation leatherette covered wooden boxes lined with satin. The case names were emblazoned on satin ribbons running diagonally across the inside lid. "The Gem" case has caused some confusion among collectors (including me). Why a Kampfe Star razor in a case labeled "The Gem"? The word GEM was first registered as a U.S. trademark for safety razors in 1888 by Henry B. Leach of Boston who claimed use since April

1886. The name was registered again in 1924 by the American Safety Razor Corp. of Brooklyn, New York who claimed use since June 1, 1898. This was probably when the Gem Cutlery Co. first used this trademark.

In 1919 the American Safety Razor Co. (makers of the Ever-Ready safety razor), acquired both Kampfe Bros. and the Gem Cutlery Co. These companies then became the Star Safety Razor Corp. and the Gem Safety Razor Corp., respectively. Although both were now subsidiaries of the A.S.R. Corporation, advertisements of the time made no mention of the fact other than using the new corporate names. A.S.R. had started out in 1903 as the Reichard & Scheuber Co. founded by Jeremiah Reichard (formerly of Kampfe Bros. and one of the founders of Gem Cutlery Co.) and August W. Scheuber. Thus, Kampfe Brothers and the two spin off companies that Mr. Reichard had helped in founding had come full circle.

As far as I have been able to determine, the last U.S. patents of the brothers Kampfe were granted to Frederic in 1907, to Reichard in 1914 and lastly to Otto in 1921.

The Star wedge blade razor made its last appearance in the Sears Roebuck catalog around 1920. The thick concave blade for the razor continued to be offered in the Sears catalog through 1926 and then it, too, disappeared. The Star wedge blade safety razor had survived for about 40 years. The Star trademark lived on and has been used on single edge blades, on a razor exactly like the the thin blade single edged Gem, and finally on double edged blades ("Famous Since 1880") and for safety razors identical to the Gillette.

The Star wedge blade safety razor in its various forms as well as its many competitors are interesting historical artifacts and certainly worthy items for collectors to search for and preserve.

Acknowledgements
Mr. Sigmund Wohl furnished information on the Torrey Safety Razor and Mr. Ernest Wittkopf described to me the 1916 Kampfe Bros./ Stoll razor. Mr. Bill Zigrang kindly gave permission to reproduce the Kampfe Bros. advertisements from his collection.

This article appeared in Knife World January, 1987.

Ward and Yale Safety Razors

by Kurt Moe

William N. Ward of Chicago, Illinois, was granted Patent number 868,588 on October 15, 1907 for his safety razor. Two weeks later he also received Patent number 869,757 for a handle to be used for stropping the thin safety razor blades. Both patents were assigned to the Yale Safety Razor Company.

In his razor patent specifications, W. Ward considered both his blade holding mechanism and the hexagonal handle ending in a ring, to be important. The six sides were to enable the operator to grasp the handle firmly without danger of it twisting. The ring at the end of the handle was to hold the little finger of the person shaving and could be used to hang the razor when it was not being used.

A black presentation case with a slide fastener holds a razor and stropper. The case is lined in purple velvet and fitted for the razor and stropper handles. A satin ribbon reads in gold, "Yale Safety Razor Co., Chicago, Ill."

The razor itself has the type of tarnish on it which suggests that it is plated with real silver. The smooth hexagon handle bears the Ward patent date, "Oct. 15, 1907." The handle has a ring on one end and a guard on the other end. Putting the little finger into this ring does seem to steady the razor.

The razor used a double edged blade with a slot on each end. One blade slot is fit into a fixed peg and a movable peg can be slid into the other slot. The movable peg can then be finger tightened with a nut.

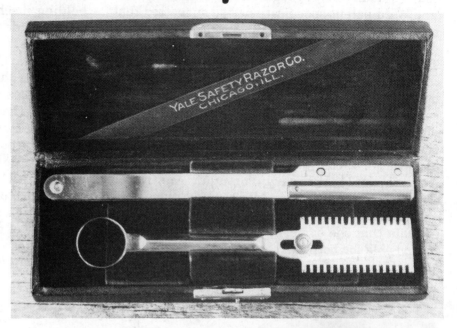

Stropper handle and silver plated Yale Safety Razor

Silver plated Ward Safety Razor and paper blade package shown next to their closed box.

The stropper appears to be nickel plated and bears the Ward "Oct 29, 1907" patent date. The stropping handle consists of a clamp or holder. The thick back of the holder ensured that a blade was held at a correct angle for stropping.

Another hinged black box with a sliding fastener is similar to the Yale box in materials and construction but is not as wide. The inside is covered in the same shade of purple velvet as is the Yale

231

box and is fitted to the razor handle. The box is marked "Ward Safety Razor, Chicago. Price $4.00."

This razor also appears to be silver plated. The round handle has a rough cross hatched surface. The Ward patent specifications had suggested that cross hatching or pebbling could be used to provide grip security. This razor handle also ends in a ring. The razor itself is stamped "Patent Apld For."

The "Ward Concave Blade" has notches punched out of the ends. A spring loaded cone shaped point centers the blade and holds it tight. The box holding extra Ward blades has twelve patent dates shown from June 11, 1907, to the U.S. patent date of April 28, 1908. Various countries listed include Austria, Italy, Hungary, Portugal, Australia, Germany, Spain, Belgium, Mexico and France.

The similarities of the Yale and Ward razors indicate that the same W.N. Ward may have been responsible for both. My search of April 28, 1908, patents, however, did not confirm this. Instead, a patent of that date was awarded to Henrie Clauss. The specifications of his patent number 886,039 show a razor very similar to the Ward razor except that it lacks a ring for the little finger. The blade holding mechanism uses a cone shaped point to hold a blade with notches in the ends just as the Ward does. I wish I knew the rest of this story and how Henrie Clauss was involved.

The fact that both the Yale and Ward razors and their boxes were found in excellent condition indicates that for some reason they were not used very long by their first owners. The design did not seem to be popular with the U.S. shaving public.

It is unfortunate that these razors are not marked with their brand name. Today's safety razor collector, however, appreciates their unusual construction and silver plating. It is a special day when one of these uncommon razors turns up at a flea market.

This article appeared in Knife World August, 1984.

Kampfe Bros. Catalogue 1906

by Robert K. Waits

On October 7, 1906, H.H. Covey, Esq., of Big Moose, New York, received a Kampfe Bros. catalogue in the mail. President Theodore Roosevelt was preparing to visit Panama to check on a construction project. There were forty-five states in the union. San Francisco was rebuilding six months after a devastating earthquake and fire. Henry Ford's automobile company was three years old. King C. Gillette's company was also three years old, had paid its first dividend, and was selling razors and disposable blades. It was a new century and times were changing.

Kampfe Bros. had been in business over 30 years. The brothers were Frederick, Richard and Otto Kampfe of 8-12 Reade Street, New York City. In June of 1880 they obtained the first U.S. patent on a device that they called a "safety razor." It used a removable 1-1/2 inch long concave wedge blade similar to a section of the traditional straight razor and had a comb-like guard beneath the blade. Their trademark was Star.

In 1906 the original Star Safety razor patents had expired and competition was getting stiff. It came not only from imitators such as the Ever-Ready made by the newly named American Safety Razor Co. and the Gem from the Gem Cutlery Co., but also from innovators like the new Gillette.

The Gillette employed a thin flexible double edge blade that could be mass produced by automated machinery. Gillette had received a British patent in 1902 and U.S. patents in 1904. During

Cover of 1906 Kampfe Bros. catalogue

The Genuine

Star Safety Razor

No. 1.

distinguishes itself from inferior goods on the market by our novel, as well as useful, new improved Combination Razor Box.

For safe-keeping and protection from rust, always place the blade in the carrier frame in the blade case connected with the combination razor box, as annexed cut will show.

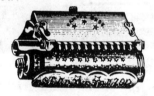

2/3 of actual size.

STAR SAFETY RAZOR COMPLETE,

with handle inside, ready for packing.

Price $1.50

This cut shows Enameled Box with Complete Razor.

The Blade Holder in which to carry the blade for protection. (Pat. Nov. 28, 1899.) Dimensions of this box, 2¼ in. long, 1⅜ wide by 1⅛ high.

6

The new model Star had been introduced in December, 1901.

1905, Gillette had sold over 270,000 razors and would sell over 300,000 more in 1906. Kampfe had been claiming "over five million users" for several years. Most Star razor advertisements concluded with the phrase: Send for catalogue.

The Kampfe Bros. catalog (to drop the 1900's spelling), has no

233

No. 5.

The Star Case.

TWO BLADES.

A neat, compact, satin-lined Morocco leather covered case, with a Doeskin covered block, containing Safety Razor complete, consisting of **two blades,** frame and handle. Handle can be used with the frame, and for stropping the blades.

Price, $3.10.

Over five million users appreciate daily the value of this marvel of simplicity, and are our best advertisers.

Dimensions of this case, 3½ in. long, 2½ in. wide by 1½ in. high.

No. 5 The Star Case

No. 14.

THE

Elite Case.

A handsome satin-lined Morocco leather covered case, with a sterling silver Safety Razor frame and a genuine ivory handle, **seven blades,** and an ivory stropping and honing handle.

Price $17.00.

Dimensions of this case, 6¼ in. long, 3⅜ in. wide by 1¾ in. high.

No. 14 The Elite Case contained a sterling silver razor with ivory handle.

date but the postmark on back of the mailing envelope is Oct. 7, 1906. The stamp had been torn off, but the mark of the destination post office had survived. We can thank those who carefully preserved the envelope, if not the stamp. The latest dates mentioned in the catalog are awards at Lewis & Clark Exposition, Portland, Oregon, 1905, (back cover) and a July 4, 1905, patent date (p.44). Together with the postmark, these dates place the catalog as being produced no earlier than late July, 1905, and no later than September 1906.

Some confusion over the age of the Kampfe Bros. enterprise is caused by the statement on the catalog cover— "Established 1875"— versus the statement on the back of the envelope— "Established 25 years." Perhaps the envelope was somewhat out of date; the razor-tin design shown was circa 1901.

The 64 page catalog is about postcard size (3-1/2" x 5-1/4") with a cover printed in shades of green. The back cover shows an array of medals awarded at various expositions: American Institute (held in 1885), Mechanics Institute, San Francisco- 1886, Exposition Univereselle Internationale- 1900, Louisiana Purchase Exposition (held in 1904), and the Pan American Exposition (held in 1901).

The first two pages of the catalog contain, under the headline, "A GLORIOUS TRIBUTE," an extensive quote from the pen of the late Dr. Oliver Wendell Holmes commending ... "the Star Razor to all who travel by land or sea, as well as to all who stay at home." It was not mentioned that Dr. Holmes had written the recommendation in March, 1887, nearly twenty years earlier. (See "Star Safety Razor," *Knife World*, December, 1986). Dr. Holmes had died in 1894; in 1872 he had written "life is a fatal complaint and an eminently contagious one." In 1902, Dr. Holmes' son and name-sake had been appointed an associate justice of the U.S. Supreme Court by President Roosevelt, so Oliver Wendell Holmes continued to be a well known name.

The catalog shows that, although Kampfe had a full line of shaving products, they were not innovating or even keeping up with the times. There were no less than 26 varieties of Star safety razor cased sets and nine frame

234

back razor sets. Prices for razor sets in "satin-lined Morocco leather covered" cases ranged from $2 for a one blade set to $17 for a seven blade set. The No.5 Star Case with two blades was $3.10. Prior to about 1902 this set was called "The Gem Case."

A one blade set in a metal "enameled box" was $1.50. This "useful, new improved Combination Razor Box" had a lid on both the top and the bottom; the razor was in a top compartment and the blade was stored in the lower one.

The Star Safety razor was the New Model with a hinged frame that could be opened for easier cleaning and drying. The "New" model was almost 5 years old. The previous "Improved Model," also having a hinged frame, was advertised as late as August, 1901. That December, advertisements announced that the New Model was "Now Ready" for Christmas giving.

The frame-back razor— Kampfe's New Star Interchangeable Razor— actually *was* new, although from our vantage point it seems a step backward, lacking even a safety guard! Related patents had been issued in May, 1905. It was an old style folding straight razor with a replaceable blade similar to the Star safety razor blade, but an inch longer— approximately 2-1/2 inches vs. 1-1/2 inches for the safety blade— with a rounded edge-corner at the handle end. The advantage over the ordinary straight razor was that the blade could be removed and stropped with a Star Stropper or Star Stropping Machine. The stropper flipped the blade at the end of each stroke. The stropping machine also turned the blade automatically and, in addition,

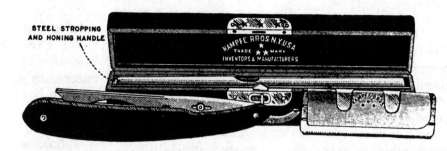

No. 130.

KAMPFE'S STAR INTERCHANGEABLE RAZOR.

STEEL STROPPING AND HONING HANDLE

This compact set contains one Interchangeable Razor (holder and handle), with one blade and a steel blade holder, which can be used for either stropping or honing the blade.

Price $2.25.

Kampfe's New Star Interchangeable Razor

No. 3M (Metal Handle).

Star Safety Razor

STROPPING MACHINE.

Read the following explanation, also see annexed cut, which, we believe, will show better than words the wonders of this astonishing machine.

BEWARE

OF SPURIOUS STROPPING DEVICES—THEY SPOIL THE BLADE.

The blade is placed into the central blade-holder between the two friction rollers, and the device placed **upon** the strop in such a manner that the blade and rollers rest on said strop, the guard downward; reverse side reads: "**this side up.**" The machine is moved backward and forward on the strop, and every time it is reversed the blade is automatically turned on its back and a fresh face or side presented to the strop.

It is absolutely impossible to turn one of our Razor Blades held in this device on its edge, and thus the blade cannot be dulled or damaged.

Any good flexible razor strop can be used with this stropping device, our Star Diagonal Strop is far superior to all others.

STROPPING MACHINE No. 3W (with a Rosewood Handle), Price $2.00.

9

Price $1.65.

Cut of Stropping Machine With Blade Inserted Ready for Stropping

No. 3M Stropping Machine

had two friction rollers that rested on the strop, helped to align the blade to the strop and limited the pressure that could be applied. To quote the catalog: "Not over one man out of twenty-five knows how to strop a razor properly, and while many prefer an old style razor in preference to a safety, still, ... the use of the old style razor has not been satisfactory... Our Interchangeable Razor Blade can be stropped with our Star Stropper, which works automatically... the operator becomes an expert in the art of stropping..." The catalog features two Star Stropper kits for the Interchangeable Razor Blades plus a similar Star Stropper for the safety blades. The Star Safety Razor Stropping Machine was available with either metal or wood handles and luxury models could be purchased with either pearl ($7.50) or ivory ($6.00) handles and "extra heavy silver plate."

A brief commercial message on page 61 was entitled: "The Reason Why The Star Safety Razor Blades Are Superior in Quality." Aimed at the competing Gillette blade, it claimed that honing by hand "is the old fashioned process; it cannot be improved upon... Would you part with the razor handed down by your grandfather?" Hardly the words of a company intent on innovation. And again alluding to Gillette: "... many manufacturers sacrifice quality to reduce the cost of production by stamping their blades from sheet metal, hardening them in lots of 200 or 300 at a time and grinding and honing by machinery. Such products are invariably of inferior quality. Extensive advertising may influence many to purchase such merchandise, but they realize after a trial that they have made a poor investment." Only three years later, in November, 1909, Kampfe would be advertising the Star Convex Safety Razor that used thin flexible blades that "are positively uniform in quality." Kampfe had perhaps decided "if you can't lick them..." Kampfe would also introduce a Gillette look-alike knurled metal handle for the Star razors at about the same time.

As Kampfe noted, Gillette's advertising also was extensive. Russell Adams, in his excellent book "King C. Gillette," (Little, Brown, Boston, 1978) stated that "from the very start it was company policy to set aside about twenty-five cents per razor for advertising..." The advertising was effective; over 445,000 packets of Gillette blades would be sold by the end of 1906 and almost double this number the next year.

Genuine Star Safety Razor Blades were 85 cents each (Gillette throw-away blades were a nickel). Referring to the blade, Kampfe ungrammatically claimed that "Owing to its hidden magnetic force they never irritate the skin or flesh..." not much different from some of today's creative advertising. In October of 1906, The Gillette Sales Co. of New York was claiming "365 Shaves Without Stropping." A silver-plated razor with 12 blades was relatively expensive at $5, but the blades were 10 for fifty cents. If you sent Gillette 25 cents and "the name of a friend who does not use the Gillette Razor" they would send you "a full deck of (Gillette) playing cards,... celluloid finish, with round corners and gold edges, in a handsome

heavy gold-embossed leatherette telescope case." Those 25 cent cards were worth hanging on to; a boxed deck of Gillette playing cards sold for $150 at auction in 1982.

The prestige safety razor kits in the Kampfe catalog were the seven blade sets. The Complete Outfit (No.190 included the automatic stropping machine. The Elite Case (No.14) had a Star safety razor with a sterling silver frame and ivory handle plus an ivory stropping and honing handle. These sets were priced at $17. To put this in perspective you have to realize that the average weekly wage in 1900 was about $15.

Razor handles in the sets were available in three varieties: the slim two piece metal tube, wood (your choice of ebony or rosewood), and ivory. These wooden handles were longer than the early wood handles which were short enough to fit inside the lather-catcher of the razor. A price list for parts and supplies on page 62 indicates that small and large pearl handles were also available at $2 and $2.75 each. The price for a sterling silver razor frame was $5.00 (vs. 50 cents for the common metal frame)— of course this would require nothing less than a pearl or ivory handle.

Three each "Army" and "Navy" safety-razor outfits are illustrated. All the razors had wooden handles. The distinction between the two branches of the service is that all the Army kits have a shaving soap stick and a badger-hair shaving brush while the Navy kits do not. Presumably the Navy was more likely than the Army to have access to soap and brushes!

Other items shown in the catalog included: The Star Honing machine for $5.00, twelve styles of Kampfe's New Improved Star Diagonal Strops, and two types of badger-hair shaving brushes designed for traveling in a sectional nickel tube or with a folding hoop handle. Finally, on the last page of the catalog, there is a list of prices for empty cases that ranged from 75 cents to $4.50.

How much did the dealer make? A separate catalog insert stated that the "wholesale discount for quantity only," F.O.B. New York, was "Less 25%." A further discount of 2% was offered for cash paid within 10 days.

During 1905-07, Kampfe Bros. advertisements appeared in the Saturday Evening Post and The Outing Magazine, among others, but in general appear to be few and far-between compared to the ubiquitous Gillette ads. The 1905 catalog of the H.H. Kiffe Company, New York, featured the

Gillette razor and five Star Outfits side-by-side on the same page. The Gillette had text to "sell" the razor; the Star sets were described simply by listing the contents. By the way, compare the original Gillette razor shown on this catalog page with the "1907 Model" shown in the October, 1906, ad. There *is* a difference!

Kampfe Bros. survived for 13 more years. The Star wedge blade razor last appeared in the Sears catalog in 1919. That year Kampfe Bros. had become the Star Safety Razor Corp., a subsidiary of the American Safety Razor Corp. In 1920 alone, Gillette sold 2 million razors and 19 million packages of blades. Times had changed.

This article appeared in Knife World April, 1990.

Santas and Shaving Stuff

by Kurt Moe

Santa, that jolly man dressed in a red suit trimmed in white, carries his sack of toys for children who have been on their best behavior. But look again, this Santa carries a bag of goodies for those old enough to shave. The bag is spilling over with Gillette shaving products. Even after all these years to fade its colors, black and white photography just does not do the beautiful display justice.

It is a challenge to determine the age of this 39-1/2 inch tall cardboard display featuring Santa. A special promotion package containing ten boxes of blades found in the bag has a calendar showing the month of December. Had the year been shown, then dating the display would have been easy. Gillette may have expected that the Santa display be used for more than one year. I am told that this is unlikely, however, as razor models, promotional packages, and prices could be expected to change from Christmas to Christmas. The Tech razor set was even priced in the display at 98¢. In any case there is no year showing. There is a clue, though, as Christmas falls on a Monday on the display's December calendar. Looking through the fine print on the back of a current calendar produces the information that Christmas was celebrated on Monday in 1933, 1939, and in leap year 1944 during the period that the Santa was probably first used.

Some of the products shown in Santa's bag help pin down the year the display was meant to be used. The Gillette Senator razor shown is said to be first manufactured in about 1938. The words "A twist its open, a twist its closed" accompany illustrations of the one piece razor. The Gillette three piece Tech razor shown also was introduced in about 1938. The Tech was said to be the first Gillette without a comb-tooth guard. The Tech razor was sold as part of a 1939 World Series promotion with five extra blades. When the cheering of the Yankee fans was over Gillette was said to have sold 2-1/2 million special Tech sets at 49¢ each.

Another product shown in Santa's bag is the King Gillette brushless shaving cream. The display packaging shown doesn't mention K-34

Gillette Safety Razor Co. display from about 1939. Santa's bag contains the Senator and Tech razors, Blue Blades, and brushless shaving cream.

facial antiseptic shown on some similar shaving cream packaging. The shaving cream was advertised as "made with costly peanut oil" and was said to have been introduced in 1936. The product was also heavily advertised in 1939 in connection with Blue Blades and the Tech razor.

Gillette Blue Blades in a blue package featuring King Gillette's portrait was a part of each gift set in the Santa display.

Since several of the Gillette Safety Razor Co.

products shown in Santa's bag were not introduced until 1936 or 1938, the 1933 calendar possibility seems to have been eliminated. Assuming that the Santa display was meant to promote new and top of the line Gillette products then my best guess would be that it dates from about 1939. Had the 1944 calendar possibility been correct, it is probable that some sort of mention would have been made of World War II.

Gillette also got Santa's elves into the act of selling shaving stuff. There is a cardboard advertising display from about the same era that shows an elf holding a carton of blades decorated with a Santa face.

Professional Blade Co. of Newark, New Jersey, had a mailing carton holding 4 boxes of Professional Gold Blades with 5 blades each. The package required only a 1-1/2¢ stamp for domestic postage and a 6¢ stamp for overseas postage. Perhaps the mailer was to be a convenient way to send blades to soldiers overseas. This package must date from the 1940 or 50's as that is when the Professional Blade Co. is said to have been active. Also, I don't remember domestic postage at only 1-1/2¢ for any letter that I've ever sent!

Some firms made year around use of Santa. The Clauss Cutlery Company of Fremont, Ohio made much of their name being as easy to remember as Santa Claus. That firm's catalog from about 1920 contained a trademark with a bearded Santa holding reins. The illustration is surrounded by

AutoStrop ad thought from about 1908 showing Santa after shaving.

the words, "If you can remember Santa Claus, you can remember that Clauss Cutlery is the best."

An advertisement thought to date from 1908 contains an illustration of Old Saint Nick with bare cheeks. "For generations 'Old Saint Nick' refused to shave, for lack of a good razor" the ad says. "He would not use the ordinary straight razor nor the old style safety." Santa was said to have shaved his characteristic whiskers using the AutoStrop Safety Razor and was "More Happy" than ever before. The shaving outfit described was a quadruple silver plated self stropping razor with 12 blades and a horse hide strop. A benefit of this razor was that there was nothing to unscrew or take apart. Even the blade was not removed from the holder for stropping or cleaning. All this was only $5 with no continual expense for new blades.

I'm sure there are many fine razors and other shaving products available still in 1991 that would make welcome Christmas gifts. So...you better be good, you better be nice, Santa Claus is coming to town!

This article appeared in Knife World December, 1991.

Professional Blade Co. mailer with Santa from about 1945. Both sides of blade boxes are shown and the blade itself in colorful paper wrapper.

Cutlery Postcards

by Kurt Moe

Does your wife, better half, or significant other get bored while you haunt flea markets? While you're dreaming of sorting through boxes of dirty old razors, knives, and smelly leather strops would she rather be attending the craft festival or watching a tractor pull? Perhaps an alternative pleasure would be to help search the postcard stacks looking for those with cutlery related subjects. After getting small inexpensive individual copper frames you may even be allowed to hang some cards in the bathroom.

Postcards come in black and white as well as in color. Some postcards have realistic photographs while others have scenes of cartoon-like figures. Keep in mind that society's sense of humor has changed since the beginning of this century. What may have been funny decades ago may now be too subtle.

Some cards may not even seem funny. A young lady with an untrustworthy "attitude" about her was holding a very large pair of scissors. If my memory serves, she was saying, "I wouldn't cut you!"

A copyrighted 1909 card is titled "The Unsafe Safety Razor." It shows a young man being shaved outdoors by a young lady. Wish we could determine the brand of razor used but neither the razor nor its box seems printed clear enough. The meaning might be that the safety razor will keep his face from being cut but may still leave him in an unsafe position. His smooth face won't allow him to be safe where the young lady is concerned. The card required postage of one cent for domestic and two cents for foreign mail.

Used postcards are certainly easier

AMAG No. 1799 postcard with cartoon scene. European? 1931?

Postmarked 1916, card shows loving couple and reads, "Try it once and you will always use it. Rex Safety Razor Co."

to date than it is to date most cutlery. The postmark date, if legible, shows the date the card was processed by the post office.

Postcard writers usually didn't have a long flowery and complicated message to send. Though one could write very small there wasn't much room on one side of these picture postcards for the address, the stamp, and the message. The writer's object may have been just to remind someone not to forget them in their absence.

A card shows "Pa's razor" which is a straight razor. It shows "Ma's raiser" which was a baby bottle. In order to get this one you must know that in about 1909 Ma used yeast to raise her bread dough. You don't learn that by watching today's television commercials!

A postcard titled "A Chip Off the Old Block" is postmarked 1910. The brown tone photograph has a nifty shaving stand. The youngster is using the shaving tools just like dad would. The card used one cent postage and was written to someone who was to send a return card when they learned how to write.

A Tough Kid Series postcard has a baby in a diaper using Dad's razor and cuts himself. "Oh, Damn! Damn! Damn! Well That's What Pappa Always Says," There is a one cent stamp and a postmark date of 1913.

Seasonal cards with Thanksgiving, Christmas, or Easter themes often feature outrageously sized knives to carve turkey or ham.

The Chicago Daily News War Postals appear to have been a whole series of cards with WWI scenes. This one shows a soldier being shaved in the field with the caption, "No Hot Towels Here." The people back home were making sacrifices for the war effort. The soldiers, however, lacked even some of the small comforts enjoyed at home like a hot towel before a shave.

Most barbershops have been thought of as a place for male companionship and barber conversation in the usual manly topics. One cartoon style card shows a gentleman settling back in the barber chair and he's saying, "No Haircut, No Shave, No Shampoo, No Tonic! Just talk to me, Tony."

Women, however, were known to wield the straight razor too. When a

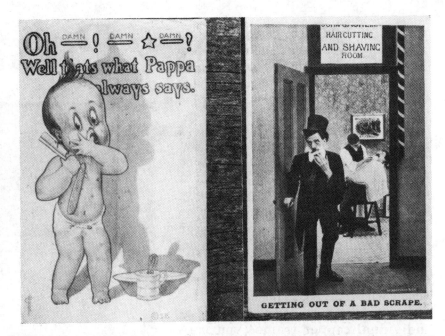

Left: Tough Kid Series postmarked 1913. Right: "Getting out of a bad scrape" card postmarked 1908. This card was addressed, stamped, and sent. There was no message written and no signature.

Left: Chicago Daily News War Postal Series of WWI scenes. G.J. Kavanaugh. "No Hot Towels Here." Right: "The Unsafe Safety Razor" copyrighted 1909.

group of young men on threshing crews hit the main street of the small North Dakota town of Windsor they wanted to look their best. They didn't want to see their Saturday night slipping away while waiting their turn for the regular barber. As told to me this was a fine opportunity for one young lady to practice the fine art of shaving, meet young men, and make money. It could also be expected that the men would be at their very best behavior while their throat was under the razor. They probably were too proud as well to complain about a nick and a small amount of blood from time to time. Some men might even say that a woman's touch tends to be lighter, while still being firm and quicker than a man's touch.

It has been said that an experienced barber is able to control the closeness of a shave. Depending on the customer's preference and daring, a real close shave might last longer before the next trip back to the barber was necessary.

Sometimes a postcard's caption may have a double meaning. A postcard shows a lady barber leaning her bust into the head of the lathered fellow in the chair. She asks "Do you like a close Shave?"

This article appeared in Knife World December, 1993.

Postmarked 1908 this card reads "You're Next," and refers to barber shop use of the phrase although it really advertises a firm's wallpaper sample books.

Postcard from Sheffield. Still another meaning for the phrase "Close Shaves."

244

Razor or Fountain Pen?

by Kurt Moe

Over the years, I've often asked antique dealers with old fountain pens whether they have any pens with safety razors instead of pen points inside of them. Conversation with the dealer was usually uncomfortable and abrupt. Perhaps there was doubt as to my sanity.

For those who have doubts that such a thing as a pen-razor exists, I present the "Arnold Fountain Safety Razor," "Reading, Penn," "Patent Oct. 23,1906". This information is marked on the black barrel case of the razor.

A narrow blade is clamped in a hinged safety guard. The guard has threads to enable it to be screwed into the pen barrel to be a complete and functional razor. The guard portion is reversed for safe storage.

There is a black plastic cap with a design that matches the barrel. The cap has an ornate gold band where it fits the barrel. The cap does not have a clip for the pocket, however, the razor looks very much like a large fountain pen. It easily fits in a vest pocket.

A pen sold by Sears, Roebuck & Co. for the usual use of writing has a very similar black body. Even the wavy design made up of small lines is very similar. This pen came with little pellets that made ink when dissolved in water.

Frederick H. Arnold applied for many razor patents involving various ways of holding blades. The patents were not granted in order of application and perhaps some of the applications were never approved. Those patents granted that show pen type razors include No.833,767 granted Oct. 23, 1906, No.834,353 granted Oct. 30, 1906, and No.838,762 granted Dec. 18, 1906. Patent

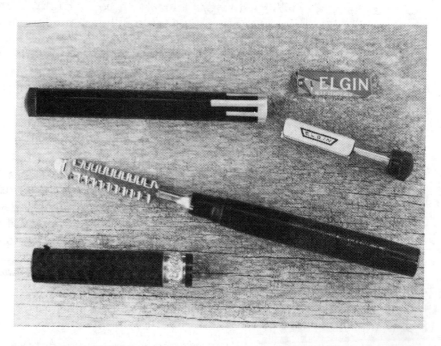

Top: Elgin Razor for Women shown for storage with paper wrapped blade. Bottom: Arnold Fountain Safety Razor patented Oct. 23, 1906.

Arnold's $ Razor with a blade holding mechanism.

No.839,447 granted on Dec. 25, 1906, shows a more ordinary straight handle.

Another razor is marked "Arnold's $ Razor," "Pat. 2-26-07," "Reading, Pa USA." The drawings for patent No.845,389 issued to F.H. Arnold and E.D. Becker on Feb 26, 1907, show another pen type razor. The blade holding mechanism shown in the patent drawing is, however, similar to that used by the "Arnold $ Razor." There is a spring lever that serves to hold or release the blade.

The "Dollar" razor is not very complex and seems to have been made from one flat piece of nickel plated metal. The finger hold and curved portion of the handle allow a secure grip on the razor.

Still another variation of blade holding mechanisms was patent No.885,422 received by F.H. Arnold on April 21, 1908.

A drawback of the Arnold razors appears to be that the blades were not interchangeable. The different patented holding mechanisms required holes or notches in the blade in specific places. The Dollar razor even required a blade wider than did the Fountain razor. More successful razor companies such as Gillette managed to standardize their blades. Blades with changes to fit their new model razors were designed so that the new blades still fit razors manufactured decades earlier. An owner of an older razor was happy that he could continue to purchase blades to fit his razor. A retail store did not have to stock extra variations.

John Goins' *"Pocketknives"* book says that the Arnold firm was located at No. 440 Court Street in Reading, Pa. The Fountain trademark was used on cutlery and tools from 1906 to 1909.

A second and more easily found brand of pen-razor was made by the Elgin American Co. of Elgin, Illinois. There are black, red, and white models of this razor which is smaller than the Arnold Fountain razor. The woman's section in old Montgomery War catalogs calls this item, "The Elgin Razor for Women." A 1937 catalog sold them for 59 cents and a 1938 catalog dropped the price to 49 cents each.

It would have been exciting to find an Arnold or an Elgin razor in a pile of old fountain pens. It hasn't happened yet so we keep looking for variations that we don't have. Some people collect large items like automobiles or steam engines and have large storage needs. The worst thing that can happen to us is that we have to find another cigar box to hold the bargain fountain pens that we couldn't resist.

This article appeared in Knife World September, 1984.